W9-ATK-128

GRACE
FOR
EACH DAY

Copyright © 2014 by Worthy Inspired, a division of Worthy Media, Inc.

ISBN 978-1-61795-384-2
ISBN 978-1-61795-416-0 (Special Edition)

Published by Worthy Inspired, a division of Worthy Media, Inc.,
134 Franklin Road, Suite 200, Brentwood, Tennessee 37027.

Scripture references marked KJV are from the Holy Bible, King James Version

Scripture references marked NKJV are from the Holy Bible, New King James Version.
Copyright © 1982 by Thomas Nelson, Inc. Used by permission.

Scripture references marked NCV are from the New Century Version®. Copyright © 1987,
1988, 1991 by Word Publishing, a division of Thomas Nelson, Inc. All rights reserved. Used
by permission.

Scripture references marked HCSB are from the Holman Christian Standard Bible™
Copyright © 1999, 2000, 2001 by Holman Bible Publishers. Used by permission.

Scripture references marked NIV are from the Holy Bible, New International Version®, NIV®
Copyright © 1973, 1978, 1984, 2011 by Biblica, Inc.® Used by permission. All rights reserved
worldwide.

Scripture references marked NLT are from the Holy Bible. New Living Translation. Copyright
© 1996 Tyndale Charitable Trust. Used by permission of Tyndale House Publishers.

Scripture references marked MSG are from the Message. Copyright © 1993, 1994, 1995,
1996, 2000, 2001, 2002. Used by permission of NavPress Publishing Group.

Cover Design by Kim Russell / Wahoo Designs
Page Layout by Bart Dawson

Printed in the United States of America

1 2 3 4 5—SBI—18 17 16 15 14

GRACE
FOR
EACH DAY

365 DEVOTIONS AND PRAYERS

WORTHY
Inspired

Introduction

Jesus is the spiritual sun that gives warmth, light, and life to the world. Christ died on the cross so that we might have eternal life. This gift, freely given from God's only Son, is the priceless possession of everyone who accepts Him as Lord and Savior.

Thankfully, God's grace is not an earthly reward for righteous behavior; it is, instead, a blessed spiritual gift. When we welcome Christ into our hearts, we are saved by His grace. The familiar words from the book of Ephesians make God's promise perfectly clear: "For it is by grace you have been saved, through faith—and this not from yourselves, it is the gift of God—not by works, so that no one can boast" (2:8-9 NIV).

As a Christian living in these troubled times, you may be easily sidetracked by the distractions and demands of everyday living. These devotional readings are intended to remind you of the priceless gift of God's grace. May you experience His grace—and may you share His Good News—with a world that desperately needs both.

This Is the Day

This is the day the LORD has made; we will rejoice and be glad in it.

Psalm 118:24 NKJV

What do you expect from the day ahead? Are you expecting God to do wonderful things, or are you living beneath a cloud of apprehension and doubt? The familiar words of Psalm 118:24 remind us of a profound yet simple truth: "This is the day which the LORD hath made; we will rejoice and be glad in it" (KJV).

For Christians, every day begins and ends with God's Son and God's promises. When we accept Christ into our hearts, God promises us the opportunity for earthly peace and spiritual abundance. But more importantly, God promises us the priceless gift of eternal life.

As we face the inevitable challenges of life-here-on-earth, we must arm ourselves with the promises of God's Holy Word. When we do, we can expect the best, not only for the day ahead, but also for all eternity.

When we meditate on God and remember the promises He has given us in His Word, our faith grows, and our fears dissolve.

Charles Stanley

Today's Prayer

Dear God, the Bible contains many promises. Let me trust Your promises, and let me live according to Your Holy Word, not just for today, but forever. Amen

Grace for Each Day

For all have sinned and fall short of the glory of God.

Romans 3:23 NKJV

Despite our shortcomings, God sent His Son so that we might be redeemed from our sins. In doing so, our Heavenly Father demonstrated His infinite mercy and His infinite love. We have received countless gifts from God, but none can compare with the gift of salvation. God's grace is the ultimate gift, and we owe Him the ultimate in thanksgiving.

Christ sacrificed His life on the cross so that we might have eternal life. This gift, freely given from God's only begotten Son, is the priceless possession of everyone who accepts Him as Lord and Savior. We return our Savior's love by welcoming Him into our hearts and sharing His message and His love. When we do so, we are blessed here on earth and throughout all eternity.

The grace of God is infinite and eternal. As it had no beginning, so it can have no end, and being an attribute of God, it is as boundless as infinitude.

A. W. Tozer

Today's Prayer

Dear Lord, You have offered Your grace freely through Christ Jesus. I praise You for that priceless gift. Let me share the good news of Your Son with a world that desperately needs His peace, His abundance, His love, and His salvation. Amen

Life Abundant

I have come that they may have life, and that they may have it more abundantly.

John 10:10 NKJV

The 10th chapter of John tells us that Christ came to earth so that our lives might be filled with abundance. But what, exactly, did Jesus mean when He promised "life . . . more abundantly"? Was He referring to material possessions or financial wealth? Hardly. Jesus offers a different kind of abundance: a spiritual richness that extends beyond the temporal boundaries of this world.

Is material abundance part of God's plan for our lives? Perhaps. But in every circumstance of life, during times of wealth or times of want, God will provide us what we need if we trust Him (Matthew 6). May we, as believers, claim the riches of Christ Jesus every day that we live, and may we share His blessings with all who cross our path.

The only way you can experience abundant life is to surrender your plans to Him.

Charles Stanley

Today's Prayer

Dear Lord, You have offered me the gift of abundance through Your Son. Thank You, Father, for the abundant life that is mine through Christ Jesus. Let me accept His gifts and use them always to glorify You. Amen

Strength for Today

So because of Christ, I am pleased in weaknesses, in insults, in catastrophes, in persecutions, and in pressures. For when I am weak, then I am strong.

2 Corinthians 12:10 HCSB

Life is a tapestry of good days and difficult days, with good days predominating. During the good days, we are tempted to take our blessings for granted (a temptation that we must resist with all our might). But, during life's difficult days, we discover precisely what we're made of. And more importantly, we discover what our faith is made of.

Has your faith been put to the test yet? If so, then you know that with God's help, you can endure life's darker days. But if you have not yet faced the inevitable trials and tragedies of life-here-on-earth, don't worry . . . you will. And when your faith is put to the test, rest assured that God is perfectly willing—and always ready—to give you strength for the struggle.

The roots grow deep when the winds are strong.

Charles Swindoll

Today's Prayer

Dear Lord, in the dark moments of my life, help me to remember that You, my Savior, are always near and that You can overcome any challenge. Keep me mindful of Your love and Your power, so that I may live courageously and faithfully today and every day. Amen

Infinite Love

For I am convinced that neither death, nor life, nor angels, nor principalities, nor things present, nor things to come, nor powers, nor height, nor depth, nor any other created thing, will be able to separate us from the love of God, which is in Christ Jesus our Lord.

Romans 8:38-39 NASB

Christ's love for you is personal. He loves you so much that He gave His life in order that you might spend all eternity with Him. Christ loves you individually and intimately; His is a love unbounded by time or circumstance. Are you willing to experience an intimate relationship with Him? Your Savior is waiting patiently; don't make Him wait a single minute longer.

———※———

Christ is like a river that is continually flowing. There are always fresh supplies of water coming from the fountain-head, so that a man may live by it and be supplied with water all his life. So Christ is an ever-flowing fountain; he is continually supplying his people, and the fountain is not spent. They who live upon Christ may have fresh supplies from him for all eternity; they may have an increase of blessedness that is new, and new still, and which never will come to an end.

Jonathan Edwards

Today's Prayer

Thank You, Lord, for Your Son. His love is boundless, infinite, and eternal. Today, let me pause and reflect upon Christ's love for me, and let me share that love with all those who cross my path. Amen

God's Assurance

I've told you all this so that trusting me, you will be unshakable and assured, deeply at peace. In this godless world you will continue to experience difficulties. But take heart! I've conquered the world.

John 16:33 MSG

Are you a confident believer, or do you live under a cloud of uncertainty and doubt? As a Christian, you have many reasons to be confident. After all, God is in His Heaven; Christ has risen; and you are the recipient of God's grace. Despite these blessings, you may, from time to time, find yourself being tormented by negative emotions—and you are certainly not alone.

Even the most faithful Christians are overcome by occasional bouts of fear and doubt. You are no different.

But even when you feel very distant from God, remember that God is never distant from you. When you sincerely seek His presence, He will touch your heart, calm your fears, and restore your confidence.

———

Believe and do what God says. The life-changing consequences will be limitless, and the results will be confidence and peace of mind.

Franklin Graham

Today's Prayer

Lord, You are my Savior and my Sustainer. I will be safe with You in Heaven, and I am safe with You here on earth. Today, I will trust in Your promises, and I will be a confident, obedient, purposeful servant to Your Son. Amen

Let God Decide

A man's heart plans his way, but the Lord directs his steps.

Proverbs 16:9 NKJV

Are you facing a difficult decision, a troubling circumstance, or a powerful temptation? If so, it's time to step back, to stop focusing on the world, and to focus, instead, on the will of your Father in Heaven. The world will often lead you astray, but God will not. His counsel leads you to Himself, which, of course, is the path He has always intended for you to take.

Everyday living is an exercise in decision-making. Today and every day you must make choices: choices about what you will do, what you will worship, and how you will think. When in doubt, make choices that you sincerely believe will bring you to a closer relationship with God. And if you're uncertain of your next step, pray about it. When you do, answers will come—the right answers for you.

———

God always gives His best to those who leave the choice with Him.

Jim Elliot

Today's Prayer

Lord, help me to make decisions that are pleasing to You. Help me to be honest, patient, thoughtful, and obedient. And above all, help me to follow the teachings of Jesus, not just today, but every day. Amen

Confident Christianity

You are my hope; O Lord GOD, You are my confidence.

Psalm 71:5 NASB

We Christians have many reasons to be confident. God is in His Heaven; Christ has risen, and we are the sheep of His flock. Yet sometimes, even the most devout Christians can become discouraged. Discouragement, however, is not God's way; He is a God of possibility not negativity.

Are you a confident Christian? You should be. God's grace is eternal and His promises are unambiguous. So count your blessings, not your hardships. And live courageously. God is the Giver of all things good, and He watches over you today and forever.

If we indulge in any confidence that is not grounded on the Rock of Ages, our confidence is worse than a dream, it will fall on us and cover us with its ruins, causing sorrow and confusion.

C. H. Spurgeon

Today's Prayer

Lord, when I place my confidence in the things of this earth, I will be disappointed. But, when I put my confidence in You, I am secure. In every aspect of my life, Father, let me place my hope and my trust in Your infinite wisdom and Your boundless grace. Amen

Living by the Book

He who despises the word will be destroyed, but he who fears the commandment will be rewarded.

Proverbs 13:13 NKJV

The Holy Bible contains thorough instructions which, if followed, lead to fulfillment, righteousness, and salvation. But, if we choose to ignore God's commandments, the results are as predictable as they are tragic.

A righteous life has many components: faith, honesty, generosity, love, kindness, humility, gratitude, and worship, to name but a few. If we seek to follow the steps of our Savior, Jesus Christ, we must seek to live according to His commandments. Let us follow God's commandments, and let us conduct our lives in such a way that we might be shining examples for those who have not yet found Christ.

Bible history is filled with people who began the race with great success but failed at the end because they disregarded God's rules.

Warren Wiersbe

Today's Prayer

Lord, Your commandments are a perfect guide for my life. Give me the wisdom to walk righteously in Your way, Father, trusting always in You. Amen

Counting Your Blessings

Finally, brethren, whatsoever things are true, whatsoever things are honest, whatsoever things are just, whatsoever things are pure, whatsoever things are lovely, whatsoever things are of good report; if there be any virtue, and if there be any praise, think on these things.

Philippians 4:8 KJV

How will you direct your thoughts today? Will you obey the words of Philippians 4:8 by dwelling upon those things that are honorable, just, and commendable? Or will you allow your thoughts to be hijacked by the negativity that seems to dominate our troubled world? Are you fearful, angry, bored, or worried? Are you so preoccupied with the concerns of this day that you fail to thank God for the promise of eternity? Are you confused, bitter, or pessimistic? If so, God wants to have a little talk with you.

God intends that you experience joy and abundance. So, today and every day hereafter, celebrate the life that God has given you by focusing your thoughts upon those things that are worthy of praise. Today, count your blessings instead of your hardships. Thank the Giver of all things good for gifts that are too numerous to count.

Developing a positive attitude means working continually to find what is uplifting and encouraging.

Barbara Johnson

Today's Prayer

Dear Lord, help me have an attitude that is pleasing to You as I count my blessings today, tomorrow, and every day. Amen

An Intensely Bright Future: Yours

I came so they can have real and eternal life, more and better life than they ever dreamed of.

John 10:10 MSG

Are you excited about the opportunities of today and thrilled by the possibilities of tomorrow? Do you confidently expect God to lead you to a place of abundance, peace, and joy? And, when your days on earth are over, do you expect to receive the priceless gift of eternal life? If you trust God's promises, and if you have welcomed God's Son into your heart, then you believe that your future is intensely and eternally bright.

It takes courage to dream big dreams. You will discover that courage when you do three things: accept the past, trust God to handle the future, and make the most of the time He has given you today. No dreams are too big for God—not even yours. So start living—and dreaming—accordingly.

Set goals so big that unless God helps you, you will be a miserable failure.

Bill Bright

Today's Prayer

Dear Lord, my hope is in You. Give me the courage to face the future with certainty, and give me the wisdom to follow in the footsteps of Your Son, today and forever. Amen

Enthusiasm for Christ

So roll up your sleeves, put your mind in gear, be totally ready to receive the gift that's coming when Jesus arrives. Don't lazily slip back into those old grooves of evil, doing just what you feel like doing. You didn't know any better then; you do now. As obedient children, let yourselves be pulled into a way of life shaped by God's life, a life energetic and blazing with holiness.

1 Peter 1:13-15 MSG

John Wesley advised, "Catch on fire with enthusiasm and people will come for miles to watch you burn." His words still ring true. When we fan the flames of enthusiasm for Christ, our faith serves as a beacon to others.

Our world desperately needs faithful believers who share the Good News of Jesus with joyful exuberance. Be such a believer. The world desperately needs your enthusiasm—now!

———◦———

We act as though comfort and luxury were the chief requirements of life, when all we need to make us really happy is something to be enthusiastic about.

Charles Kingsley

Today's Prayer

Dear Lord, let me be an enthusiastic participant in life. And let my enthusiasm bring honor and glory to You. Amen

We Are All Role Models

You are the light of the world. A city on a hill cannot be hidden. Neither do people light a lamp and put it under a bowl. Instead they put it on its stand, and it gives light to everyone in the house. In the same way, let your light shine before men, that they may see your good deeds and praise your Father in heaven.

Matthew 5:14-16 NIV

Whether we like it or not, we are role models. Hopefully, the lives we lead and the choices we make will serve as enduring examples of the spiritual abundance that is available to all who worship God and obey His commandments.

Ask yourself this question: Are you the kind of role model that you would want to emulate? If so, congratulations. But if certain aspects of your behavior could stand improvement, the best day to begin your self-improvement regimen is this one. Because whether you realize it or not, people you love are watching your behavior, and they're learning how to live. You owe it to them—and to yourself—to live righteously and well.

———

The sermon of your life in tough times ministers to people more powerfully than the most eloquent speaker.

Bill Bright

Today's Prayer

Dear Lord, help me be a honorable role model to others. Let the things that I say and the things that I do show everyone what it means to be a follower of Your Son. Amen

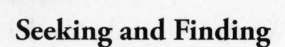

Seeking and Finding

Ask, and God will give to you. Search, and you will find. Knock, and the door will open for you. Yes, everyone who asks will receive. Everyone who searches will find. And everyone who knocks will have the door opened.

Matthew 7:7-8 NCV

Where is God? He is everywhere you have ever been and everywhere you will ever go. He is with you night and day; He knows your every thought; He hears your every heartbeat.

Sometimes, in the crush of your daily duties, God may seem far away. Or sometimes, when the disappointments and sorrows of life leave you brokenhearted, God may seem distant, but He is not. When you earnestly seek God, you will find Him because He is here, waiting patiently for you to reach out to Him . . . right here . . . right now.

—※—

O God. You are always the same. Let me know myself and know You.

St. Augustine

Today's Prayer

How comforting it is, dear Lord, to know that if I seek You, I will find You. You are with me, Father, every step that I take. Let me reach out to You, and let me praise You for revealing Your Word, Your way, and Your love. Amen

God Wants to Use You

To everything there is a season, a time for every purpose under heaven.

Ecclesiastes 3:1 NKJV

God has things He wants you to do and places He wants you to go. The most important decision of your life is your commitment to accept Jesus Christ as your personal Lord and Savior. And, once your eternal destiny is secured, you will undoubtedly ask yourself the question "What's next?" If you earnestly seek God's will for your life, you will find it . . . in time.

You may be certain that God is planning to use you in surprising, wonderful ways. And you may be certain that He intends to lead you along a path of His choosing. Your task is to watch for His signs, to listen to His words, to obey His commandments, and to follow where He leads.

———

It is important to set goals because if you do not have a plan, a goal, a direction, a purpose, and a focus, you are not going to accomplish anything for the glory of God.

Bill Bright

Today's Prayer

Dear Lord, let Your purposes be my purposes. Let Your priorities be my priorities. Let Your will be my will. Let Your Word be my guide. And, let me grow in faith and in wisdom today and every day. Amen

Compassionate Servants

Finally, all of you be of one mind, having compassion for one another; love as brothers, be tenderhearted, be courteous.

1 Peter 3:8 NKJV

God's Word commands us to be compassionate, generous servants to those who need our support. As believers, we have been richly blessed by our Creator. We, in turn, are called to share our gifts, our possessions, our testimonies, and our talents.

Concentration camp survivor Corrie ten Boom correctly observed, "The measure of a life is not its duration but its donation." These words remind us that the quality of our lives is determined not by what we are able to take from others, but instead by what we are able to share with others.

The thread of compassion is woven into the very fabric of Christ's teachings. If we are to be disciples of Christ, we, too, must be zealous in caring for others. Our Savior expects no less from us. And He deserves no less.

Our Lord worked with people as they were, and He was patient—not tolerant of sin, but compassionate.

Vance Havner

Today's Prayer

Lord, make me a loving, encouraging, compassionate Christian. And, let my love for Christ be reflected through the kindness that I show to my family, to my friends, and to all who need the healing touch of the Master's hand. Amen

Your Plans and God's Plans

People may make plans in their minds, but the Lord decides what they will do.

Proverbs 16:9 NCV

If you're like most people, you like being in control. Period. You want things to happen according to your wishes and according to your timetable. But sometimes, God has other plans . . . and He always has the final word. Are you embittered by a personal tragedy that you did not deserve and cannot understand? If so, it's time to make peace with life. It's time to forgive others, and, if necessary, to forgive yourself. It's time to accept the unchangeable past, to embrace the priceless present, and to have faith in the promise of tomorrow. It's time to trust God completely. And it's time to reclaim the peace—His peace—that can and should be yours.

So if you've encountered unfortunate circumstances that are beyond your power to control, accept those circumstances . . . and trust God. When you do, you can be comforted in the knowledge that your Creator is both loving and wise, and that He understands His plans perfectly, even when you do not.

Today's Prayer

Lord, when I am discouraged, give me hope. When I am impatient, give me peace. When I face circumstances that I cannot change, give me a spirit of acceptance. In all things great and small, let me trust in Your plans, Dear Lord, knowing that You are the Giver of life and the Giver of all things good, today and forever. Amen

Acknowledging Your Blessings

The Lord bless you and keep you; the Lord make His face shine upon you, and be gracious to you.

Numbers 6:24-25 NKJV

Today, you will take one more step on your life's journey. Today offers one more opportunity to be genuinely thankful for your blessings. The coming day is a canvass upon which you can compose a beautiful work of art if you choose to do so.

Norman Vincent Peale observed, "The life of stress is difficult. But the life of thanksgiving—a life that comes from a positive attitude—is the easiest type of existence." And those words apply to you.

So today, look for things to be thankful for. If you look carefully, you won't need to look very far. And remember: when it comes time to count your blessings, nobody can count them for you.

———◆———

God's kindness is not like the sunset—brilliant in its intensity, but dying every second. God's generosity keeps coming and coming and coming.

Bill Hybels

Today's Prayer

Lord, I have more blessings than I can count, and I praise You for Your gifts. Let me use my talents and my possessions for Your glory and for Your Son. Amen

Conquering Everyday Frustrations

A hot-tempered man stirs up conflict, but a man slow to anger calms strife.

Proverbs 15:18 HCSB

Life is full of frustrations: some great and some small. On occasion, you, like Jesus, will confront evil, and when you do, you may respond as He did: vigorously and without reservation. But, more often your frustrations will be of the more mundane variety. As long as you live here on earth, you will face countless opportunities to lose your temper over small, relatively insignificant events: a traffic jam, a spilled cup of coffee, an inconsiderate comment, a broken promise. When you are tempted to lose your temper over the minor inconveniences of life, don't. Turn away from anger, hatred, bitterness, and regret. Turn instead to God. When you do, you'll be following His commandments and giving yourself a priceless gift . . . the gift of peace.

Today's Prayer

Dear Lord, when I am angry, I cannot feel the peace that You intend for my life. When I am bitter, I cannot sense Your love. Heavenly Father, keep me mindful that forgiveness is Your commandment and Your will for my life. Let me turn away from anger and instead claim the spiritual abundance that You offer through the priceless gift of Your Son Jesus. Amen

Your Real Riches

Naked I came from my mother's womb, and naked I will leave this life. The Lord gives, and the Lord takes away. Praise the name of the Lord.

Job 1:21 HCSB

Martin Luther observed, "Many things I have tried to grasp and have lost. That which I have placed in God's hands I still have." How true. Earthly riches are transitory; spiritual riches are not.

In our demanding world, financial security can be a good thing, but spiritual prosperity is profoundly more important. Certainly we all need the basic necessities of life, but once we've acquired those necessities, enough is enough. Why? Because our real riches are not of this world. We are never really rich until we are rich in spirit.

───◈───

The characteristic of the life of a saint is essentially elemental simplicity.

Oswald Chambers

Today's Prayer

Dear Lord, all I have belongs to You. When I leave this world I take nothing with me. Help me to value my relationship with You—and my relationships with others—more than I value my material possessions. Amen

The Wisdom to Celebrate

A miserable heart means a miserable life; a cheerful heart fills the day with a song.

Proverbs 15:15 MSG

The Christian life is a cause for celebration, but sometimes we don't feel much like celebrating. In fact, when the weight of the world seems to bear down upon our shoulders, celebration may be the last thing on our minds . . . but it shouldn't be. As God's children, we are all blessed beyond measure on good days and bad. This day is a non-renewable resource—once it's gone, it's gone forever. We should give thanks for this day while using it for the glory of God.

What will be your attitude today? Will you be fearful, angry, bored, or worried? Will you be cynical, bitter or pessimistic? If so, God wants to have a little talk with you.

God created you in His own image, and He wants you to experience joy and abundance. But, God will not force His joy upon you; you must claim it for yourself. So today, and every day thereafter, celebrate the life that God has given you. Think optimistically about yourself and your future. Give thanks to the One who has given you everything, and trust in your heart that He wants to give you so much more.

Today's Prayer

Dear Lord, I pray for an attitude that pleases You. In every circumstance, I will strive to celebrate the life You have given me . . . and I will praise You for Your priceless gifts. Amen

The Guidebook

All Scripture is given by inspiration of God, and is profitable for doctrine, for reproof, for correction, for instruction in righteousness, that the man of God may be complete, thoroughly equipped for every good work.

2 Timothy 3:16-17 NKJV

God has given us a guidebook for righteous living called the Holy Bible. It contains thorough instructions which, if followed, lead to fulfillment, righteousness, and salvation. But, if we choose to ignore God's commandments, the results are as predictable as they are tragic.

God has given us the Bible for the purpose of knowing His promises, His power, His commandments, His wisdom, His love, and His Son. As we study God's teachings and apply them to our lives, we live by the Word that shall never pass away.

Today, let us follow God's commandments, and let us conduct our lives in such a way that we might be shining examples to our families, and, most importantly, to those who have not yet found Christ.

Today's Prayer

As I journey through this life, Lord, help me always to consult the true road map: Your Holy Word. I know that when I turn my heart and my thoughts to You, Father, You will lead me along the path that is right for me. Today, dear Lord, let me know Your will and study Your Word so that I might know Your plan for my life. Amen

New and Improved

Therefore if any man be in Christ, he is a new creature: old things are passed away; behold, all things are become new.

2 Corinthians 5:17 KJV

Think, for a moment, about the "old" you, the person you were before you invited Christ to reign over your heart. Now, think about the "new" you, the person you have become since then. Is there a difference between the "old" you and the "new and improved" version? There should be! And that difference should be noticeable not only to you but also to others.

The Bible clearly teaches that when we welcome Christ into our hearts, we become new creations through Him. Our challenge, of course, is to behave ourselves like new creations. When we do, God fills our hearts, He blesses our endeavors, and transforms our lives . . . forever.

No man is ever the same after God has laid His hand upon him.

A. W. Tozer

Today's Prayer

Lord, when I accepted Jesus as my personal Savior, You changed me forever and made me whole. Let me share Your Son's message with my friends, with my family, and with the world. You are a God of love, redemption, conversion, and salvation. I will praise You today and forever. Amen

The Cornerstone

Let us fix our eyes on Jesus, the author and perfecter of our faith, who for the joy set before him endured the cross, scorning its shame, and sat down at the right hand of the throne of God.

Hebrews 12:2 NIV

Is Christ the focus of your life? Are you fired with enthusiasm for Him? Are you an energized Christian who allows God's Son to reign over every aspect of your day? Make no mistake: that's exactly what God intends for you to do.

God has given you the gift of eternal life through His Son. In response to God's priceless gift, you are instructed to focus your thoughts, your prayers, and your energies upon God and His only begotten Son. To do so, you must resist the subtle yet powerful temptation to become a "spiritual dabbler." A person who dabbles in the Christian faith is unwilling to place God above all other things. Resist that temptation; make God the cornerstone and the touchstone of your life. When you do, He will give you all the strength and wisdom you need to live victoriously for Him.

Today's Prayer

Lord, You have told me to give thanks always and to rejoice in Your marvelous creation. Let me be a joyful Christian, Lord, and let me focus my thoughts upon Your blessings and Your love. Amen

His Promises

Let us hold on to the confession of our hope without wavering, for He who promised is faithful.

Hebrews 10:23 HCSB

The Christian faith is founded upon promises that are contained in a unique book. That book is the Holy Bible. The Bible is a roadmap for life here on earth and for life eternal. As Christians, we are called upon to study its meaning, to trust its promises, to follow its commandments, and to share its Good News. God's Holy Word is, indeed, a transforming, life-changing, one-of-a-kind treasure. And, a passing acquaintance with the Good Book is insufficient for Christians who seek to obey God's Word and understand His will.

God has made promises to you, and He intends to keep them. So take God at His word: trust His promises and share them with your family, with your friends, and with the world.

We can have full confidence in God's promises because we can have full faith in His character.

Franklin Graham

Today's Prayer

Lord, Your Holy Word contains promises, and I will trust them. I will use the Bible as my guide, and I will trust You, Lord, to speak to me through Your Holy Spirit and through Your Holy Word, this day and forever. Amen

Saying Yes to God

Fear thou not; for I am with thee.

Isaiah 41:10 KJV

Your decision to seek a deeper relationship with God will not remove all problems from your life; to the contrary, it will bring about a series of personal crises as you constantly seek to say "yes" to God, while the world encourages you to do otherwise. Each time you are tempted to distance yourself from the Creator, you will face a spiritual crisis. A few of these crises may be monumental in scope, but most will be the small, everyday decisions of life. In fact, life here on earth can be seen as one test after another—and with each crisis comes yet another opportunity to grow closer to God . . . or to distance yourself from His plan for your life.

Today, you will face many opportunities to say "yes" to your Creator—and you will also encounter many opportunities to say "no" to Him. Your answers will determine the quality of your day and the direction of your life, so answer carefully . . . very carefully.

The Christian life is not a playground; it is a battleground.

Warren Wiersbe

Today's Prayer

Dear Lord, when life seems chaotic, remind me of Your love and protection. Difficult times provide opportunities for me to grow closer to You. Thank You for all that this day has to offer. Amen

Courtesy Matters

Out of respect for Christ, be courteously reverent to one another.

Ephesians 5:21 MSG

Did Christ instruct us in matters of etiquette and courtesy? Of course He did. Christ's instructions are clear: "In everything, therefore, treat people the same way you want them to treat you, for this is the Law and the Prophets" (Matthew 7:12 NASB). Jesus did not say, "In some things, treat people as you wish to be treated." And, He did not say, "From time to time, treat others with kindness." Christ said that we should treat others as we wish to be treated in every aspect of our daily lives. This, of course, is a tall order indeed, but as Christians, we are commanded to do our best.

Today, be a little kinder than necessary to family members, friends, and total strangers. And, as you consider all the things that Christ has done in your life, honor Him with your words and with your deeds. He expects no less, and He deserves no less.

───────

Only the courteous can love, but it is love that makes them courteous.

C. S. Lewis

Today's Prayer

Guide me, Lord, to treat all those I meet with courtesy and respect. You have created each person in Your own image; let me honor those who cross my path with the dignity that You have bestowed upon them. We are all Your children, Lord; let me show kindness to all. Amen

A Positive Influence

Be an example to the believers in word, in conduct, in love, in spirit, in faith, in purity.

1 Timothy 4:12 NKJV

As followers of Christ, we must each ask ourselves an important question: "What kind of example am I?" The answer to that question determines, in large part, whether or not we are positive influences on our own little corners of the world.

Are you the kind of person whose life serves as a powerful example of righteousness? Are you a person whose behavior serves as a positive role model for young people? Are you the kind of Christian whose actions, day in and day out, are based upon integrity, fidelity, and a love for the Lord? If so, you are not only blessed by God, you are also a powerful force for good in a world that desperately needs positive influences such as yours.

———⬧———

For one man who can introduce another to Jesus Christ by the way he lives and by the atmosphere of his life, there are a thousand who can only talk jargon about him.

Oswald Chambers

Today's Prayer

Lord, I am aware that my behavior will influence others. Let my influence be positive. Let me follow in the footsteps of Your Son, and let others see Him through me. Amen

A Place of Worship

For where two or three come together in my name, there am I with them.

Matthew 18:20 NIV

The Bible teaches that we should worship God in our hearts and in our churches (Acts 20:28). We have clear instructions to "feed the church of God" and to worship our Creator in the presence of fellow believers.

We live in a world that is teeming with temptations and distractions—a world where good and evil struggle in a constant battle to win our minds, our hearts, and our souls. Our challenge, of course, is to ensure that we cast our lot on the side of God. One way that we remain faithful to Him is through the practice of regular, purposeful worship with our families. When we worship the Father faithfully and fervently, we are blessed.

The Church, as announced by Christ, seen in the book of Acts, and explained by Paul, is a thing of great simplicity and rare beauty. The church, as we see it today, is unsymmetrical, highly complex, and anything but beautiful.

A. W. Tozer

Today's Prayer

Dear Lord, today I pray for Your church. Let me help to feed Your flock by helping to build Your church so that others, too, might experience Your enduring love and Your eternal grace. Amen

Standing on the Rock

He heals the brokenhearted and binds up their wounds.

Psalm 147:3 HCSB

God loves us and protects us. In times of trouble, He comforts us; in times of sorrow, He dries our tears. Psalm 147 promises, "He heals the brokenhearted, and binds their wounds" (v. 3, NASB). When we are troubled, we must call upon God, and—in His own time and according to His own plan—He will heal us.

Do you feel fearful, or weak, or sorrowful? Are you discouraged or bitter? Do you feel "stuck" in a place that is uncomfortable for you? If so, remember that God is as near as your next breath. So trust Him and turn to Him for solace, for security, and for salvation. And build your life on the rock that cannot be shaken . . . that rock is God.

God will never let you sink under your circumstances. He always provides a safety net and His love always encircles.

Barbara Johnson

Today's Prayer

Lord, sometimes, I am worried, weary, or heartbroken. And sometimes, I encounter powerful temptations to disobey Your commandments. But, when I lift my eyes to You, Father, You strengthen me. Today, I will turn to You for strength, for hope, for direction, and for deliverance. Amen

Up for the Challenge

I will be your God throughout your lifetime—until your hair is white with age. I made you, and I will care for you. I will carry you along and save you.

Isaiah 46:4 NLT

God has promised to lift you up and guide your steps if you let Him do so. God has promised that when you entrust your life to Him completely and without reservation, He will give you the strength to meet any challenge, the courage to face any trial, and the wisdom to live in His righteousness.

God's hand uplifts those who turn their hearts and prayers to Him. Will you count yourself among that number? Will you accept God's peace and wear God's armor against the temptations and distractions of our dangerous world? If you do, you can live courageously and optimistically, knowing that you have been forever touched by the loving, unfailing, uplifting hand of God.

When we face an impossible situation, all self-reliance and self-confidence must melt away; we must be totally dependent on Him for the resources.

Anne Graham Lotz

Today's Prayer

Dear Lord, as I face the challenges of this day, You protect me. I thank You, Father for Your love and for Your strength. I will lean upon You today and forever. Amen

Beyond Grief

The Lord is near to those who have a broken heart.

Psalm 34:18 NKJV

When you find yourself caught in the emotional quicksand called grief, you may wonder if you'll ever recover. When the feelings of sorrow are intense, you may think—mistakenly—that the pain will never subside. But the good news is this: while time heals many wounds, God has the power to heal them all.

Have you sincerely asked God for His help as you begin the healing process? Have you asked Him to lead you on the first step back to recovery? Have you prayed for the peace that passes all understanding? If so, you're on the right track. If not, it's time to abandon your doubts and reclaim your faith in God's promises.

God's Holy Word makes it clear: absolutely nothing is impossible for Him. And since the Bible means what it says, you can be comforted in the knowledge that the Creator of the universe can do miraculous things in your own life and in the lives of your loved ones. Your challenge, as a believer, is to take God at His word, and to wait patiently for Him to bless you with peace that flows from His miraculous healing touch.

Today's Prayer

Dear Lord, when I grieve, I will turn to You. When I am weak, I will seek Your strength. When I am discouraged, Father, I will be mindful of Your love and Your grace. I will ask You for the things I need, Father, and I will trust Your answers, today and forever. Amen

He Reigns

In all your ways acknowledge Him, and He shall direct your paths.

Proverbs 3:6 NKJV

God is sovereign. He reigns over the entire universe and He reigns over your little corner of that universe. Your challenge is to recognize God's sovereignty and live in accordance with His commandments. Sometimes, of course, this is easier said than done.

Your Heavenly Father may not always reveal Himself as quickly (or as clearly) as you would like. But rest assured: God is in control, God is here, and God intends to use you in wonderful, unexpected ways. He desires to lead you along a path of His choosing. Your challenge is to watch, to listen, to learn . . . and to follow.

He proves His sovereignty, not by intervening constantly and preventing these events, but by ruling and overruling them so that even tragedies end up accomplishing His ultimate purposes.

Warren Wiersbe

Today's Prayer

Dear Lord, You rule over our world, and I will allow You to rule over my heart. I will obey Your commandments, I will study Your Word, and I will seek Your will for my life, today and every day of my life. Amen

Living in an Anxious World

Cast all your anxiety on him because he cares for you.

1 Peter 5:7 NIV

We live in a world that often breeds anxiety and fear. When we come face-to-face with tough times, we may fall prey to discouragement, doubt, or depression. But our Father in Heaven has other plans. God has promised that we may lead lives of abundance, not anxiety. In fact, His Word instructs us to "be anxious for nothing" (Philippians 4:6). But how can we put our fears to rest? By taking those fears to God and leaving them there.

As you face the challenges of daily life, you may find yourself becoming anxious, troubled, discouraged, or fearful. If so, turn every one of your concerns over to your Heavenly Father. The same God who created the universe will comfort you if you ask Him… so ask Him and trust Him. And then watch in amazement as your anxieties melt into the warmth of His loving hands.

Worry is a complete waste of energy. It solves nothing. And it won't solve that anxiety on your mind either.

Charles Swindoll

Today's Prayer

Father, sometimes troubles and distractions preoccupy thoughts and trouble my soul. When I am anxious, Lord, let me turn my prayers to You. When I am worried, give me faith in You. Let me live courageously, Dear God, knowing that You love me and that You will protect me, today and forever. Amen

The Right Kind of Attitude

May the words of my mouth and the meditation of my heart be acceptable to You, Lord, my rock and my Redeemer.

Psalm 19:14 HCSB

What is your attitude today? Are you fearful or worried? Are you more concerned about pleasing your friends than about pleasing your God? Are you bitter, confused, cynical or pessimistic? If so, it's time to have a little chat with your Father in Heaven.

God intends that your life be filled with spiritual abundance and joy—but God will not force His joy upon you—you must claim it for yourself. So do yourself this favor: accept God's gifts with a smile on your face, a song on your lips, and joy in your heart. Think optimistically about yourself and your future. Give thanks to the One who has given you everything, and trust in your heart that He wants to give you so much more.

The things we think are the things that feed our souls. If we think on pure and lovely things, we shall grow pure and lovely like them; and the converse is equally true.

Hannah Whitall Smith

Today's Prayer

Lord, I pray for an attitude that is Christlike. Whatever my situation, whether good or bad, happy or sad, let me respond with an attitude of optimism, faith, and love for You. Amen

The Storms of Life

But Jesus quickly spoke to them, "Have courage! It is I. Do not be afraid."

Matthew 14:27 NCV

A storm rose quickly on the Sea of Galilee, and the disciples were afraid. Although they had seen Jesus perform many miracles, the disciples feared for their lives, so they turned to their Savior, and He calmed the waters and the wind.

Sometimes, we, like the disciples, feel threatened by the inevitable storms of life. And when we are fearful, we, too, can turn to Christ for courage and for comfort.

The next time you're afraid, remember that the One who calmed the wind and the waves is also your personal Savior. And remember that the ultimate battle has already been won at Calvary. We, as believers, can live courageously in the promises of our Lord . . . and we should.

The fear of God is the death of every other fear.

C. H. Spurgeon

Today's Prayer

Dear Lord, sometimes I face disappointments and challenges that leave me worried and afraid. When I am fearful, let me seek Your strength. Keep me mindful, Lord, that You are my God. With You by my side, Lord, I have nothing to fear. Help me to be Your grateful and courageous servant this day and every day. Amen

His Joy . . . and Ours

Rejoice in the Lord . . . again I say, Rejoice.

Philippians 4:4 KJV

Christ made it clear: He intends that His joy should become our joy. Yet sometimes, amid the inevitable hustle and bustle of life-here-on-earth, we can forfeit—albeit temporarily—the joy of Christ as we wrestle with the challenges of daily living.

Billy Graham correctly observed, "When Jesus Christ is the source of our joy, no words can describe it." And C. S. Lewis noted that, "Joy is the serious business of Heaven." So here's a prescription for better spiritual health: Open the door of your soul to Christ. When you do, He will give you peace and joy.

Our joy ends where love of the world begins.

C. H. Spurgeon

Today's Prayer

Dear Lord, You have created a glorious universe that is far beyond my understanding. You have given me the gift of Your Son and the gift of salvation. Let me be a joyful Christian, Lord, this day and every day. Today is Your gift to me. Let me use it to Your glory as I give all the praise to You. Amen

Foolish Pride

Do nothing out of rivalry or conceit, but in humility consider others as more important than yourselves.

Philippians 2:3 HCSB

Sometimes our faith is tested more by prosperity than by adversity. Why? Because in times of plenty, we are tempted to stick out our chests and say, "I did that." But nothing could be further from the truth. All of our blessings start and end with God, and whatever "it" is, He did it. And He deserves the credit.

Who are the greatest among us? Are they the proud and the powerful? Hardly. The greatest among us are the humble servants who care less for their own glory and more for God's glory. If we seek greatness in God's eyes, we must forever praise God's good works, not our own.

God exalts humility. When God works in our lives, helping us to become humble, he gives us a permanent joy. Humility gives us a joy that cannot be taken away.

Max Lucado

Today's Prayer

Lord, give me a humble heart. Keep me mindful, dear God, that all my gifts come from You. When I feel prideful, remind me that You sent Your Son to be a humble carpenter and that Jesus was ridiculed on a cross. Let me grow beyond my need for earthly praise, Lord, and when I seek approval, let me look only to You. Amen

Seeking God and Finding Happiness

But happy are those . . . whose hope is in the LORD their God.

Psalm 146:5 NLT

Happiness depends less upon our circumstances than upon our thoughts. When we turn our thoughts to God, to His gifts, and to His glorious creation, we experience the joy that God intends for His children. But, when we focus on the negative aspects of life, we suffer needlessly.

Do you sincerely want to be a happy Christian? Then set your mind and your heart upon God's love and His grace. The fullness of life in Christ is available to all who seek it and claim it. Count yourself among that number. Seek first the salvation that is available through a personal relationship with Jesus Christ, and then claim the joy, the peace, and the spiritual abundance that the Shepherd offers His sheep.

God has charged Himself with full responsibility for our eternal happiness and stands ready to take over the management of our lives the moment we turn in faith to Him.

A. W. Tozer

Today's Prayer

Dear Lord, I am thankful for all the blessings You have given me. Let me be a happy Christian, Father, as I share Your joy with friends, with family, and with the world. Amen

Compassionate Christianity

So, as those who have been chosen of God, holy and beloved, put on a heart of compassion, kindness, humility, gentleness and patience.

Colossians 3:12 NASB

The instructions of Colossians 3:12 are unambiguous: as Christians, we are to be compassionate, humble, gentle, and kind. But sometimes, we fall short. In the busyness and confusion of daily life, we may neglect to share a kind word or a kind deed. This oversight hurts others, but it hurts us most of all.

Today, slow yourself down and be alert for those who need your smile, your kind words, or your helping hand. Make kindness a centerpiece of your dealings with others. They will be blessed, and you will be too. Today, honor Christ by following obeying His Golden Rule. He deserves no less, and neither, for that matter, do your friends.

———

When you extend hospitality to others, you're not trying to impress people, you're trying to reflect God to them.

Max Lucado

Today's Prayer

Dear Lord, help me see the needs of those around me. Today, let me spread kind words in honor of Your Son. Let forgiveness rule my heart, and let my love for Christ be reflected through the acts of kindness that I extend to those who need the healing touch of the Master's hand. Amen

The Joys of Friendship

I thank my God upon every remembrance of you.

Philippians 1:3 NKJV

What is a friend? The dictionary defines the word friend as "a person who is attached to another by feelings of affection or personal regard." This definition is accurate, as far as it goes, but when we examine the deeper meaning of friendship, so many more descriptors come to mind: trustworthiness, loyalty, helpfulness, kindness, encouragement, humor, and cheerfulness, to mention but a few.

Today, as you consider the many blessings that God has given you, remember to thank Him for the friends He has chosen to place along your path. May you be a blessing to them, and may they richly bless you today, tomorrow, and every day that you live.

True friends don't spend time gazing into each other's eyes. They show great tenderness toward each other, but they face in the same direction, toward common projects, interest, goals, and above all, toward a common Lord.

C. S. Lewis

Today's Prayer

Dear Lord, I thank You for my friends. You have brought wonderful Christian friends into my life. Let our friendships honor You as we walk in the footsteps of Your Son. Amen

So Laugh!

A happy heart makes the face cheerful. . . .

Proverbs 15:13 NIV

Laughter is God's gift, and He intends that we enjoy it. Yet sometimes, because of the inevitable stresses of everyday life, laughter seems only a distant memory. As Christians we have every reason to be cheerful and to be thankful. Our blessings from God are beyond measure, starting, of course, with a gift that is ours for the asking, God's gift of salvation through Christ Jesus.

Few things in life are more absurd than the sight of a grumpy Christian. So today, as you go about your daily activities, approach life with a grin and a chuckle. After all, God created laughter for a reason . . . to use it. So laugh!

It is pleasing to the dear God whenever you rejoice or laugh from the bottom of your heart.

Martin Luther

Today's Prayer

Lord, when I begin to take myself or my life too seriously, let me laugh. When I rush from place to place, slow me down, Lord, and let me laugh. Put a smile on my face, dear Lord, and let me share that smile with all who cross my path . . . and let me laugh. Amen

A Terrific Tomorrow

"For I know the plans I have for you"—[this is] the Lord's declaration—
"plans for [your] welfare, not for disaster, to give you a future and a
hope."

Jeremiah 29:11 HCSB

How bright do you believe your future to be? Well, if you're a faithful believer, God has plans for you that are so bright that you'd better pack several pairs of sunglasses and a lifetime supply of sunblock!

The way that you think about your future will play a powerful role in determining how things turn out (it's called the "self-fulfilling prophecy," and it applies to everybody, including you). So here's another question: Are you expecting a terrific tomorrow, or are you dreading a terrible one? The answer to that question will have a powerful impact on the way tomorrow unfolds.

Today, as you live in the present and look to the future, remember that God has an amazing plan for you. Act—and believe—accordingly. And one more thing: don't forget the sunblock.

The pages of your past cannot be rewritten, but the pages of your tomorrows are blank.

Zig Ziglar

Today's Prayer

Dear Lord, sometimes when I think about the future, I worry. Today, I will do a better job of trusting You. You are my Father, and I will place my hope and my faith in You. Amen

A Helping Hand

Then a Samaritan traveling down the road came to where the hurt man was. When he saw the man, he felt very sorry for him. The Samaritan went to him, poured olive oil and winen on his wounds, and bandaged them. Then he put the hurt man on his own donkey and took him to an inn where he cared for him.

Luke 10:33-34 NCV

Sometimes we would like to help make the world a better place, but we're not sure how to do it. Jesus told the story of the "Good Samaritan," a man who helped a fellow traveler when no one else would. We, too, should be good Samaritans when we find people who need our help.

When bad things happen in our world, there's always something we can do. So what can you do to make God's world a better place? You can start by making your own corner of the world a little nicer place to live (by sharing kind words and good deeds). And then, you can take your concerns to God in prayer. Whether you've offered a helping hand or a heartfelt prayer, you've done a lot.

When you add value to others, you do not take anything away from yourself.

John Maxwell

Today's Prayer

Dear Lord, let me help others in every way that I can. Jesus served others; I can too. I will serve other people with my good deeds and with my prayers, today and every day. Amen

Beyond Materialism

For what will it profit a man if he gains the whole world, and loses his own soul? Or what will a man give in exchange for his soul?

Mark 8:36-37 NKJV

In our modern society, we need money to live. But as Christians, we must never make the acquisition of money the central focus of our lives. Money is a tool, but it should never overwhelm our sensibilities. The focus of life must be squarely on things spiritual, not things material.

Whenever we place our love for material possessions above our love for God—or when we yield to the countless other temptations of everyday living—we find ourselves engaged in a struggle between good and evil. Let us respond to this struggle by freeing ourselves from that subtle yet powerful temptation: the temptation to love the world more than we love God.

———

The cross is laid on every Christian. It begins with the call to abandon the attachments of this world.

Dietrich Bonhoeffer

Today's Prayer

Lord, my greatest possession is my relationship with You through Jesus Christ. You have promised that, when I first seek Your kingdom and Your righteousness, You will give me whatever I need. Let me trust You completely, Lord, for my needs, both material and spiritual, this day and always. Amen

Discipline Yourself

Discipline yourself for the purpose of godliness.

1 Timothy 4:7 NASB

Are you a self-disciplined person? If so, congratulations . . . your disciplined approach to life can help you build a more meaningful relationship with God. Why? Because God expects all His believers (including you) to lead lives of disciplined obedience to Him . . . and He rewards those believers who do.

Sometimes, it's hard to be dignified and disciplined. Why? Because you live in a world where many prominent people want you to believe that dignified, self-disciplined behavior is going out of style. But don't deceive yourself: self-discipline never goes out of style.

Your greatest accomplishments will probably require plenty of work and a heaping helping of self-discipline—which, by the way, is perfectly fine with God. After all, He knows that you're up to the task, and He has big plans for you. God will do His part to fulfill those plans, and the rest, of course, depends upon you.

Nothing of value is ever acquired without discipline.

Gordan MacDonald

Today's Prayer

Dear Lord, I want to be a disciplined believer. Let me use my time wisely, let me obey Your commandments faithfully, and let me worship You joyfully, today and every day. Amen

Keep an Eternal Perspective

And the world is passing away, and the lust of it; but he who does the will of God abides forever.

1 John 2:17 NKJV

For most of us, life is busy and complicated. Amid the rush and crush of the daily grind, it is easy to lose perspective . . . easy, but wrong. When our world seems to be spinning out of control, we can regain perspective by slowing ourselves down and then turning our thoughts and prayers toward God.

Do you carve out quiet moments each day to offer thanksgiving and praise to your Creator? You should. During these moments of stillness, you will often sense the love and wisdom of our Lord.

The familiar words of Psalm 46:10 remind us to "Be still, and know that I am God" (NKJV). When we do so, we encounter the awesome presence of our loving Heavenly Father, and we are blessed beyond words. But, when we ignore the presence of our Creator, we rob ourselves of His perspective, His peace, and His joy.

Today and every day, make time to be still before God. When you do, you can face the day's complications with the wisdom and power that only He can provide.

Today's Prayer

Dear Lord, when the pace of my life becomes frantic, slow me down and give me perspective. Give me the wisdom to realize that the problems of today are only temporary but that Your love is eternal. When I become discouraged, keep me steady and sure, so that I might do Your will. Amen

A Passionate Pursuit of God's Truth

But grow in the grace and knowledge of our Lord and Savior Jesus Christ. To Him be the glory both now and forever. Amen.

2 Peter 3:18 NKJV

Have you established a passionate relationship with God's Holy Word? Hopefully so. The words of Matthew 4:4 remind us that, "Man shall not live by bread alone but by every word that proceedeth out of the mouth of God" (KJV). As believers, we must study the Bible and meditate upon its meaning for our lives. Otherwise, we deprive ourselves of a priceless gift from our Creator.

Martin Luther observed, "The Bible is alive, it speaks to me; it has feet, it runs after me; it has hands, it lays hold of me. The Bible is not antique or modern. It is eternal." God's Holy Word is, indeed, an eternal, transforming, one-of-a-kind treasure. And, a passing acquaintance with the Good Book is insufficient for Christians who seek to obey God's Word and to understand His will—passionate believers must never live by bread alone . . .

Today's Prayer

Dear Lord, the Bible is Your gift to me; let me use it. When I place Your Word at the very center of my life, I am blessed. Make me a faithful student of Your Word so that I might be a faithful servant in Your world this day and every day. Amen

Building Fellowship

How good and pleasant it is when brothers can live together!

Psalm 133:1 HCSB

Fellowship with other believers should be an integral part of your everyday life. Your association with fellow Christians should be uplifting, enlightening, encouraging, and consistent.

Are you an active member of your own fellowship? Are you a builder of bridges inside the four walls of your church and outside it? Do you contribute to God's glory by contributing your time and your talents to a close-knit band of believers? Hopefully so. The fellowship of believers is intended to be a powerful tool for spreading God's Good News and uplifting His children. And God intends for you to be a fully contributing member of that fellowship. Your intentions should be the same.

———

Christian brotherhood is not an ideal which we must realize; it is rather a reality created by God in Christ in which we may participate.

Dietrich Bonhoeffer

Today's Prayer

Heavenly Father, You have given me a community of supporters called the church. Let our fellowship be a reflection of the love we feel for each other and the love we feel for You. Amen

Beyond Bitterness

Don't insist on getting even; that's not for you to do. "I'll do the judging," says God. "I'll take care of it."

Romans 12:19 MSG

Bitterness is a spiritual sickness. It will consume your soul; it is dangerous to your emotional health. It can destroy you if you let it . . . so don't let it!

If you are caught up in intense feelings of anger or resentment, you know all too well the destructive power of these emotions. How can you rid yourself of these feelings? First, you must prayerfully ask God to cleanse your heart. Then, you must learn to catch yourself whenever thoughts of bitterness or hatred begin to attack you. Your challenge is this: You must learn to resist negative thoughts before they hijack your emotions.

Matthew 5:22 teaches us that if we judge our brothers and sisters, we, too, will be subject to judgement. Let us refrain, then, from judging our neighbors. Instead, let us forgive them and love them, while leaving their judgement to a far more capable authority: the One who sits on His throne in Heaven.

Today's Prayer

Dear Lord, free me from the poison of bitterness and the futility of blame. Let me turn away from destructive emotions so that I may know the perfect peace and the spiritual abundance that can, and should, be mine. Amen

The Futility of Blaming Others

Walking down the street, Jesus saw a man blind from birth. His disciples asked, "Rabbi, who sinned: this man or his parents, causing him to be born blind?" Jesus said, "You're asking the wrong question. You're looking for someone to blame. There is no such cause-effect here. Look instead for what God can do."

John 9:1-3 MSG

To blame others for our own problems is the height of futility. Yet blaming others is a favorite human pastime. Why? Because blaming is much easier than fixing, and criticizing others is so much easier than improving ourselves. So instead of solving our problems legitimately (by doing the work required to solve them) we are inclined to fret, to blame, and to criticize, while doing precious little else. When we do, our problems, quite predictably, remain unsolved.

So, instead of looking for someone to blame, look for something to fix, and then get busy fixing it. And as you consider your own situation, remember this: God has a way of helping those who help themselves, but He doesn't spend much time helping those who don't.

Today's Prayer

Dear Lord, when I make a mistake, I want to admit it. Help me not blame others for the mistakes that I make. And when I make a mistake, help me to learn from it. Amen

You Are Blessed

I will bless them and the places surrounding my hill. I will send down showers in season; there will be showers of blessings.

Ezekiel 34:26 NIV

If you sat down and began counting your blessings, how long would it take? A very, very long time! Your blessings include life, freedom, family, friends, talents, and possessions, for starters. But, your greatest blessing—a gift that is yours for the asking—is God's gift of salvation through Christ Jesus.

Today, begin making a list of your blessings. You most certainly will not be able to make a complete list, but take a few moments and jot down as many blessings as you can. Then give thanks to the giver of all good things: God. His love for you is eternal, as are His gifts. And it's never too soon—or too late—to offer Him thanks.

———————

Blessings can either humble us and draw us closer to God or allow us to become full of pride and self-sufficiency.

Jim Cymbala

Today's Prayer

Lord, I have more blessings than I can possibly count; make me mindful of Your precious gifts. You have cared for me, Lord, and You have saved me. I will give thanks and praise You always. Today, let me share Your blessings with others, just as You first shared them with me. Amen

Ultimate Accountability

We encouraged, comforted, and implored each one of you to walk worthy of God, who calls you into His own kingdom and glory.

1 Thessalonians 2:12 HCSB

For most of us, it is a daunting thought: one day, perhaps soon, we'll come face-to-face with our Heavenly Father, and we'll be called to account for our actions here on earth. Our personal histories will certainly not be surprising to God; He already knows everything about us. But the full scope of our activities may be surprising to us: some of us will be pleasantly surprised; others will not be.

Today, do whatever you can to ensure that your thoughts and your deeds are pleasing to your Creator. Because you will, at some point in future, be called to account for your actions. And the future may be sooner than you think.

The measure of a man is not what he does on Sunday, but rather who he is Monday through Saturday.

Anonymous

Today's Prayer

Dear Lord, let my words and actions show the world the changes that You have made in my life. You sent Your Son so that I might have abundant life and eternal life. Thank You, Father, for my Savior, Christ Jesus. I will follow Him, honor Him, and share His Good News, this day and every day. Amen

Born Again

You have been born again, and this new life did not come from something that dies, but from something that cannot die. You were born again through God's living message that continues forever.

1 Peter 1:23 NCV

Why did Christ die on the cross? Christ sacrificed His life so that we might be born again. This gift, freely given from God's only begotten Son, is the priceless possession of everyone who accepts Him as Lord and Savior.

Let us claim Christ's gift today. Let us walk with the Savior, let us love Him, let us praise Him, and let us share His message of salvation with all those who cross our paths.

The comforting words of Ephesians 2:8 make God's promise clear: "For by grace you have been saved through faith, and that not of yourselves; it is the gift of God" (NKJV). Thus, we are saved not because of our good deeds but because of our faith in Christ. May we, who have been given so much, praise our Savior for the gift of salvation, and may we share the joyous news of our Master's limitless love with our families, with our friends, and with the world.

Today's Prayer

Lord, when I accepted Jesus as my personal Savior, You changed me forever and made me whole. I was born again. Help me to share Your Son's message with my friends. You are a God of love, redemption, conversion, and salvation. I will praise You today and forever. Amen

A Walk with God

I have set you an example that you should do as I have done for you.

John 13:15 NIV

Each day, we are confronted with countless opportunities to serve God and to follow in the footsteps of His Son. When we do, our Heavenly Father guides our steps and blesses our endeavors. As citizens of a fast-changing world, we face challenges that sometimes leave us feeling overworked, overcommitted, and overwhelmed. But God has different plans for us. He intends that we slow down long enough to praise Him and to glorify His Son. When we do, He lifts our spirits and enriches our lives.

Today provides a glorious opportunity to place yourself in the service of the One who is the Giver of all blessings. May you seek His will, may you trust His word, and may you walk in the footsteps of His Son.

Teach a man a rule and you help him solve a problem; teach a man to walk with God and you help him solve the rest of his life.

John Eldredge

Today's Prayer

Dear Jesus, because I am Your disciple, I will trust You, I will obey Your teachings, and I will share Your Good News. You have given me life abundant and life eternal, and I will follow You today and forever. Amen

Doers of the Word

But prove yourselves doers of the word, and not merely hearers who delude themselves.

James 1:22 NASB

The old saying is both familiar and true: actions speak louder than words. And as believers, we must beware: our actions should always give credence to the changes that Christ can make in the lives of those who walk with Him.

God calls upon each of us to act in accordance with His will and with respect for His commandments. If we are to be responsible believers, we must realize that it is never enough simply to hear the instructions of God; we must also live by them. And it is never enough to wait idly by while others do God's work here on earth; we, too, must act. Doing God's work is a responsibility that each of us must bear, and when we do, our loving Heavenly Father rewards our efforts with a bountiful harvest.

Action springs not from thought, but from a readiness for responsibility.

Dietrich Bonhoeffer

Today's Prayer

Dear Lord, I have heard Your Word, and I have felt Your presence in my heart; let me act accordingly. Let my words and deeds serve as a testimony to the changes You have made in my life. Let me praise You, Father, by following in the footsteps of Your Son, and let others see Him through me. Amen

The Right Kind of Behavior

This is how we are sure that we have come to know Him: by keeping His commands.

1 John 2:3 HCSB

When we seek righteousness in our own lives—and when we seek the companionship of those who do likewise—we reap the spiritual rewards that God intends for us to enjoy. When we behave ourselves as godly men, we honor God. When we live righteously and according to God's commandments, He blesses us in ways that we cannot fully understand.

Today, as you fulfill your responsibilities, hold fast that which is good, and associate yourself with believers who behave themselves in like fashion. When you do, your good works will serve as a powerful example for others and as a worthy offering to your Creator.

A pure theology and a loose morality will never mix.

C. H. Spurgeon

Today's Prayer

Dear Lord, this world has countless temptations, distractions, interruptions, and frustrations. When I allow my focus to drift away from You and Your Word, I suffer. But, when I turn my thoughts and my prayers to You, Heavenly Father, You guide my path. Let me discover the right thing to do—and let me do it—this day and every day that I live. Amen

A Man of Prayer

Rejoice always, pray without ceasing, in everything give thanks; for this is the will of God in Christ Jesus for you.

1 Thessalonians 5:16-18 NKJV

Is prayer an integral part of your daily life, or is it a hit-or-miss habit? Do you "pray without ceasing," or is your prayer life an afterthought? Do you regularly pray in the solitude of the early morning darkness, or do you lower your head only when others are watching? The answer to these questions will determine the direction of your day—and your life.

So here's your challenge: pray without ceasing. Begin your prayers early in the morning and continue them throughout the day. And remember this: God does answer your prayers, but He's not likely to answer those prayers until you've prayed them.

Prayer is the most important tool for your mission to the world. People may refuse our love or reject our message, but they are defenseless against our prayers.

Rick Warren

Today's Prayer

Lord, give me the wisdom to consult You often; give me the insight to hear Your voice; and give me the courage to follow Your path, this day and every day. Amen

Rejoice!

Rejoice in the Lord always. Again I will say, rejoice!

Philippians 4:4 NKJV

Oswald Chambers correctly observed, "Joy is the great note all throughout the Bible." But, even the most dedicated Christians can, on occasion, forget to celebrate each day for what it is: a priceless gift from God.

Today, let us celebrate life as God intended. Today, let us share the Good News of Jesus Christ. Today, let us put smiles on our faces, kind words on our lips, and songs in our hearts. Let us be generous with our praise and free with our encouragement. And then, when we have celebrated life to the full, let us invite others to do likewise. After all, this is God's day, and He has given us clear instructions for its use. We are commanded to rejoice and be glad. So, with no further ado, let the celebration begin.

———

Let God have you, and let God love you—and don't be surprised if your heart begins to hear music you've never heard and your feet learn to dance as never before.

Max Lucado

Today's Prayer

Dear Lord, let me celebrate this moment and every moment of life. Let me celebrate You and Your marvelous creation, Father, and let me give thanks for this day. Today is Your gift to me, Lord. Let me use it to Your glory while giving all the praise to You. Amen

Eternal Perspective

Our Savior Jesus poured out new life so generously. God's gift has restored our relationship with him and given us back our lives. And there's more life to come—an eternity of life!

Titus 3:6-7 MSG

As mere mortals, our vision for the future, like our lives here on earth, is limited. God's vision is not burdened by such limitations: His plans extend throughout all eternity. Thus, God's plans for you are not limited to the ups and downs of everyday life. Your Heavenly Father has bigger things in mind . . . much bigger things.

Christ sacrificed His life on the cross so that we might have eternal life. This gift, freely given by God's only begotten Son, is the priceless possession of everyone who accepts Him as Lord and Savior. So, when you encounter troubles, keep things in perspective. Although you will experience occasional defeats in this world, you'll have all eternity to celebrate the ultimate victory in the next.

All that is not eternal is eternally out of date.

C. S. Lewis

Today's Prayer

I know, Lord, this world is not my home; I am only here for a short time. You have given me the priceless gift of eternal life through Your Son Jesus. Keep the promise of Heaven in my heart, and help me to pass through this world with joy, with perspective, with thanksgiving, and with praise on my lips for You. Amen

In His Hands

For whatever is born of God overcomes the world. And this is the victory that has overcome the world—our faith.

1 John 5:4 NKJV

The first element of a successful life is faith: faith in God, faith in His Son, and faith in His promises. If we place our lives in God's hands, our faith is rewarded in ways that we—as human beings with clouded vision and limited understanding—can scarcely comprehend. But, if we seek to rely solely upon our own resources, or if we seek earthly success outside the boundaries of God's commandments, we reap a bitter harvest for ourselves and for our loved ones.

Do you desire the abundance and success that God has promised? Then trust Him today and every day that you live. Then, when you have entrusted your future to the Giver of all things good, rest assured that your future is secure, not only for today, but also for all eternity.

Every man lives by faith, the nonbeliever as well as the saint; the one by faith in natural laws and the other by faith in God.

A. W. Tozer

Today's Prayer

Father, in the dark moments of my life, help me to remember that You are always near and that You can overcome any challenge. Keep me mindful of Your love and Your power, so that I may live courageously and faithfully today and every day. Amen

Courage During Times of Change

Therefore don't worry about tomorrow, because tomorrow will worry about itself. Each day has enough trouble of its own.

Matthew 6:34 HCSB

Are you anxious about situations that you cannot control? Take your anxieties to God. Are you troubled about changes that threaten to disrupt your life? Take your troubles to Him. Does your corner of the world seem to be trembling beneath your feet? Seek protection from the One who cannot be moved.

The same God who created the universe will protect you if you ask Him . . . so ask Him . . . and then serve Him with willing hands and a trusting heart. And rest assured that the world may change moment by moment, but God's love endures—unfathomable and unchanging—forever.

When we are young, change is a treat, but as we grow older, change becomes a threat. But when Jesus Christ is in control of your life, you need never fear change or decay.

Warren Wiersbe

Today's Prayer

Dear Lord, help me become the person I can be and should be. Guide me along a path of Your choosing, and let me follow in the footsteps of Your Son, today and every day. Amen

God's Voice

For this is commendable, if because of conscience toward God one endures grief, suffering wrongfully.

1 Peter 2:19 NKJV

Billy Graham correctly observed, "Most of us follow our conscience as we follow a wheelbarrow. We push it in front of us in the direction we want to go." To do so, of course, is a profound mistake. Yet all of us, on occasion, have failed to listen to the voice that God planted in our hearts, and all of us have suffered the consequences.

God gave you a conscience for a very good reason: to make your path conform to His will. Wise believers make it a practice to listen carefully to that quiet internal voice. Count yourself among that number. When your conscience speaks, listen and learn. In all likelihood, God is trying to get His message through. And in all likelihood, it is a message that you desperately need to hear.

The beginning of backsliding means your conscience does not answer to the truth.

Oswald Sanders

Today's Prayer

Dear Lord, You speak to me through the gift of Your Holy Word. And, Father, You speak to me through that still small voice that tells me right from wrong. Let me follow Your way, Lord, and, in these quiet moments, show me Your plan for this day, that I might serve You. Amen

The Love of Money

For the love of money is a root of all kinds of evil, for which some have strayed from the faith in their greediness, and pierced themselves through with many sorrows.

1 Timothy 6:10 NKJV

Our society is in love with money and the things that money can buy. God is not. God cares about people, not possessions, and so must we. We must, to the best of our abilities, love our neighbors as ourselves, and we must, to the best of our abilities, resist the mighty temptation to place possessions ahead of people.

Money, in and of itself, is not evil; worshipping money is. So today, as you prioritize matters of importance for you and yours, remember that God is almighty, but the dollar is not. If we worship God, we are blessed. But if we worship "the almighty dollar," we are inevitably punished because of our misplaced priorities—and our punishment inevitably comes sooner rather than later.

When money is in your possession, what you do with it screams loudly who you are.

Dave Ramsey

Today's Prayer

Dear Lord, I will earn money and I will use money, but I will not worship money. Give me the wisdom and the discipline to be a responsible steward of my financial resources, and let me use those resources for glory of Your kingdom. Amen

Calming Your Fears

Be not afraid; only believe.

Mark 5:36 NKJV

Most of the things we worry about will never come to pass, yet we worry still. We worry about the future and the past; we worry about finances and relationships. As we survey the landscape of our lives, we observe all manner of molehills and imagine them to be mountains.

Are you concerned about the inevitable challenges that make up the fabric of everyday life? If so, why not ask God to help you regain a clear perspective about the problems (and opportunities) that confront you? When you petition your Heavenly Father sincerely and seek His guidance, He can touch your heart, clear your vision, renew your mind, and calm your fears.

Despair is a greater sin than any of the sins which provoke it.

C. S. Lewis

Today's Prayer

Your Word reminds me, Lord, that even when I walk through the valley of the shadow of death, I need fear no evil, for You are with me. Thank You, Lord, for a perfect love that casts out fear. Let me live courageously and faithfully this day and every day. Amen

The Gift of Cheerfulness

Anxiety in a man's heart weighs it down, but a good word cheers it up.

Proverbs 12:25 HCSB

Cheerfulness is a gift that we give to others and to ourselves. And, as believers who have been saved by a risen Christ, why shouldn't we be cheerful? The answer, of course, is that we have every reason to honor our Savior with joy in our hearts, smiles on our faces, and words of celebration on our lips.

Christ promises us lives of abundance and joy if we accept His love and His grace. Yet sometimes, even the most righteous among us are beset by fits of ill temper and frustration. During these moments, we may not feel like turning our thoughts and prayers to Christ, but that's precisely what we should do. When we do so, we simply can't stay grumpy for long.

The people whom I have seen succeed best in life have always been cheerful and hopeful people who went about their business with a smile on their faces.

Charles Kingsley

Today's Prayer

Dear Lord, You have given me so many reasons to celebrate. Today, let me choose an attitude of cheerfulness. Let me be a joyful Christian, Lord, quick to smile and slow to anger. And, let me share Your goodness with all whom I meet so that Your love might shine in me and through me. Amen

Taking Risks

Is anything too hard for the Lord?

Genesis 18:14 NKJV

As we consider the uncertainties of the future, we are confronted with a powerful temptation: the temptation to "play it safe." Unwilling to move mountains, we fret over molehills. Unwilling to entertain great hopes for tomorrow, we focus on the unfairness of today. Unwilling to trust God completely, we take timid half-steps when God intends that we make giant leaps.

Today, ask God for the courage to step beyond the boundaries of your doubts. Ask Him to guide you to a place where you can realize your full potential—a place where you are freed from the fear of failure. Ask Him to do His part, and promise Him that you will do your part. Don't ask Him to lead you to a "safe" place; ask Him to lead you to the "right" place . . . and remember: those two places are seldom the same.

God is teaching me to become more and more "teachable": To keep evolving. To keep taking the risk of learning something new . . . or unlearning something old and off base.

Beth Moore

Today's Prayer

Heavenly Father, I don't want to be reckless, but I want to be totally committed to Your kingdom's work. Sometimes that will involve risk. Help me to know when I need to take sensible risks in service to my family and my service to You. Amen

A Wing and a Prayer

Be cheerful. Keep things in good repair. Keep your spirits up. Think in harmony. Be agreeable. Do all that, and the God of love and peace will be with you for sure.

2 Corinthians 13:11 MSG

Mrs. Charles E. Cowman, the author of the classic devotional text *Streams in the Desert*, wrote, "Two wings are necessary to lift our souls toward God: prayer and praise. Prayer asks. Praise accepts the answer." That's why we should find the time to lift our concerns to God in prayer, and to praise Him for all that He has done.

John Wesley observed, "Sour godliness is the devil's religion." These words remind us that pessimism and doubt are some of the most important tools that Satan uses to achieve his objectives. Our challenge, of course, is to ensure that Satan cannot use these tools on us.

Are you a cheerful Christian? You should be! And what is the best way to attain the joy that is rightfully yours? By giving Christ what is rightfully His: your heart, your soul, and your life.

Today's Prayer

Dear Lord, Your Word reminds me that this is the day that You have created; let me rejoice in it. Today, let me choose an attitude of celebration. Let me be joyful, Lord, quick to smile and slow to anger, so that others will see Your goodness in me. Amen

Choosing to Please God

I have set before you life and death, blessing and curse. Choose life so that you and your descendants may live, love the Lord your God, obey Him, and remain faithful to Him. For He is your life, and He will prolong your life in the land the Lord swore to give to your fathers Abraham, Isaac, and Jacob.

Deuteronomy 30:19-20 HCSB

Sometimes, because you're an imperfect human being, you may become so wrapped up in meeting society's expectations that you fail to focus on God's expectations. To do so is a mistake of major proportions—don't make it. Instead, seek God's guidance as you focus your energies on becoming the best "you" that you can possibly be. And, when it comes to matters of conscience, seek approval not from your peers, but from your Creator.

Whom will you try to please today: God or man? Your primary obligation is not to please imperfect men and women. Your obligation is to strive diligently to meet the expectations of an all-knowing and perfect God. Trust Him always. Love Him always. Praise Him always. And make choices that please Him. Always.

Faith is not a feeling; it is action. It is a willed choice.

Elisabeth Elliot

Today's Prayer

Dear Lord, today, I will choose to please You and only You. I will obey Your commandments, and I will praise You for Your gifts, for Your love, and for Your Son. Amen

God Is Love

He who does not love does not know God, for God is love.

1 John 4:8 NKJV

God loves you. He loves you more than you can imagine; His affection is deeper than you can fathom. God made you in His own image and gave you salvation through the person of His Son Jesus Christ. And as a result, you have an important decision to make. You must decide what to do about God's love: you can return it . . . or not.

When you accept the love that flows from the heart of God, you are transformed. When you embrace God's love, you feel differently about yourself, your neighbors, your community, your church, and your world. When you open your heart to God's love, you will feel compelled to share God's message—and His compassion—with others. God's heart is overflowing—accept His love; return His love; and share His love. Today.

Often, in the midst of great problems, we stop short of the real blessing God has for us, which is a fresh vision of who He is.

Anne Graham Lotz

Today's Prayer

Lord, the Bible tells me that You are my loving Father. I thank You for Your love and for Your Son. I will praise You, I will worship You, and I will love You, dear Lord, today, tomorrow, and forever. Amen

A Relationship that Honors God

I am always praising you; all day long I honor you.

Psalm 71:8 NCV

As you think about the nature of your relationship with God, remember this: you will always have some type of relationship with Him—it is inevitable that your life must be lived in relationship to God. The question is not if you will have a relationship with Him; the burning question is whether or not that relationship will be one that seeks to honor Him.

Are you willing to place God first in your life? And, are you willing to welcome God's Son into your heart? Unless you can honestly answer these questions with a resounding yes, then your relationship with God isn't what it could be or should be. Thankfully, God is always available, He's always ready to forgive, and He's waiting to hear from you now. The rest, of course, is up to you.

A faith that hasn't been tested can't be trusted.

Adrian Rogers

Today's Prayer

Lord, I praise You from the depths of my heart, and I give thanks for Your goodness, for Your mercy, and for Your Son. Let me honor You every day of my life through my words and my deeds. Let me honor You, Father, with all that I have and all that I am. Amen

Our Ultimate Savior

And we have seen and testify that the Father has sent the Son as Savior of the world.

1 John 4:14 NKJV

Thomas Brooks spoke for believers of every generation when he observed, "Christ is the sun, and all the watches of our lives should be set by the dial of his motion." Christ, indeed, is the ultimate Savior of mankind and the personal Savior of those who believe in Him. As His servants, we should place Him at the very center of our lives. And, every day that God gives us breath, we should share Christ's love and His message with a world that needs both.

Christ is no Moses, no exactor, no giver of laws, but a giver of grace, a Savior; he is infinite mercy and goodness, freely and bountifully given to us.

Martin Luther

Today's Prayer

Dear Lord, keep me mindful of Your priceless gift: my personal Savior, Christ Jesus. Father, You loved me before I was ever born, and You will love me throughout eternity. In return, let me offer my life to You so that I might live according to Your commandments and according to Your plan. Let me always praise You, Lord, as I give thanks for Your Son Jesus and for Your everlasting love. Amen

Obedience Now

This is how we are sure that we have come to know Him: by keeping His commands.

1 John 2:3 HCSB

In order to enjoy a deeper relationship with God, you must strive diligently to live in accordance with His commandments. But there's a problem—you live in a world that seeks to snare your attention and lead you away from God.

Because you are an imperfect mortal being, you cannot be perfectly obedient, nor does God expect you to be. What is required, however, is a sincere desire to be obedient coupled with an awareness of sin and a willingness to distance yourself from it as soon as you encounter it.

Are you willing to conform your behavior to God's rules? Hopefully, you can answer that question with a resounding yes. Otherwise, you'll never experience a full measure of the blessings that the Creator gives to those who obey Him.

We grow spiritually as our Lord grew physically: by a life of simple, unobtrusive obedience.

Oswald Chambers

Today's Prayer

Heavenly Father, I want to grow closer to You each day. I know that obedience to Your will strengthens my relationship with You, so help me to follow Your commandments and obey Your Word today . . . and every day of my life. Amen

His Rightful Place

You shall have no other gods before Me.

Exodus 20:3 NKJV

When Jesus was tempted by Satan, the Master's response was unambiguous. Jesus chose to worship the Lord and serve Him only. We, as followers of Christ, must follow in His footsteps by placing God first.

When we place God in a position of secondary importance, we do ourselves great harm. When we allow temptations or distractions to come between us and our Creator, we suffer. But, when we imitate Jesus and place the Lord in His rightful place—at the center of our lives—then we claim spiritual treasures that will endure forever.

I am of the opinion that we should not be concerned about working for God until we have learned the meaning and delight of worshipping Him.

A. W. Tozer

Today's Prayer

Lord, You have commanded that I have no gods before You. Let me place You first in my heart, Father, and let me accept the salvation of Your Son Jesus. Then, let me encourage others to accept Your love and Your grace. Amen

Blessed Beyond Measure

May the Lord bless you and keep you. May the Lord show you his kindness and have mercy on you.

Numbers 6:24-25 NCV

Have you counted your blessings lately? You should. Of course, God's gifts are too numerous to count, but as a grateful Christian, you should attempt to count them nonetheless. Your blessings include life, family, friends, talents, and possessions, for starters. And your greatest gift—a treasure that was paid for on the cross and is yours for the asking—is God's gift of salvation through Christ Jesus.

As believing Christians, we have all been blessed beyond measure. Thus, thanksgiving should become a habit, a regular part of our daily routines. Today, let us pause and thank our Creator for His blessings. And let us demonstrate our gratitude to the Giver of all things good by using His gifts for the glory of His kingdom.

We prevent God from giving us the great spiritual gifts He has in store for us, because we do not give thanks for daily gifts.

Dietrich Bonhoeffer

Today's Prayer

Lord, You have given me so much, and I am thankful. I know that every good thing You give me is to be shared with others. I give thanks for Your gifts . . . and I will share them. Amen

Believing Makes a Difference

You love Him, though you have not seen Him. And though not seeing Him now, you believe in Him and rejoice with inexpressible and glorious joy, because you are receiving the goal of your faith, the salvation of your souls.

1 Peter 1:8-9 HCSB

If you'd like to partake in the peace that only God can give, make certain that your actions are guided by His Word. And while you're at it, pay careful attention to the conscience that God, in His infinite wisdom, has placed in your heart. Don't treat your faith as if it were separate from your everyday life. Weave your beliefs into the very fabric of your day. When you do, God will honor your good works, and your good works will honor God.

If you seek to be a responsible believer, you must realize that it is never enough to hear the instructions of God; you must also live by them. And it is never enough to wait idly by while others do God's work here on earth; you, too, must act. Doing God's work is a responsibility that every Christian (including you) should bear. And when you do, your loving Heavenly Father will reward your efforts with a bountiful harvest.

Today's Prayer

Dear Lord, I will stand up for my beliefs, and I will honor You with my thoughts, my actions, and my prayers. And I will worship You, Father, with thanksgiving in my heart, this day and forever. Amen

The Simple Life

Whoever becomes simple and elemental again, like this child, will rank high in God's kingdom.

Matthew 18:4 MSG

You live in a world where simplicity is in short supply. Think for a moment about the complexity of your everyday life and compare it to the lives of your ancestors. Certainly, you are the beneficiary of many technological innovations, but those innovations have a price: in all likelihood, your world is highly complex.

Unless you take firm control of your time and your life, you may be overwhelmed by an ever-increasing tidal wave of complexity that threatens your happiness. But your Heavenly Father understands the joy of living simply, and so should you. So do yourself a favor: keep your life as simple as possible. Simplicity is, indeed, genius. By simplifying your life, you are destined to improve it.

It is part of Satan's program to make our faith complicated and involved. Now and then, we need a rediscovery of the simplicity that is in Christ and in our faith in Him.

Vance Havner

Today's Prayer

Lord, help me keep it simple. When I complicate my life, give me the wisdom to simplify. The world values complexity, Father, but You do not. Today, I will strive to keep my thoughts focused intently on Your Word, on Your love, and on Your Son. Amen

Honoring God

Honor the Lord with your possessions, and with the firstfruits of all your increase; so your barns will be filled with plenty.

Proverbs 3:9-10 NKJV

Whom will you choose to honor today? If you honor God and place Him at the center of your life, every day is a cause for celebration. But if you fail to honor your Heavenly Father, you're asking for trouble, and lots of it.

At times, your life is probably hectic, demanding, and complicated. When the demands of life leave you rushing from place to place with scarcely a moment to spare, you may fail to pause and thank your Creator for the blessings He has bestowed upon you. But that's a big mistake. So honor God for who He is and for what He has done for you. And don't just honor Him on Sunday morning. Praise Him all day long, every day, for as long as you live . . . and then for all eternity.

God shows unbridled delight when He sees people acting in ways that honor Him.

Bill Hybels

Today's Prayer

I praise You, Lord, from the depths of my heart, and I give thanks for Your goodness, for Your mercy, and for Your Son. Let me honor You every day of my life through my words and my deeds. Let me honor You, Father, with all that I am. Amen

Living in Christ's Love

So now, little children, remain in Him, so that when He appears we
may have boldness and not be ashamed before Him at His coming.

1 John 2:28-29 HCSB

Even though we are imperfect, fallible human beings, even though we have fallen far short of God's commandments, Christ loves us still. His love is perfect and steadfast; it does not waver—it does not change. Our task, as believers, is to accept Christ's love and to encourage others to do likewise.

In today's troubled world, we all need the love and the peace that is found through the Son of God. Thankfully, Christ's love has no limits; it can encircle all of us. And it's up to each of us to ensure that it does.

If you come to Christ, you will always have the option of an ever-present friend. You don't have to dial long-distance. He'll be with you every step of the way.

Bill Hybels

Today's Prayer

Dear Jesus, I know that You love me today and that You will love me forever. And I thank You for Your love . . . today and forever. Amen

His Power and Yours

Therefore we were buried with Him by baptism into death, in order that, just as Christ was raised from the dead by the glory of the Father, so we too may walk in a new way of life.

Romans 6:4 HCSB

When you invite Christ to rule over your heart, you avail yourself of His power. And make no mistake about it: You and Christ, working together, can do miraculous things. In fact, miraculous things are exactly what Christ intends for you to do, but He won't force you to do great things on His behalf. The decision to become a full-fledged participant in His power is a decision that you must make for yourself.

The words of John 14:12 make this promise: when you put absolute faith in Christ, you can share in His power. Today, trust the Savior's promise and expect a miracle in His name.

The Christian life is not simply following principles but being empowered to fulfill our purpose: knowing and exalting Christ.

Franklin Graham

Today's Prayer

Dear Lord, Your Son died for the salvation of all men, and He died for me. Through the power of Christ, I can be compassionate, courageous, and strong. Help me use that power, Father, for the glory of Your kingdom, today and forever. Amen

Praise Him

Praise the Lord! Oh, give thanks to the Lord, for He is good! For His mercy endures forever.

Psalm 106:1 NKJV

Sometimes, in our rush "to get things done," we simply don't stop long enough to pause and thank our Creator for the countless blessings He has bestowed upon us. But when we slow down and express our gratitude to the One who made us, we enrich our own lives and the lives of those around us.

Thanksgiving should become a habit, a regular part of our daily routines. God has blessed us beyond measure, and we owe Him everything, including our eternal praise. Let us praise Him today, tomorrow, and throughout eternity.

Most of the verses written about praise in God's Word were voiced by people faced with crushing heartaches, injustice, treachery, slander, and scores of other difficult situations.

Joni Eareckson Tada

Today's Prayer

Heavenly Father, today and every day I will praise You. I will praise You with my thoughts, my prayers, my words, and my deeds . . . now and forever. Amen

Building His Church

For we are God's fellow workers; you are God's field, you are God's building.

1 Corinthians 3:9 NKJV

The church belongs to God; it is His just as certainly as we are His. When we help build God's church, we bear witness to the changes that He has made in our lives.

Today and every day, let us worship God with grateful hearts and helping hands as we support the church that He has created. Let us witness to our friends, to our families, and to the world. When we do so, we bless others—and we are blessed by the One who sent His Son to die so that we might have eternal life.

Only participation in the full life of a local church builds spiritual muscle.

Rick Warren

Today's Prayer

Lord, wherever it is that we worship, You are there. Let me support Your church, let me help build Your church, and let me remember that church is not only a place, it is also a state of mind and a state of grace. Amen

Friends and Family

Iron sharpens iron, and one man sharpens another.

Proverbs 27:17 HCSB

A loving family is a treasure from God; so is a trustworthy friend. If you are a member of a close knit, supportive family, offer a word of thanks to your Creator. And if you have a close circle of trustworthy friends, consider yourself richly blessed.

Today, let us praise God for our family and for our friends. God has placed these people along our paths. Let us love them and care for them. And, let us give thanks to the Father for all the people enrich our lives. These people are, in a very real sense, gifts from God; we should treat them as such.

Perhaps the greatest treasure on earth and one of the only things that will survive this life is human relationships: old friends. We are indeed rich if we have friends. Friends who have loved us through the problems and heartaches of life. Deep, true, joyful friendships. Life is too short and eternity too long to live without old friends.

Gloria Gaither

Today's Prayer

Heavenly Father, thank You for my friends and family. Let me be a trustworthy friend to all, and let my love for You be reflected in my genuine love for them. Amen

A Life of Fulfillment

For You, O God, have tested us; You have refined us as silver is refined
. . . we went through fire and through water; but You brought us out to
rich fulfillment.

Psalm 66:10–12 NKJV

Everywhere we turn, or so it seems, the world promises fulfillment, contentment, and happiness. But the contentment that the world offers is fleeting and incomplete. Thankfully, the fulfillment that God offers is all encompassing and everlasting.

Sometimes, amid the inevitable hustle and bustle of life-here-on-earth, we can forfeit—albeit temporarily—the joy of Christ as we wrestle with the challenges of daily living. Yet God's Word is clear: fulfillment through Christ is available to all who seek it and claim it. Count yourself among that number. Seek first a personal, transforming relationship with Jesus, and then claim the joy, the fulfillment, and the spiritual abundance that the Shepherd offers His sheep.

We are never more fulfilled than when our longing for God is met by His presence in our lives.

Billy Graham

Today's Prayer

Dear Lord, when I turn my thoughts and prayers to You, I feel peace and fulfillment. But sometimes, when I am distracted by the busyness of the day, fulfillment seems far away. Today, let me trust Your will, let me follow Your commands, and let me accept Your peace. Amen

Not Enough Hours?

It is good to give thanks to the Lord, to sing praises to the Most High. It is good to proclaim your unfailing love in the morning, your faithfulness in the evening.

Psalm 92:1-2 NLT

Each day has 1,440 minutes—do you value your relationship with God enough to spend a few of those minutes with Him? He deserves that much of your time and more—is He receiving it from you? Hopefully so. But if you find that you're simply "too busy" for a daily chat with your Father in Heaven, it's time to take a long, hard look at your priorities and your values.

As you consider your plans for the day ahead, here's a tip: organize your life around this simple principle: "God first." When you place your Creator where He belongs—at the very center of your day and your life—the rest of your priorities will fall into place.

———◦———

A person with no devotional life generally struggles with faith and obedience.

Charles Stanley

Today's Prayer

Dear Lord, every day of my life is a journey with You. I will take time today to think, to pray, and to study Your Word. Guide my steps, Father, and keep me mindful that today offers yet another opportunity to celebrate Your blessings, Your love, and Your Son. Amen

Measuring Your Words

The heart of the wise teaches his mouth, and adds learning to his lips.

Proverbs 16:23 NKJV

God's Word reminds us that "Reckless words pierce like a sword, but the tongue of the wise brings healing" (Proverbs 12:18 NIV). If you seek to be a source of encouragement to friends, to family members and to coworkers, then you must measure your words carefully. And that's exactly what God wants you to do.

Today, make this promise to yourself: vow to be an honest, effective, encouraging communicator at work, at home, and everyplace in between. Speak wisely, not impulsively. Use words of kindness and praise, not words of anger or derision. Learn how to be truthful without being cruel. Remember that you have the power to heal others or to injure them, to lift others up or to hold them back. And when you learn how to lift them up, you'll soon discover that you've lifted yourself up, too.

We should ask ourselves three things before we speak: Is it true? Is it kind? Does it glorify God?

Billy Graham

Today's Prayer

Lord, You have warned me that I will be judged by the words I speak. Keep me mindful, Lord, that I have influence on many people; make me an influence for good. And, may the words that I speak today be worthy of the One who has saved me forever. Amen

Mankind's Treasure Hunt

For where your treasure is, there your heart will be also.

Luke 12:34 NKJV

All of mankind is engaged in a colossal, worldwide treasure hunt. Some people seek treasure from earthly sources, treasures such as material wealth or public acclaim; others seek God's treasures by making Him the cornerstone of their lives.

What kind of treasure hunter are you? Are you so caught up in the demands of everyday living that you sometimes allow the search for worldly treasures to become your primary focus? If so, it's time to think long and hard about what you value, and why. All the items on your daily to-do list are not created equal. That's why you must put first things first by placing God in His rightful place: first place. The world's treasures are difficult to find and difficult to keep; God's treasures are ever-present and everlasting. Which treasures, then, will you claim as your own?

The Scriptures also reveal warnings that if we are consumed with greed, not only do we disobey God, but we will miss the opportunity to allow Him to use us as instruments for others.

Charles Stanley

Today's Prayer

Heavenly Father, when I focus intently upon You, I am blessed. When I focus too intently on the acquisition of material possessions, I am troubled. Make my priorities pleasing to You, Father, and make me a worthy servant of Your Son. Amen

No Complaints

Do everything without complaining or arguing. Then you will be innocent and without any wrong.

Philippians 2:14-15 NCV

Because we are imperfect human beings, we often lose sight of our blessings. Ironically, most of us have more blessings than we can count, but we may still find reasons to complain about the minor frustrations of everyday life. To do so, of course, is not only wrong; it is also the pinnacle of shortsightedness and a serious roadblock on the path to spiritual abundance.

Are you tempted to complain about the inevitable minor frustrations of everyday living? Don't do it! Today and every day, make it a practice to count your blessings, not your hardships. It's the truly decent way to live.

I am sure it is never sadness—a proper, straight, natural response to loss—that does people harm, but all the other things, all the resentment, dismay, doubt and self-pity with which it is usually complicated.

C. S. Lewis

Today's Prayer

Lord, I know that the choice is mine—I can either count my blessings or recount my disappointments. Today, help me to focus my thoughts upon my blessings, my gifts, and my opportunities. Amen

Christ's Love Changes Everything

Your old life is dead. Your new life, which is your real life—even though invisible to spectators—is with Christ in God. He is your life.

Colossians 3:3 MSG

What does the love of Christ mean to His believers? It changes everything. His love is perfect and steadfast. Even though we are fallible, and wayward, the Good Shepherd cares for us still. Even though we have fallen far short of the Father's commandments, Christ loves us with a power and depth that is beyond our understanding. And, as we accept Christ's love and walk in Christ's footsteps, our lives bear testimony to His power and to His grace. Yes, Christ's love changes everything; may we invite Him into our hearts so it can then change everything in us.

⸻

As we are reminded through our burden of our utter weakness without Christ, we are given the strength to go on.

Mary Morrison Suggs

Today's Prayer

Dear Jesus, my life has been changed forever by Your love and sacrifice. Today I will praise You, I will honor You, and I will walk with You. Amen

The Wisdom of Moderation

Moderation is better than muscle, self-control better than political power.

Proverbs 16:32 MSG

Moderation and wisdom are traveling companions. If we are wise, we must learn to temper our appetites, our desires, and our impulses. When we do, we are blessed, in part, because God has created a world in which temperance is rewarded and intemperance is inevitably punished.

Would you like to improve your life? Then harness your appetites and restrain your impulses. Moderation is difficult, of course; it is especially difficult in a prosperous society such as ours. But the rewards of moderation are numerous and long-lasting. Claim those rewards today. No one can force you to moderate your appetites. The decision to live temperately (and wisely) is yours and yours alone. And so are the consequences.

To many, total abstinence is easier than perfect moderation.

St. Augustine

Today's Prayer

Dear Lord, give me the wisdom to be moderate and self-disciplined. Let me strive to do Your will here on earth, and as I do, let me find contentment and balance. Let me be a disciplined believer, Father, today and every day. Amen

The Voice Inside Your Head

I always do my best to have a clear conscience toward God and men.

Acts 24:16 HCSB

When you're about to do something that you know is wrong, a little voice inside your head has a way of speaking up. That voice, of course, is your conscience: an early-warning system designed to keep you out of trouble. If you listen to that voice, you'll be okay; if you ignore it, you're asking for headaches, or heartbreaks, or both.

Whenever you're about to make an important decision, you should listen carefully to the quiet voice inside. Sometimes, of course, it's tempting to do otherwise. From time to time you'll be tempted to abandon your better judgement by ignoring your conscience. But remember: a conscience is a terrible thing to waste. So instead of ignoring that quiet little voice, pay careful attention to it. If you do, your conscience will lead you in the right direction—in fact, it's trying to lead you right now. So listen . . . and learn.

———

To go against one's conscience is neither safe nor right. Here I stand. I cannot do otherwise.

Martin Luther

Today's Prayer

Dear God, You've given me a conscience that tells me right from wrong. Let me trust my conscience, and let me live according to Your teachings, not just for today, but forever. Amen

Need Courage?
God Can Handle It

Do not be afraid or discouraged, for the LORD is the one who goes before you. He will be with you; he will neither fail you nor forsake you.

Deuteronomy 31:8 NLT

Life-here-on-earth can be difficult and discouraging at times. During our darkest moments, God offers us courage and strength if we turn our hearts and our prayers to Him.

As believing Christians, we have every reason to live courageously. After all, the ultimate battle has already been fought and won on the cross at Calvary. But sometimes, because we are imperfect human beings who possess imperfect faith, we fall prey to fear and doubt. The answer to our fears, of course, is God.

The next time you find your courage tested to the limit, remember that God is as near as your next breath. He is your shield and your strength; He is your protector and your deliverer. Call upon Him in your hour of need and then be comforted. Whatever your challenge, whatever your trouble, God can handle it . . . and will!

Today's Prayer

Lord, let me turn to You for courage and for strength. You are with me always, Father, and I will face the challenges of this day with trust and assurance in You. Amen

His Awesome Creation

And to every beast of the earth and to every bird of the sky and to every thing that moves on the earth which has life . . . God saw all that He had made, and behold, it was very good.

Genesis 1:30-31 NASB

When we consider God's glorious universe, we marvel at the miracle of nature. The smallest seedlings and grandest stars are all part of God's infinite creation. God has placed His handiwork on display for all to see, and if we are wise, we will make time each day to celebrate the world that surrounds us.

Today, as you fulfill the demands of everyday life, pause to consider the majesty of Heaven and earth. It is as miraculous as it is beautiful, as incomprehensible as it is breathtaking.

The Psalmist reminds us that the heavens are a declaration of God's glory (Psalm 19:1). May we never cease to praise the Father for a universe that stands as an awesome testimony to His presence and His power.

Today you will encounter God's creation. When you see the beauty around you, let each detail remind you to lift your head in praise.

Max Lucado

Today's Prayer

Dear Lord, You have created a universe that is glorious to behold yet impossible to comprehend. I praise You for Your creation, Father, and for the sense of awe and wonder that You have placed in my heart. Amen

Contented in Him

The LORD will give strength to His people; the LORD will bless His people with peace.

Psalm 29:11 NKJV

Everywhere we turn, or so it seems, the world promises us contentment and happiness. But the contentment that the world offers is fleeting and incomplete. Thankfully, the contentment that God offers is all encompassing and everlasting.

Happiness depends less upon our circumstances than upon our thoughts. When we turn our thoughts to God, to His gifts, and to His glorious creation, we experience the joy that God intends for His children. But, when we focus on the negative aspects of life we cause ourselves needless suffering.

Do you sincerely want to be a contented Christian? Then set your mind and your heart upon God's love and His grace. Seek first the salvation that is available through a personal relationship with Jesus Christ, and then claim the joy, the contentment, and the spiritual abundance that the Shepherd offers His sheep.

Real contentment hinges on what's happening inside us, not around us.

Charles Stanley

Today's Prayer

Dear Lord, You offer me contentment and peace; let me accept Your peace. Help me to trust Your Word, to follow Your commandments, and to welcome the peace of Jesus into my heart, today and forever. Amen

Troubled Times

He shall not be afraid of evil tidings: his heart is fixed, trusting in the LORD.

Psalm 112:7 KJV

We live in a fear-based world, a world where bad new travels at light speed and good news doesn't. These are troubled times, times when we have legitimate fears for the future of our nation, our world, and our families. But as Christians, we have every reason to live courageously.

Perhaps you, like countless other believers, have found your courage tested by the anxieties and fears that are an inevitable part of 21st-century life. If so, God wants to have a little chat with you. The next time you find your courage tested to the limit, God wants to remind you that He is not just near, He is here.

Your Heavenly Father is your Protector and your Deliverer. Call upon Him in your hour of need, and be comforted. Whatever your challenge, whatever your trouble, God can handle it. And will.

Fear lurks in the shadows of every area of life. The future may look very threatening. Jesus says, "Stop being afraid. Trust me!"

Charles Swindoll

Today's Prayer

Dear Lord, when I am fearful, keep me mindful that You are my salvation. Because of You, Father, I can live courageously and faithfully this day and every day. Amen

How to Treat Others:
A Simple Rule of Thumb

Therefore, whatever you want others to do for you, do also the same for them—this is the Law and the Prophets.

Matthew 7:12 HCSB

Would you like to make the world a better place? If so, you can start by practicing the Golden Rule.

Is the Golden Rule your rule, or is it just another Bible verse that goes in one ear and out the other? Jesus made Himself perfectly clear: He instructed you to treat other people in the same way that you want to be treated. But sometimes, especially when you're feeling the pressures of everyday living, obeying the Golden Rule can seem like an impossible task—but it's not. So if you want to know how to treat other people, ask the person you see every time you look into the mirror. The answer you receive will tell you exactly what to do.

———

Good will is written into the constitution of things; ill will is sand in the machinery.

E. Stanley Jones

Today's Prayer

Lord, I thank You for friends and family members who practice the Golden Rule. Because I expect to be treated with kindness, let me be kind. Because I wish to be loved, let me be loving. In all things, Lord, let me live by the Golden Rule, and let me express my gratitude to those who offer kindness to me. Amen

Priorities . . . Moment by Moment

You can't go wrong when you love others. When you add up everything in the law code, the sum total is love. But make sure that you don't get so absorbed and exhausted in taking care of all your day-by-day obligations that you lose track of the time and doze off, oblivious to God.

Romans 13:10-11 MSG

Each waking moment holds the potential to think a creative thought or offer a heartfelt prayer. So even if you're a person with too many demands and too few hours in which to meet them, don't panic. Instead, be comforted in the knowledge that when you sincerely seek to discover God's priorities for your life, He will provide answers in marvelous and surprising ways.

Remember: this is the day that God has made and that He has filled it with countless opportunities to love, to serve, and to seek His guidance. Seize those opportunities. And as a gift to yourself, to your family, and to the world, slow down and claim the inner peace that is your spiritual birthright: the peace of Jesus Christ. It is yours for the asking. So ask . . . and be thankful.

Today's Prayer

Dear Lord, when the demands of the day leave me distracted and discouraged, let me accept the spiritual abundance that is mine through Christ, let me share His message and His love with all who cross my path. Amen

The Battle Has Been Won

Cast your burden upon the Lord and He will sustain you: He will never allow the righteous to be shaken.

Psalm 55:22 NASB

Christians have every reason to live courageously. After all, the ultimate battle has already been won on the cross at Calvary. But even dedicated followers of Christ may find their courage tested by the inevitable disappointments and fears that visit the lives of believers and non-believers alike.

When you find yourself worried about the challenges of today or the uncertainties of tomorrow, you must ask yourself whether or not you are ready to place your concerns and your life in God's all-powerful, all-knowing, all-loving hands. If the answer to that question is yes—as it should be—then you can draw courage today from the source of strength that never fails: your Heavenly Father.

Seeing that a Pilot steers the ship in which we sail, who will never allow us to perish even in the midst of shipwrecks, there is no reason why our minds should be overwhelmed with fear and overcome with weariness.

John Calvin

Today's Prayer

Lord, sometimes, this world can be a fearful place, but You have promised me that You are with me always. Today, Lord, I will live courageously as I place my trust in Your everlasting power and my faith in Your everlasting love. Amen

God's Timetable

Therefore humble yourselves under the mighty hand of God, that He may exalt you in due time.

1 Peter 5:6 NKJV

Sometimes, the hardest thing to do is to wait. This is especially true when we're in a hurry and when we want things to happen now, if not sooner! But God's plan does not always happen in the way that we would like or at the time of our own choosing. Our task—as believing Christians who trust in a benevolent, all knowing Father—is to wait patiently for God to reveal Himself.

We human beings are, by nature, impatient. We know what we want, and we know exactly when we want it: RIGHT NOW! But, God knows better. He has created a world that unfolds according to His own timetable, not ours . . . thank goodness!

He has the right to interrupt your life. He is Lord. When you accepted Him as Lord, you gave Him the right to help Himself to your life anytime He wants.

Henry Blackaby

Today's Prayer

Dear Lord, Your timing is always right for me. You have a plan for my life that is grander than I can imagine. When I am impatient, remind me that You are never early or late. You are always on time, Father, so let me trust in You . . . always. Amen

Mountaintops and Valleys

I sought the Lord, and He answered me and delivered me from all my fears.

Psalm 34:4 HCSB

Every life (including yours) is an unfolding series of events: some fabulous, some not-so-fabulous, and some downright disheartening. When you reach the mountaintops of life, praising God is easy. But, when the storm clouds form overhead, your faith will be tested, sometimes to the breaking point. As a believer, you can take comfort in this fact: Wherever you find yourself, whether at the top of the mountain or the depths of the valley, God is there, and because He cares for you, you can live courageously.

The next time you find your courage tested to the limit, remember that God is your shield and your strength; He is your protector and your deliverer. Call upon Him in your hour of need and He will protect you.

There comes a time when we simply have to face the challenges in our lives and stop backing down.

John Eldredge

Today's Prayer

Dear Lord, when I am fearful or worried, give me courage, perspective, and wisdom. In every circumstance, I will trust You to guide me and protect me, now and forever. Amen

Happiness and Holiness

Happy are the people who live at your Temple . . . . Happy are those whose strength comes from you.

Psalm 84:4-5 NKJV

Do you seek happiness, abundance, and contentment? If so, here are some things you should do: Love God and His Son; depend upon God for strength; try, to the best of your abilities, to follow God's will; and strive to obey His Holy Word. When you do these things, you'll discover that happiness goes hand-in-hand with righteousness. The happiest people are not those who rebel against God; the happiest people are those who love God and obey His commandments.

What does life have in store for you? A world full of possibilities (of course it's up to you to seize them), and God's promise of abundance (of course it's up to you to accept it). Your Creator has blessed you beyond measure. Honor Him with your prayers, your words, your deeds, and your joy.

God saved us to make us holy, not happy.

Vance Havner

Today's Prayer

Dear Lord, You are my strength and my joy. I will rejoice in the day that You have made, and I will give thanks for the countless blessings that You have given me. Let me be a joyful Christian, Father, as I share the Good News of Your Son. Amen

Hope for the Journey

That is why we can say with confidence, "The Lord is my helper, so I will not be afraid. What can mere mortals do to me?"

Hebrews 13:6 NLT

Because we are saved by a risen Christ, we can have hope for the future, no matter how desperate our circumstances may seem. After all, God has promised that we are His throughout eternity. And, He has told us that we must place our hopes in Him.

Today, summon the courage to follow God. Even if the path seems difficult, even if your heart is fearful, trust your Heavenly Father and follow Him. Trust Him with your day and your life. Do His work, care for His children, and share His Good News. Let Him guide your steps. He will not lead you astray.

Why rely on yourself and fall? Cast yourself upon His arm. Be not afraid. He will not let you slip. Cast yourself in confidence. He will receive you and heal you.

St. Augustine

Today's Prayer

Dear Lord, when I am fearful, I will lean upon You. Keep me ever mindful, Lord, that You are my God, my strength, and my shield. With You by my side, I have nothing to fear. And, with Your Son Jesus as my Savior, I have received the priceless gift of eternal life. Help me to be a grateful and courageous servant this day and every day. Amen

Temporary Setbacks

A time to weep, and a time to laugh; a time to mourn, and a time to dance....

Ecclesiastes 3:4 KJV

The occasional disappointments and failures of life are inevitable. Such setbacks are simply the price that we must occasionally pay for our willingness to take risks as we follow our dreams. But even when we encounter bitter disappointments, we must never lose faith.

When we encounter the inevitable difficulties of life-here-on-earth, God stands ready to protect us. Our responsibility, of course, is to ask Him for protection. When we call upon Him in heartfelt prayer, He will answer—in His own time and according to His own plan—and He will heal us. And, while we are waiting for God's plans to unfold and for His healing touch to restore us, we can be comforted in the knowledge that our Creator can overcome any obstacle, even if we cannot.

Goals are worth setting and worth missing. We learn from non-successes.

Bill Bright

Today's Prayer

Dear Lord, even when I'm afraid of failure, give me the courage to try. Remind me that with You by my side, I really have nothing to fear. So today, Father, I will live courageously as I place my faith in You. Amen

The Morning Watch

He awakens [Me] each morning; He awakens My ear to listen like those being instructed. The Lord God has opened My ear, and I was not rebellious; I did not turn back.

Isaiah 50:4-5 HCSB

Each new day is a gift from God, and if you are wise, you will spend a few quiet moments each morning thanking the Giver.

Warren Wiersbe writes, "Surrender your mind to the Lord at the beginning of each day." And that's sound advice. When you begin each day with your head bowed and your heart lifted, you are reminded of God's love, His protection, and His commandments. Then, you can align your priorities for the coming day with the teachings and commandments that God has placed upon your heart.

So, if you've acquired the unfortunate habit of trying to "squeeze" God into the corners of your life, it's time to reshuffle the items on your to-do list by placing God first. And if you haven't already done so, form the habit of spending quality time with your Father in hevaen. He deserves it . . . and so do you.

———◦◦◦———

Meditation is as silver; but tribulation is as fine gold.

C. H. Spurgeon

Today's Prayer

Lord, help me to hear Your direction for my life in the quiet moments of each day. Let everything that I say and do be in Your perfect will. Amen

Comforting Others

Carry one another's burdens; in this way you will fulfill the law of Christ.

Galatians 6:2 HCSB

We live in a world that is, on occasion, a frightening place. Sometimes, we sustain life-altering losses that are so profound and so tragic that it seems we could never recover. But, with God's help and with the help of encouraging family members and friends, we can recover.

In times of need, God's Word is clear: as believers, we must offer comfort to those in need by sharing not only our courage but also our faith. As the renowned revivalist Vance Havner observed, "No journey is complete that does not lead through some dark valleys. We can properly comfort others only with the comfort wherewith we ourselves have been comforted of God." Enough said.

When action-oriented compassion is absent, it's a tell-tale sign that something's spiritually amiss.

Bill Hybels

Today's Prayer

Dear Lord, this world can be a difficult place, a place full of suffering and tears. Let me give comfort to those in need, and let me share Your love with those who grieve. When I meet those who mourn, guide my speech. And when I, too, become discouraged, keep me mindful of Your infinite love. Amen

During Dark Days

I have heard your prayer, I have seen your tears; surely I will heal you.

2 Kings 20:5 NKJV

The sadness that accompanies any significant loss is an inevitable fact of life. In time, sadness runs its course and gradually abates. Depression, on the other hand, is a physical and emotional condition that is highly treatable.

If you find yourself feeling "blue," perhaps it's a logical reaction to the ups and downs of daily life. But if you or someone close to you have become dangerously depressed, it's time to seek professional help.

Some days are light and happy, and some days are not. When we face the inevitable dark days of life, we must choose how we will respond. Will we allow ourselves to sink even more deeply into our own sadness, or will we do the difficult work of pulling ourselves out? We bring light to the dark days of life by turning first to God, and then to trusted family members, friends, and medical professionals. When we do, the clouds will eventually part, and the sun will shine once more upon our souls.

Today's Prayer

Heavenly Father, Your Word promises that You will not give us more than we can bear; You have promised to lift us out of our grief and despair. Today, Lord, I pray for those who mourn, and I thank You for sustaining all of us in our dark days. Amen

A Worthy Disciple

He has told you men what is good and what it is the Lord requires of you: Only to act justly, to love faithfulness, and to walk humbly with your God.

Micah 6:8 HCSB

When Jesus addressed His disciples, He warned that each one must, "take up his cross and follow Me." The disciples must have known exactly what the Master meant. In Jesus' day, prisoners were forced to carry their own crosses to the location where they would be put to death. Thus, Christ's message was clear: in order to follow Him, Christ's disciples must deny themselves and, instead, trust Him completely. Nothing has changed since then.

If we are to be disciples of Christ, we must trust Him and place Him at the very center of our beings. Jesus never comes "next." He is always first.

Do you seek to be a worthy disciple of Christ? Then pick up His cross today and every day that you live. When you do, He will bless you now and forever.

Today's Prayer

Dear Lord, thank You for the gift of Your Son Jesus, my personal Savior. Let me be a worthy disciple of Christ, and let me be ever grateful for His love. I will praise You always, Father, as I give thanks for Your Son and for Your everlasting love. Amen

Spending Time with God Every Day

Thou shalt have no other gods before me.

Exodus 20:3 KJV

When it comes to spending time with God, are you a "squeezer" or a "pleaser"? Are you a person who squeezes God into your busy schedule with an occasional prayer before meals (and maybe with a quick visit to church on Sunday)? Or do you please God by talking to Him far more often than that? If you're wise, you'll form the habit of spending time with God every day. When you do, it will change your life.

When you begin each day with your head bowed and your heart lifted, you remind yourself of God's love, His protection, and His commandments. And if you are wise, you will use your morning prayer time to align your priorities for the coming day with the teachings and commandments of God's Holy Word.

Even if you're the busiest person on Planet Earth, you can still carve out a little time for God. And when you think about it, isn't that the very least you should do?

Today's Prayer

Dear Lord, Your love is eternal and Your laws are everlasting. When I obey Your commandments, I am blessed. Today, I invite You to reign over every corner of my heart. I will have faith in You, Father. I will sense Your presence; I will accept Your love; I will trust Your will; and I will praise You for the Savior of my life: Jesus. Amen

Serenity Now

Do not remember the former things, nor consider the things of old. Behold, I will do a new thing.

Isaiah 43:18-19 NKJV

The American theologian Reinhold Niebuhr composed a profoundly simple verse that came to be known as the Serenity Prayer: "God, grant me the serenity to accept the things I cannot change, the courage to change the things I can, and the wisdom to know the difference." Niebuhr's words are far easier to recite than they are to live by, especially for people who are fighting a serious illness. After all, most of us want life to unfold in accordance with our own wishes and timetables. But sometimes God has other plans.

If you've encountered unfortunate circumstances that seem beyond your power to control, don't give up, don't give in, and don't lose faith. Turn all your concerns over to God, and trust Him to manage the things that you can't. When you do, you can be comforted in the knowledge that your Creator is both loving and wise, and that He understands His plans perfectly, even when you do not.

Today's Prayer

Father, the events of this world unfold according to a plan that I cannot fully understand. But You understand. Help me to trust You, Lord, even when I am grieving. Help me to trust You even when I am confused. Today, in whatever circumstances I find myself, let me trust Your will and accept Your love . . . completely. Amen

Above and Beyond Our Circumstances

Should we accept only good from God and not adversity?

Job 2:10 HCSB

All of us face difficult days. Sometimes even the most devout Christians can become discouraged, and you are no exception. After all, you live in a world where expectations can be high and demands can be even higher.

If you find yourself enduring difficult circumstances, remember that God remains in His Heaven. If you become discouraged with the direction of your day or your life, turn your thoughts and prayers to Him. He is a God of possibility, not negativity. He will guide you through your difficulties and beyond them . . . far beyond.

Crisis brings us face to face with our inadequacy and our inadequacy in turn leads us to the inexhaustible sufficiency of God.

Catherine Marshall

Today's Prayer

Dear Heavenly Father, when I am troubled, You heal me. When I am afraid, You protect me. When I am discouraged, You lift me up. During the difficult days of my life, I will me trust You. And whatever my circumstances, Lord, I thank You for Your blessings, for Your love, and for Your Son. Amen

Energized for Life

Be energetic in your life of salvation, reverent and sensitive before God.
That energy is God's energy, an energy deep within you, God himself
willing and working at what will give him the most pleasure.

Philippians 2:12-13 MSG

Are you fired with enthusiasm for Christ? If so, congratulations, and keep up the good work! But, if your spiritual batteries are running low, then perhaps you're spending too much energy working for yourself and not enough energy working for God.

If you're feeling tired, or troubled, or both, don't despair. Instead, seek strength from the source that never fails; that source, of course, is your Heavenly Father. And rest assured—when you sincerely petition Him, He will give you all the strength you need to live victoriously for Him.

Where there is much prayer, there will be much of the Spirit; where there is much of the Spirit, there will be ever-increasing power.

Andrew Murray

Today's Prayer

Lord, let me find my strength in You. When I am weary, give me rest. When I feel overwhelmed, let me look to You for my priorities. Let Your power be my power, Lord, and let Your way be my way, today and forever. Amen

The Shepherd's Care

*Your righteousness reaches heaven, God, You who have done great
things; God, who is like You?*

Psalm 71:19 HCSB

It's a promise that is made over and over again in the Bible:
Whatever "it" is, God can handle it.

Life isn't always easy. Far from it! Sometimes, life can be very,
very difficult. But even then, even during our darkest moments,
we're protected by a loving Heavenly Father. When we're worried,
God can reassure us; when we're sad, God can comfort us. When
our hearts are broken, God is not just near, He is here. So we must
lift our thoughts and prayers to Him. When we do, He will answer
our prayers. Why? Because He is our shepherd, and He has promised to protect us now and forever.

He is always thinking about us. We are before his eyes. The Lord's
eye never sleeps, but is always watching out for our welfare. We are
continually on His heart.

C. H. Spurgeon

Today's Prayer

Dear Lord, when I obey Your commandments, I am blessed. Today,
I invite You to reign over my heart. I will sense Your presence,
Father; I will accept Your love; and I will praise You for the Savior
of my life: Your Son Jesus. Amen

Seeking His Will

Teach me to do Your will, for You are my God; Your Spirit is good. Lead me in the land of uprightness.

Psalm 143:10 NKJV

God has a plan for our world and our lives. God does not do things by accident; He is willful and intentional. Unfortunately for us, we cannot always understand the will of God. Why? Because we are mortal beings with limited understanding. Although we cannot fully comprehend the will of God, we should always trust the will of God.

As this day unfolds, seek God's will and obey His Word. When you entrust your life to Him without reservation, He will give you the courage to meet any challenge, the strength to endure any trial, and the wisdom to live in His righteousness and in His peace.

"If the Lord will" is not just a statement on a believer's lips; it is the constant attitude of his heart.

Warren Wiersbe

Today's Prayer

Heavenly Father, I will study Your Word and seek Your guidance. Give me the wisdom to know Your will for my life and the courage to follow wherever You may lead me, today and forever. Amen

His Generosity . . . and Yours

But God demonstrates his own love for us in this: While we were still sinners, Christ died for us.

Romans 5:8 NIV

Christ showed His love for us by willingly sacrificing His own life so that we might have eternal life. We, as Christ's followers, are challenged to share His love. And, when we walk each day with Jesus—and obey the commandments found in God's Holy Word—we are worthy ambassadors for Him.

Just as Christ has been—and will always be—the ultimate friend to His flock, so should we be Christlike in our love and generosity to those in need. When we share the love of Christ, we share a priceless gift. As His servants, we must do no less.

If we have the true love of God in our hearts, we will show it in our lives. We will not have to go up and down the earth proclaiming it. We will show it in everything we say or do.

D. L. Moody

Today's Prayer

Father, Your gifts are priceless. You gave Your Son Jesus to save us, and Your motivation was love. I pray that the gifts I give to others will come from an overflow of my heart, and that they will echo the great love You have for all of Your children. Amen

Today's Opportunities

But encourage one another day after day, as long as it is still called "Today," so that none of you will be hardened by the deceitfulness of sin.

Hebrews 3:13 NASB

The 118th Psalm reminds us, "This is the day which the Lord hath made; we will rejoice and be glad in it" (v. 24 KJV). As we rejoice in this day that the Lord has given us, let us remember that an important part of today's celebration is the time we spend celebrating others. Each day provides countless opportunities to encourage others and to praise their good works. When we do, we not only spread seeds of joy and happiness, we also follow the commandments of God's Holy Word.

How can we build others up? By celebrating their victories and their accomplishments. So look for the good in others and celebrate the good that you find. When you do, you'll be a powerful force of encouragement in the world . . . and a worthy servant to your God.

━━━━━━

A lot of people have gone further than they thought they could because someone else thought they could.

Zig Ziglar

Today's Prayer

Dear Lord, You have blessed all of Your children with special gifts and talents. Today, help me to use the talents You have given me, and in turn, let me help others find the strength and courage to use their gifts according to Your master plan. Amen

Filled with the Spirit

Don't be drunk with wine, because that will ruin your life. Instead, let the Holy Spirit fill and control you.

Ephesians 5:18 NLT

When you are filled with the Holy Spirit, your words and deeds will reflect a love and devotion to Christ. When you are filled with the Holy Spirit, the steps of your life's journey are guided by the Lord. When you allow God's Spirit to work in you and through you, you will be energized and transformed.

Today, allow yourself to be filled with the Spirit of God. And then stand back in amazement as God begins to work miracles in your own life and in the lives of those you love.

———

The Holy Spirit is like a living and continually flowing fountain in believers. We have the boundless privilege of tapping into that fountain every time we pray.

Shirley Dobson

Today's Prayer

Dear Lord, You are my sovereign God. Your Son defeated death; Your Holy Spirit comforts and guides me. Let me celebrate all Your gifts, Father, and let me be a hope-filled Christian today and every day. Amen

Richly Blessed

So let each one give as he purposes in his heart, not grudgingly or of necessity; for God loves a cheerful giver.

2 Corinthians 9:7 NKJV

God's Word commands us to be generous, compassionate servants to those who need our support. As believers, we have been richly blessed by our Creator. We, in turn, are called to share our gifts, our possessions, our testimonies, and our talents.

The theme of generosity is one of the cornerstones of Christ's teachings. If we are to be disciples of Christ, we, too, must be cheerful, generous, courageous givers. Our Savior expects no less from us. And He deserves no less.

———⚬———

Think of the blessings we so easily take for granted: Life itself; preservation from danger; every bit of health we enjoy; every hour of liberty; the ability to see, to hear, to speak, to think, and to imagine all this comes from the hand of God.

Billy Graham

Today's Prayer

Lord, You loved me before I was ever born; You sent Your Son Jesus to redeem me from my sins; You have given me the gift of eternal life. Today, I will share the priceless blessings that I have received: I will share my joy, my possessions, and my faith with others. Amen

Defeating Discouragement

The LORD himself goes before you and will be with you; he will never leave you nor forsake you. Do not be afraid; do not be discouraged.

Deuteronomy 31:8 NIV

When we fail to meet the expectations of others (or, for that matter, the expectations that we have set for ourselves), we may be tempted to abandon hope. Thankfully, on those cloudy days when our strength is sapped and our faith is shaken, there exists a source from which we can draw courage and wisdom. That source is God.

When we seek to form a more intimate and dynamic relationship with our Creator, He renews our spirits and restores our souls. God's promise is made clear in Isaiah 40:31: "But those who wait on the Lord shall renew their strength; they shall mount up with wings like eagles, they shall run and not be weary, they shall walk and not faint" (NKJV). And upon this promise we can—and should—depend.

Today's Prayer

Dear Lord, when I am discouraged, give me perspective and faith. When I am weak, give me strength. When I am fearful, give me courage for the day ahead. I will trust in Your promises, Father, and I will live with the assurance that You are with me not only for this day, but also throughout all eternity. Amen

Dream Big

With God's power working in us, God can do much, much more than anything we can ask or imagine.

Ephesians 3:20 NCV

Are you willing to entertain the possibility that God has big plans in store for you? Hopefully so. Yet sometimes, especially if you've recently experienced a life-altering disappointment, you may find it difficult to envision a brighter future for yourself and your family. If so, it's time to reconsider your own capabilities . . . and God's.

Your Heavenly Father created you with unique gifts and un-tapped talents; your job is to tap them. When you do, you'll begin to feel an increasing sense of confidence in yourself and in your future. So even if you're experiencing difficult days, don't abandon your dreams. Instead, trust that God is preparing you for greater things.

To make your dream come true, you have to stay awake.

Dennis Swanberg

Today's Prayer

Dear Lord, give me the courage to dream and the faithfulness to trust in Your perfect plan. When I am worried or weary, give me strength for today and hope for tomorrow. Keep me mindful of Your healing power, Your infinite love, and Your eternal salvation. Amen

The Remedy for Uncertainty

He replied, "You of little faith, why are you so afraid?" Then he got up and rebuked the winds and the waves, and it was completely calm.

Matthew 8:26 NIV

Sometimes, like Jesus' disciples, we feel threatened by the storms of life. During these moments, when we our hearts are flooded with uncertainty, we must remember that God is not simply near, He is here.

Have you ever felt your faith in God slipping away? If so, you are in good company. Even the most faithful Christians are, at times, beset by occasional bouts of discouragement and doubt. But even when you feel far removed from God, God never leaves your side. He is always with you, always willing to calm the storms of life. When you sincerely seek His presence—and when you genuinely seek to establish a deeper, more meaningful relationship with His Son—God will calm your fears, answer your prayers, and restore your soul.

Today's Prayer

Dear God, sometimes this world can be a puzzling place, filled with uncertainty and doubt. When I am unsure of my next step, keep me mindful that You are always near and that You can overcome any challenge. With Your love and Your power, Father, I can live courageously and faithfully, today and every day. Amen

Saying Yes to God

Cast your burden on the Lord, and He will support you; He will never allow the righteous to be shaken.

Psalm 55:22 HCSB

Your decision to seek a deeper relationship with God will not remove all problems from your life; to the contrary, it will bring about a series of personal crises as you constantly seek to say "yes" to God although the world encourages you to do otherwise. You live in a world that seeks to snare your attention and lead you away from God. Each time you are tempted to distance yourself from the Creator, you will face a spiritual crisis. A few of these crises may be monumental in scope, but most will be the small, everyday decisions of life. In fact, life here on earth can be seen as one test after another—and with each crisis comes yet another opportunity to grow closer to God . . . or to distance yourself from His plan for your life.

Today, as you serve on the front lines of life, you will face many opportunities to say "yes" to your Creator—and you will also encounter many opportunities to say "no" to Him. Your answers will determine the quality of your day and the direction of your life, so answer carefully . . . very carefully.

Today's Prayer

Dear Lord, thank You for loving me. And thank You for sending Your Son Jesus to this earth so that I can receive Your gift of eternal love and eternal life. I will praise You, dear God, today, tomorrow, and forever. Amen

Enthusiastic Service

Do your work with enthusiasm. Work as if you were serving the Lord, not as if you were serving only men and women.

Ephesians 6:7 NCV

Do you see each day as a glorious opportunity to serve God and to do His will? Are you enthused about life, or do you struggle through each day giving scarcely a thought to God's blessings? Are you constantly praising God for His gifts, and are you sharing His Good News with the world? And are you excited about the possibilities for service that God has placed before you, whether at home, at work, at church, or at school? You should be.

You are the recipient of Christ's sacrificial love. Accept it enthusiastically and share it fervently. Jesus deserves your enthusiasm; the world deserves it; and you deserve the experience of sharing it.

We must go out and live among them, manifesting the gentle, loving spirit of our Lord. We need to make friends before we can hope to make converts.

Lottie Moon

Today's Prayer

Dear Lord, the Christian life is a glorious adventure—let me share my excitement with others. Let me be an enthusiastic believer, Father, and let me share my enthusiasm today and every day. Amen

Our Children, Our Hope

Let the little children come to Me; don't stop them, for the kingdom of God belongs to such as these.

Mark 10:14 HCSB

Every child is different, but every child is similar in this respect: he or she is a priceless gift from the Father above. And, with the Father's gift comes immense responsibilities.

Our children are our nation's most precious resource. And, as responsible parents, we must create homes in which the future generation can grow and flourish.

Today, let us pray for our children . . . all of them. Let us pray for children here at home and for children around the world. Every child is God's child. May we, as concerned adults, behave—and pray—accordingly.

Let us look upon our children; let us love them and train them as children of the covenant and children of the promise. These are the children of God.

Andrew Murray

Today's Prayer

Today, Dear Lord, I pray for all Your children. This world holds countless dangers and temptations. I pray that our children may be protected from harm, and that they may discover Your will, Your love, and Your Son. Amen

Neighbors in Need

Each one of us needs to look after the good of the people around us, asking ourselves, "How can I help?" That's exactly what Jesus did.

Romans 15:2-3 MSG

Neighbors. We know that we are instructed to love them, and yet there's so little time . . . and we're so busy. No matter. As Christians, we are commanded by our Lord and Savior Jesus Christ to love our neighbors just as we love ourselves. Period.

This very day, you will encounter someone who needs a word of encouragement, or a pat on the back, or a helping hand, or a heartfelt prayer. And, if you don't reach out to your friend, who will? If you don't take the time to understand the needs of your neighbors, who will? If you don't love your brothers and sisters, who will? So, today, look for a neighbor in need . . . and then do something to help. Father's orders.

Encouraging others means helping people, looking for the best in them, and trying to bring out their positive qualities.

John Maxwell

Today's Prayer

Heavenly Father, help me be a Good Samaritan to the people You place along my path, today and every day. Amen

Discovering God's Plans

It is God who is at work in you, both to will and to work for His good pleasure.

Philippians 2:13 NASB

If you seek to live in accordance with God's will for your life—and you should—then you will live in accordance with His commandments. You will study God's Word, and you will be watchful for His signs. You will associate with fellow Christians who will encourage your spiritual growth, and you will listen to that inner voice that speaks to you in the quiet moments of your daily devotionals.

God intends to use you in wonderful, unexpected ways if you let Him. The decision to seek God's plan and to follow it is yours and yours alone. The consequences of that decision have implications that are both profound and eternal, so choose carefully.

If not a sparrow falls upon the ground without your Father, you have reason to see that the smallest events of your career and your life are arranged by him.

C. H. Spurgeon

Today's Prayer

Dear Lord, You created me for a reason. Give me the wisdom to follow Your direction for my life's journey. Let me do Your work here on earth by seeking Your will and living it, knowing that when I trust in You, Father, I am eternally blessed. Amen

The Power of Faith

Have faith in the LORD your God and you will be upheld; have faith in his prophets and you will be successful.

2 Chronicles 20:20 NIV

Every life—including yours—is a series of successes and failures, celebrations and disappointments, joys and sorrows. Every step of the way, through every triumph and tragedy, God will stand by your side and strengthen you . . . if you have faith in Him. Jesus taught His disciples that if they had faith, they could move mountains. You can too.

When you place your faith, your trust, indeed your life in the hands of Christ Jesus, you'll be amazed at the marvelous things He can do with you and through you. So strengthen your faith through praise, through worship, through Bible study, and through prayer. And trust God's plans. With Him, all things are possible, and He stands ready to open a world of possibilities to you . . . if you have faith.

Today's Prayer

Dear God, sometimes this world can be a fearful place, full of uncertainty and doubt. But You are always near and You can overcome any challenge. Give me faith, and let me remember always that with Your love and Your power, I can live courageously and faithfully today and every day. Amen

Critics Beware

*Don't pick on people, jump on their failures, criticize their faults—
unless, of course, you want the same treatment. Don't condemn those
who are down; that hardness can boomerang. Be easy on people; you'll
find life a lot easier.*

Luke 6:37 MSG

From experience, we know that it is easier to criticize than to correct. And we know that it is easier to find faults than solutions. Yet the urge to criticize others remains a powerful temptation for most of us. Our task, as obedient believers, is to break the twin habits of negative thinking and critical speech.

Negativity is highly contagious: we give it to others who, in turn, give it back to us. This cycle can be broken by positive thoughts, heartfelt prayers, and encouraging words. As thoughtful servants of a loving God, we can use the transforming power of Christ's love to break the chains of negativity. And we should.

Never be afraid of the world's censure; it's praise is much more to be dreaded.

C. H. Spurgeon

Today's Prayer

Help me, Lord, rise above the need to criticize others. May my own shortcomings humble me, and may I always be a source of genuine encouragement to my family and friends. Amen

God Never Leaves You

And he said: "The Lord is my rock and my fortress and my deliverer; the God of my strength, in whom I will trust."

2 Samuel 22:2-3 NKJV

Being a godly believer in this difficult world is no easy task. Ours is a time of uncertainty and danger, a time when even the most courageous have legitimate cause for concern. But as believers we can live courageously, knowing that we have been saved by a loving Father and His only begotten Son.

Are you anxious? Take those anxieties to God. Are you troubled? Take your troubles to Him. Seek protection from the One who cannot be moved. And then live courageously, knowing that even in these troubled times, God is always as near as your next breath—and you are always protected.

⸻

Have courage for the great sorrows of life and patience for the small ones; and when you have laboriously accomplished your daily task, go to sleep in peace. God is awake.

Victor Hugo

Today's Prayer

Lord, You are my Shepherd. You care for me; You comfort me; You watch over me; and You have saved me. I will praise You, Father, for Your glorious works, for Your protection, for Your love, and for Your Son. Amen

Decision-Making 101

Such doubters are thinking two different things at the same time, and they cannot decide about anything they do. They should not think they will receive anything from the Lord.

James 1:8 NCV

From the instant you wake in the morning until the moment you nod off to sleep at night, you have the opportunity to make countless decisions: decisions about the things you do, decisions about the words you speak, and decisions about the thoughts you choose to think.

If you're facing one of life's major decisions, here are some things you can do: 1. Gather as much information as you can. 2. Don't be too impulsive. 3. Rely on the advice of trusted friends and mentors. 4. Pray for guidance. 5. Trust the quiet inner voice of your conscience. 6. When the time for action arrives, act. Procrastination is the enemy of progress; don't let it defeat you.

People who can never quite seem to make up their minds usually make themselves miserable. So when in doubt, be decisive. It's the decent way to live.

There is no need to fear the decisions of life when you know Jesus Christ, for His name is Counselor.

Warren Wiersbe

Today's Prayer

Dear Lord, give me the insight to make wise decisions and the courage to act upon the decisions that I make. Amen

The Power of Words

Watch the way you talk. Let nothing foul or dirty come out of your mouth. Say only what helps, each word a gift.

Ephesians 4:29 MSG

The words that we speak have the power to do great good or great harm. If we speak words of encouragement and hope, we can lift others up. And that's exactly what God commands us to do!

Sometimes, when we feel uplifted and secure, it is easy to speak kind words. Other times, when we are discouraged or tired, we can scarcely summon the energy to uplift ourselves, much less anyone else. God intends that we speak words of kindness, wisdom, and truth, no matter our circumstances, no matter our emotions. When we do, we share a priceless gift with the world, and we give glory to the One who gave His life for us. As believers, we must do no less.

We urgently need people who encourage and inspire us to move toward God and away from the world's enticing pleasures.

Jim Cymbala

Today's Prayer

Lord, make me mindful of my words. Make me a powerful source of encouragement to those in need, and let my words and deeds be worthy of Your Son, the One who gives me courage and strength for this day and for all eternity. Amen

When People Behave Badly

Bad temper is contagious—don't get infected.

Proverbs 22:25 MSG

Face it: sometimes people can be rude . . . very rude. When other people are unkind to you, you may be tempted to strike back, either verbally or in some other way. Don't do it! Instead, remember that God corrects other people's behaviors in His own way, and He doesn't need your help (even if you're totally convinced that He does).

So, when other people behave cruelly, foolishly, or impulsively—as they will from time to time—don't be hotheaded. Instead, speak up for yourself as politely as you can, and walk away. Then, forgive everybody as quickly as you can, and leave the rest up to God.

For us the salve, the ointment that soothes the irritations of life, is Jesus Christ, the Great Physician. And we have instant communication with Him through times of prayerful solitude.

Franklin Graham

Today's Prayer

Dear Lord, sometimes people behave badly. When other people upset me, help me to calm myself down, and help me to forgive them as quickly as I can. Amen

Character Counts

But also for this very reason, giving all diligence, add to your faith virtue, to virtue knowledge.

2 Peter 1:5 NKJV

Character is built slowly over a lifetime. It is the sum of every right decision, every honest word, every noble thought, and every heartfelt prayer. It is forged on the anvil of honorable work and polished by the twin virtues of generosity and humility. Character is a precious thing—difficult to build but easy to tear down. As believers in Christ, we must seek to live each day with discipline, honesty, and faith. When we do, integrity becomes a habit. And God smiles.

God cannot build character without our cooperation. If we resist Him, then He chastens us into submission. But, if we submit to Him, then He can accomplish His work. He is not satisfied with a halfway job. God wants a perfect work; He wants a finished product that is mature and complete.

Warren Wiersbe

Today's Prayer

Heavenly Father, Your Word instructs me to walk in righteousness and in truth. Make me Your worthy servant, Lord. Let my words be true, and let my actions lead others to You. Amen

A Growing Relationship with God

But grow in the grace and knowledge of our Lord and Savior Jesus Christ. To Him be the glory both now and to the day of eternity.

2 Peter 3:18 HCSB

Your relationship with God is ongoing; it unfolds day by day, and it offers countless opportunities to grow closer to Him . . . or not. As each new day unfolds, you are confronted with a wide range of decisions: how you will behave, where you will direct your thoughts, with whom you will associate, and what you will choose to worship. These choices, along with many others like them, are yours and yours alone. How you choose determines how your relationship with God will unfold.

Are you continuing to grow in your love and knowledge of the Lord, or are you "satisfied" with the current state of your spiritual health? Hopefully, you're determined to make yourself a growing Christian. Your Savior deserves no less, and neither, by the way, do you.

Today's Prayer

Dear Lord, thank You for the opportunity to walk with Your Son. And, thank You for the opportunity to grow closer to You each day. I thank You for the person I am . . . and for the person I can become. Amen

The Gift of Salvation

For by grace you are saved through faith, and this is not from yourselves;
it is God's gift—not from works, so that no one can boast.

Ephesians 2:8-9 HCSB

God has given us so many gifts, but none can compare with the gift of eternal life. We have not earned our salvation; it is a blessing from God. When we accept Christ into our hearts, we are saved by His grace.

God's grace is the ultimate gift, and we owe to Him the ultimate in thanksgiving. Let us praise the Creator for His priceless gift, and let us share the Good News with all who cross our paths. We return our Father's love by accepting His grace and by sharing His message and His love. When we do, we are eternally blessed . . . and the Father smiles.

Christianity helps us face the music even when we don't like the tune.

Phillips Brooks

Today's Prayer

Accepting Your grace can be hard, Lord. Somehow, I feel that I must earn Your love and Your acceptance. Yet, the Bible promises that You love me and save me by Your grace. It is a gift I can only accept and cannot earn. Thank You for Your priceless gift. Amen

Contagious Faith

Whatever you do, work at it with all your heart, as working for the Lord, not for men. . . .

Colossians 3:23 NIV

Genuine, heartfelt Christianity is contagious. If you enjoy a life-altering relationship with God, that relationship will have an impact on others—perhaps a profound impact.

Are you genuinely excited about your faith? And do you make your enthusiasm known to those around you? Or are you a "silent ambassador" for Christ? God's preference is clear: He intends that you stand before others and proclaim your faith.

Does Christ reign over your life? Then share your testimony and your excitement. The world needs both.

———

There seems to be a chilling fear of holy enthusiasm among the people of God. We try to tell how happy we are—but we remain so well-controlled that there are very few waves of glory experienced in our midst.

A. W. Tozer

Today's Prayer

Dear Lord, I know that others are watching the way that I live my life. Help me to be an enthusiastic Christian with a faith that is contagious. Amen.

The Choice to Forgive

You have heard that it was said, You shall love your neighbor and hate your enemy. But I tell you, love your enemies, and pray for those who persecute you, so that you may be sons of your Father in heaven.

Matthew 5:43-45 HCSB

Forgiveness is a choice. We can either choose to forgive those who have injured us, or not. When we obey God by offering forgiveness to His children, we are blessed. But when we allow bitterness and resentment to poison our hearts, we are tortured by our own shortsightedness.

Do you harbor resentment against anyone? If so, you are faced with an important decision: whether or not to forgive the person who has hurt you. God's instructions are clear: He commands you to forgive. And the time to forgive is now because tomorrow may be too late . . . for you.

Two works of mercy set a man free: forgive and you will be forgiven, and give and you will receive.

St. Augustine

Today's Prayer

Dear Lord, today I will choose to forgive those who have hurt me. I will empty my heart of bitterness, and I will obey Your Word by offering love and mercy to others, just as You have offered mercy and love to me. Amen

The Need for Self-Discipline

Do you not know that the runners in a stadium all race, but only one receives the prize? Run in such a way that you may win. Now everyone who competes exercises self-control in everything. However, they do it to receive a perishable crown, but we an imperishable one.

1 Corinthians 9:24-25 HCSB

God is clear: we must exercise self-discipline in all matters. Self-discipline is not simply a proven way to get ahead, it's also an integral part of God's plan for our lives. If we genuinely seek to be faithful stewards of our time, our talents, and our resources, we must adopt a disciplined approach to life. Otherwise, our talents are wasted and our resources are squandered.

Our greatest rewards result from hard work and perseverance. May we, as disciplined believers, be willing to work for the rewards we so earnestly desire.

God is the perfect Parent to strong-willed children. We need to thank Him for His constant training. And learn from it.

Charles Stanley

Today's Prayer

Heavenly Father, let me teach others by the faithfulness of my conduct, and let me follow Your will and Your Word, today and every day. Amen

Healthy Choices

I shall yet praise him, who is the health of my countenance, and my God.

Psalm 42:11 KJV

The journey toward improved health is not only a common-sense exercise in personal discipline, it is also a spiritual journey ordained by our Creator. God does not intend that we abuse our bodies by giving in to excessive appetites or to slothful behavior. To the contrary, God has instructed us to protect our physical bodies to the greatest extent we can. To do otherwise is to disobey Him.

God's plan for you includes provisions for your spiritual, physical, and emotional health. But, He expects you to do your fair share of the work! In a world that is chock-full of tasty temptations, you may find it all too easy to make unhealthy choices. Your challenge, of course, is to resist those unhealthy temptations by every means you can, including prayer. And rest assured: when you ask for God's help, He will give it.

———————

Laughter is the language of the young at heart and the antidote to what ails us.

Barbara Johnson

Today's Prayer

Lord, when I am ill, or weak, or troubled, You heal me. Renew me, Father, and let me trust Your will for my life. Let me welcome Your unending love and Your healing touch, now and forever. Amen

Infinite Forgiveness

And forgive us our sins, for we ourselves also forgive everyone in debt to us.

Luke 11:4 NKJV

God's power to forgive, like His love, is infinite. Despite your shortcomings, despite your sins, God offers you immediate forgiveness and eternal life when you accept Christ as your Savior.

As a believer who is the recipient of God's forgiveness, how should you behave towards others? Should you forgive them (just as God has forgiven you), or should you remain embittered and resentful? The answer, of course, is found in God's Word: you are instructed to forgive others. When you do, you not only obey God's command, you also free yourself from a prison of your own making.

The love of God is revealed in that He laid down His life for His enemies.

Oswald Chambers

Today's Prayer

Dear Lord, when I ask for forgiveness, You give it. Thank You, Father, for forgiving me when I make mistakes. Today, I will be quick to forgive others, just as You have forgiven me. Amen

Life Eternal

In a little while the world will see Me no longer, but you will see Me. Because I live, you will live too.

John 14:19 HCSB

How marvelous it is that God became a man and walked among us. Had He not chosen to do so, we might feel removed from a distant Creator. But ours is not a distant God. Ours is a God who understands—far better than we ever could—the essence of what it means to be human.

God understands our hopes, our fears, and our temptations. He understands what it means to be angry and what it costs to forgive. He knows the heart, the conscience, and the soul of every person who has ever lived, including you. And God has a plan of salvation that is intended for you. Accept it. Accept God's gift through the person of His Son Christ Jesus, and then rest assured: God walked among us so that you might have eternal life; amazing though it may seem, He did it for you.

Today's Prayer

I know, Lord, that this world is not my home; I am only here for a brief while. And, You have given me the priceless gift of eternal life through Your Son Jesus. Keep the hope of Heaven fresh in my heart, and, while I am in this world, help me to pass through it with faith in my heart and praise on my lips . . . for You. Amen

Beyond Envy

Therefore, laying aside all malice, all deceit, hypocrisy, envy, and all evil speaking, as newborn babes, desire the pure milk of the word, that you may grow thereby.

1 Peter 2:1-2 NKJV

Because we are frail, imperfect human beings, we are sometimes envious of others. But God's Word warns us that envy is sin. Thus, we must guard ourselves against the natural tendency to feel resentment and jealousy when other people experience good fortune. As believers, we have absolutely no reason to be envious of any people on earth. After all, as Christians we are already recipients of the greatest gift in all creation: God's grace. We have been promised the gift of eternal life through God's only begotten Son, and we must count that gift as our most precious possession.

So here's a simple suggestion that is guaranteed to bring you happiness: fill your heart with God's love, God's promises, and God's Son . . . and when you do so, leave no room for envy, hatred, bitterness, or regret.

———————

Discontent dries up the soul.

Elisabeth Elliot

Today's Prayer

Dear Lord, when I am envious of others, redirect my thoughts to the blessings I have received from You. Make me a thankful Christian, Father, and deliver me from envy. Amen

Too Many Possessions

Love not the world, neither the things that are in the world. If any man love the world, the love of the Father is not in him.

1 John 2:15 KJV

On the grand stage of a well-lived life, material possessions should play a rather small role. Of course, we all need the basic necessities of life, but once we meet those needs for ourselves and for our families, the piling up of possessions creates more problems than it solves. Our real riches, of course, are not of this world. We are never really rich until we are rich in spirit.

How much stuff is too much stuff? Well, if your desire for stuff is getting in the way of your desire to know God, then you've got too much stuff—it's as simple as that. So, if you find yourself wrapped up in the concerns of the material world, it's time to reorder your priorities. And, it's time to begin storing up riches that will endure throughout eternity—the spiritual kind.

Greed is evil because it substitutes material things for the place of honor that the Creator ought to have in an individual's life.

Charles Stanley

Today's Prayer

Dear Lord, keep me mindful that material possessions cannot bring me joy—my joy comes from You. I will share that joy with family, with friends, and with neighbors, this day and every day. Amen

A Godly Leader

But a noble person plans noble things; he stands up for noble causes.

Isaiah 32:8 HCSB

Our world needs Christian leaders who willingly honor God with their words and their deeds, but not necessarily in that order.

If you seek to be a godly leader, then you must begin by being a worthy example to your family, to your friends, to your church, and to your community. After all, your words of instruction will never ring true unless you yourself are willing to follow them.

Are you the kind of leader whom you would want to follow? If so, congratulations. But if the answer to that question is no, then it's time to improve your leadership skills, beginning with the words that you speak and the example that you set, but not necessarily in that order.

Great leaders understand that the right attitude will set the right atmosphere, which enables the right response from others.

John Maxwell

Today's Prayer

Dear Lord, when I find myself in a position of leadership, let me seek Your will and obey Your commandments. Let me be a Christ-centered leader, and let me turn to You, Father, for guidance, for courage, for wisdom, and for love. Amen

Moving On

You have heard that the law of Moses says, "Love your neighbor" and hate your enemy. But I say, love your enemies! Pray for those who persecute you! In that way, you will be acting as true children of your Father in heaven.

Matthew 5:43-45 NLT

Sometimes, people can be discourteous and cruel. Sometimes people can be unfair, unkind, and unappreciative. Sometimes people get angry and frustrated. So what's a Christian to do? God's answer is straightforward: forgive, forget, and move on. In Luke 6:37, Jesus instructs, "Do not judge, and you will not be judged. Do not condemn, and you will not be condemned. Forgive, and you will be forgiven" (HCSB).

Today and every day, make sure that you're quick to forgive others for their shortcomings. And when other people misbehave (as they most certainly will from time to time), don't pay too much attention. Just forgive those people as quickly as you can, and try to move on . . . as quickly as you can.

———

You can be sure you are abiding in Christ if you are able to have a Christlike love toward the people that irritate you the most.

Vonette Bright

Today's Prayer

Heavenly Father, make me a kind person even to those who don't treat me kindly. Let me forgive others, just as You have forgiven me. Amen

Considering the Cross

But God forbid that I should boast except in the cross of our Lord Jesus Christ, by whom the world has been crucified to me, and I to the world.

Galatians 6:14 NKJV

As we consider Christ's sacrifice on the cross, we should be profoundly humbled and profoundly grateful. And today, as we come to Christ in prayer, we should do so in a spirit of quiet, heartfelt devotion to the One who gave His life so that we might have life eternal.

He was the Son of God, but He wore a crown of thorns. He was the Savior of mankind, yet He was put to death on a rough-hewn cross made of wood. He offered His healing touch to an unsaved world, and yet the same hands that had healed the sick and raised the dead were pierced with nails.

Christ humbled Himself on a cross—for you. As you approach Him today in prayer, think about His love and His sacrifice. And be grateful.

Today's Prayer

Dear Jesus, You are my Savior and my protector. You suffered on the cross for me, and I will give You honor and praise every day of my life. I will honor You with my words, my thoughts, and my prayers. And I will live according to Your commandments, so that through me, others might come to know Your perfect love. Amen

New Beginnings

Do not remember the former things, nor consider the things of old. Behold, I will do a new thing.

Isaiah 43:18-19 NKJV

Each new day offers countless opportunities to serve God, to seek His will, and to obey His teachings. But each day also offers countless opportunities to stray from God's commandments and to wander far from His path.

Sometimes, we wander aimlessly in a wilderness of our own making, but God has better plans of us. And, whenever we ask Him to renew our strength and guide our steps, He does so.

Consider this day a new beginning. Consider it a fresh start, a renewed opportunity to serve your Creator with willing hands and a loving heart. Ask God to renew your sense of purpose as He guides your steps. Today is a glorious opportunity to serve your Father in Heaven. Seize that opportunity while you can; tomorrow may indeed be too late.

———

No matter how badly we have failed, we can always get up and begin again. Our God is the God of new beginnings.

Warren Wiersbe

Today's Prayer

O Lord, my Creator, conform me to Your image. Create in me a clean heart, a new heart that reflects Your love for me. When I need to change, change me, Lord, and make me new. Amen

A Foundation of Honesty

The honest person will live in safety, but the dishonest will be caught.

Proverbs 10:9 NCV

Lasting relationships are built upon a foundation of honesty and trust. It has been said on many occasions that honesty is the best policy. For believers, it is far more important to note that honesty is God's policy. And if we are to be servants worthy of our Savior, Jesus Christ, we must be honest and forthright in all our communications with others.

Sometimes, honesty is difficult; sometimes, honesty is painful; sometimes, honesty makes us feel uncomfortable. Despite these temporary feelings of discomfort, we must make honesty the hallmark of all our relationships; otherwise, we invite needless suffering into our own lives and into the lives of those we love.

The commandment of absolute truthfulness is really only another name for the fullness of discipleship.

Dietrich Bonhoeffer

Today's Prayer

Lord, You instruct Your children to seek truth and to live righteously. Help me always to live according to Your commandments. Sometimes, Lord, speaking the truth is difficult, but let me always speak truthfully and forthrightly. Amen

Look Up and Move On

All bitterness, anger and wrath, insult and slander must be removed from you, along with all wickedness. And be kind and compassionate to one another, forgiving one another, just as God also forgave you in Christ.

Ephesians 4:31-32 HCSB

Are you mired in the quicksand of bitterness or regret? If so, you are not only disobeying God's Word, you are also wasting your time. The world holds few if any rewards for those who remain angrily focused upon the past. Still, the act of forgiveness is difficult for all but the most saintly men and women.

Being frail, fallible, imperfect human beings, most of us are quick to anger, quick to blame, slow to forgive, and even slower to forget. Yet as Christians, we are commanded to forgive others, just as we, too, have been forgiven.

If there exists even one person—alive or dead—against whom you hold bitter feelings, it's time to forgive. Or, if you are embittered against yourself for some past mistake or shortcoming, it's finally time to forgive yourself and move on. Hatred, bitterness, and regret are not part of God's plan for your life. Forgiveness is.

Today's Prayer

Heavenly Father, free me from anger and bitterness. When I am angry or bitter, I cannot sense Your presence. Keep me mindful that forgiveness is Your commandment. Let me turn away from bitterness and instead claim the spiritual abundance that You offer through the gift of Your Son. Amen

A Prescription for Panic

Anxiety in the heart of man causes depression, but a good word makes it glad.

Proverbs 12:25 NKJV

We live in a world that sometimes seems to shift beneath our feet. We live in an uncertain world, a world where tragedies can befall even the most godly among us. And we are members of an anxious society, a society in which the changes we face threaten to outpace our abilities to make adjustments. No wonder we sometimes find ourselves beset by feelings of anxiety and panic.

At times, our anxieties may stem from physical causes—chemical imbalances in the brain that result in severe emotional distress or relentless panic attacks. In such cases, modern medicine offers hope to those who suffer. But oftentimes, our anxieties result from spiritual deficits, not physical ones. And when we're spiritually depleted, the best prescription is found not in the medicine cabinet but deep inside the human heart. What we need is a higher daily dose of God's love, God's peace, God's assurance, and God's presence. And how do we acquire these blessings from our Creator? Through prayer, through meditation, through worship, and through trust.

Today's Prayer

Lord, when I am tempted to lose faith in the future, touch my heart with Your enduring love. And, keep me mindful, Lord, that nothing, absolutely nothing, will happen this day that You and I cannot handle together. Amen

God Is Here

Draw close to God, and God will draw close to you.

James 4:8 NLT

God is constantly making Himself available to you; therefore, when you approach Him obediently and sincerely, You will most certainly find Him: God is always available to you. Whenever it seems to you that God is distant, disinterested, or altogether absent, you may rest assured that your feelings are a reflection of your own emotional state, not an indication of God's absence.

If, during life's darker days, you seek to establish a closer relationship with Him, you can do so because God is not just near, He is here.

———◦———

Christianity says we were created by a righteous God to flourish and be exhilarated in a righteous environment. God has "wired" us in such a way that the more righteous we are, the more we'll actually enjoy life.

Bill Hybels

Today's Prayer

Dear Lord, thank You for Your constant presence and Your constant love. I draw near to You this day with the confidence that You are ready to guide me. Help me walk closely with You, Father, and help me share Your Good News with all who cross my path. Amen

Building Self-esteem

And let us not grow weary while doing good, for in due season we shall reap if we do not lose heart.

Galatians 6:9 NKJV

Would you like to make the world a better place and feel better about yourself at the same time? If so, you can start by practicing the Golden Rule.

The Bible teaches us to treat other people with respect, kindness, courtesy, and love. When we do, we make other people happy, we make God happy, and we feel better about ourselves.

So if you're wondering how to make the world—and your world—a better place, here's a great place to start: let the Golden Rule be your rule. And if you want to know how to treat other people, ask the person you see every time you glance in the mirror.

When you launch an act of kindness out into the crosswinds of life, it will blow kindness back to you.

Dennis Swanberg

Today's Prayer

Dear God, help me remember to treat other people in the same way that I would want to be treated. The Golden Rule is Your rule, Father; I'll make it my rule, too. Amen

God's Forgiveness

If we confess our sins, He is faithful and righteous to forgive us our sins and to cleanse us from all unrighteousness.

1 John 1:9 NASB

The Bible promises you this: When you ask God for forgiveness, He will give it. No questions asked; no explanations required.

God's power to forgive, like His love, is infinite. Despite your sins, God offers immediate forgiveness. And it's time to take Him up on His offer.

When it comes to forgiveness, God doesn't play favorites and neither should you. You should forgive all the people who have harmed you (not just the people who have asked for forgiveness or the ones who have made restitution). Complete forgiveness is God's way, and it should be your way, too. Anything less is not enough.

When God forgives, He forgets. He buries our sins in the sea and puts a sign on the shore saying, "No Fishing Allowed."

Corrie ten Boom

Today's Prayer

Lord, when it is difficult to forgive those who have hurt me, I will draw strength from You. When forgiveness is hard work, I will persevere. You have given me the gift of forgiveness, Father; I will share that gift today, tomorrow, and forever. Amen

Actions That Reflect Our Beliefs

If the way you live isn't consistent with what you believe, then it's wrong.

Romans 14:23 MSG

As Christians, we must do our best to ensure that our actions are accurate reflections of our beliefs. Our theology must be demonstrated, not only by our words but, more importantly, by our actions. In short, we should be practical believers, quick to act whenever we see an opportunity to serve God.

Are you the kind of practical Christian who is willing to dig in and do what needs to be done when it needs to be done? If so, congratulations: God acknowledges your service and blesses it. But if you find yourself more interested in the fine points of theology than in the needs of your neighbors, it's time to rearrange your priorities. God needs believers who are willing to roll up their sleeves and go to work for Him. Count yourself among that number. Theology is a good thing unless it interferes with God's work. And it's up to you to make certain that your theology doesn't.

Today's Prayer

Heavenly Father, I believe in You, and I believe in Your Word. Help me to live in such a way that my actions validate my beliefs—and let the glory be Yours forever. Amen

Trust Him

Trust the Lord your God with all your heart and lean not on your own understanding; in all your ways acknowledge him, and he will make your paths straight.

Proverbs 3:5-6 NIV

Sometimes the future seems bright, and sometimes it does not. Yet even when we cannot see the possibilities of tomorrow, God can. As believers, our challenge is to trust an uncertain future to an all-powerful God.

When we trust God, we should trust Him without reservation. We should steel ourselves against the inevitable disappointments of the day, secure in the knowledge that our Heavenly Father has a plan for the future that only He can see.

Can you place your future into the hands of a loving and all-knowing God? Can you live amid the uncertainties of today, knowing that God has dominion over all your tomorrows? If you can, you are wise and you are blessed. When you trust God with everything you are and everything you have, He will bless you now and forever.

Today's Prayer

Lord, when I trust in things of this earth, I will be disappointed. But, when I put my faith in You, I am secure. You are my rock and my shield. Upon Your firm foundation I will build my life. When I am worried, Lord, let me trust in You. You will love me and protect me, and You will share Your boundless grace today, tomorrow, and forever. Amen

Shouting the Good News

As you go, preach this message: "The kingdom of heaven is near."

Matthew 10:7 NIV

The Good News of Jesus Christ should be shouted from the rooftops by believers the world over. But all too often, it is not. For a variety of reasons, many Christians keep their beliefs to themselves, and when they do, the world suffers because of their failure to speak up.

As believers, we are called to share the transforming message of Jesus with our families, with our neighbors, and with the world. Jesus commands us to become fishers of men. And, the time to go fishing is now. We must share the Good News of Jesus Christ today—tomorrow may indeed be too late.

The evangelistic harvest is always urgent. The destiny of men and of nations is always being decided. Every generation is strategic. We are not responsible for the past generation, and we cannot bear the full responsibility for the next one, but we do have our generation. God will hold us responsible as to how well we fulfill our responsibilities to this age and take advantage of our opportunities.

Billy Graham

Today's Prayer

Lord, even if I never leave home, make me a missionary for You. Let me share the Good News of Your Son, and let me tell of Your love and of Your grace. Make me a faithful servant for You, Father, now and forever. Amen

God and Family

Let the Word of Christ—the Message—have the run of the house. Give it plenty of room in your lives.

Colossians 3:16 MSG

These are difficult days for our nation and for our families. But, thankfully, God is bigger than all of our challenges. God loves us and protects us. In times of trouble, He comforts us; in times of sorrow, He dries our tears. When we are troubled, or weak, or sorrowful, God is as near as our next breath.

Are you concerned for the well-being of your family? You are not alone. We live in a world where temptation and danger seem to lurk on every street corner. Parents and children alike have good reason to be watchful. But, despite the evils of our time, God remains steadfast. Even in these difficult days, no problem is too big for God.

———◇———

As the first community to which a person is attached and the first authority under which a person learns to live, the family established society's most basic values.

Charles Colson

Today's Prayer

Dear Lord, I am blessed to be part of the family of God where I find love and acceptance. You have also blessed me with my earthly family. Let me show love and acceptance for my own family so that through me, they might come to know You. Amen

Sharing Words of Hope

Let's see how inventive we can be in encouraging love and helping out, not avoiding worshipping together as some do but spurring each other on.

Hebrews 10:24-25 MSG

Hope, like other human emotions, is contagious. When we associate with hope-filled Christians, we are encouraged by their faith and optimism. But, if we spend too much time in the company of naysayers and pessimists, our attitudes, like theirs, tend to be cynical and negative.

Are you a hopeful, optimistic, encouraging believer? And do you associate with like-minded people? Hopefully so. As a faithful follower of the One from Galilee, you have every reason to be hopeful, and you have every reason to share your hopes with others. So today, look for reasons to celebrate God's endless blessings. And while you're at it, look for people who will join you in the celebration. You'll be better for their company, and they'll be better for yours.

Today's Prayer

Dear Lord, make me a source of genuine, lasting encouragement to my family and friends. Today, I will celebrate Your blessings, and I will share your Good News with those who cross my path. Let my words and deeds be worthy of Your Son, the One who gives me strength and salvation. Amen

The Last Word

*For God has not given us a spirit of timidity, but of power and love and
discipline. Therefore do not be ashamed of the testimony of our Lord....*

2 Timothy 1:7-8 NASB

All of us may find our courage tested by the inevitable
disappointments and tragedies of life. After all, ours is a world
filled with uncertainty, hardship, sickness, and danger. Old Man
Trouble, it seems, is never too far from the front door.

When we focus upon our fears and our doubts, we may find
many reasons to lie awake at night and fret about the uncertainties
of the coming day. A better strategy, of course, is to focus not upon
our fears, but instead upon our God.

God is your shield and your strength; you are His forever. So
don't focus your thoughts upon the fears of the day. Instead, trust
God's plan and His eternal love for you. And remember: God is
good, and He has the last word.

Fear is a self-imposed prison that will keep you from becoming
what God intends for you to be.

Rick Warren

Today's Prayer

Father, even when I walk through the valley of the shadow of death,
I will fear no evil because You are with me. Thank You, Lord, for
Your perfect love, a love that casts out fear and gives me strength
and courage to meet the challenges of this world. Amen

In Focus

Keep your eyes focused on what is right, and look straight ahead to what is good.

Proverbs 4:25 NCV

What is your focus today? Are you willing to focus your thoughts and energies on God's blessings and upon His will for your life? Or will you turn your thoughts to other things? This day—and every day hereafter—is a chance to celebrate the life that God has given you. It's also a chance to give thanks to the One who has offered you more blessings than you can possibly count.

Today, why not focus your thoughts on the joy that is rightfully yours in Christ? Why not take time to celebrate God's glorious creation? Why not trust your hopes instead of your fears? When you do, you will think optimistically about yourself and your world . . . and you can then share your optimism with others. They'll be better for it, and so will you.

———◦———

Jesus challenges you and me to keep our focus daily on the cross of His will if we want to be His disciples.

Anne Graham Lotz

Today's Prayer

Dear Lord, help me to face this day with a spirit of optimism and thanksgiving. And let me focus my thoughts on You and Your incomparable gifts. Amen

Accepting His Gifts

What father among you, if his son asks for a fish, will, instead of a fish, give him a snake? Or if he asks for an egg, will give him a scorpion? If you then, who are evil, know how to give good gifts to your children, how much more will the heavenly Father give the Holy Spirit to those who ask Him?

Luke 11:11-13 HCSB

God gives the gifts; we, as believers, should accept them—but oftentimes, we don't. Why? Because we fail to trust our Heavenly Father completely, and because we are, at times, surprisingly stubborn. Luke 11 teaches us that God does not withhold spiritual gifts from those who ask. Our obligation, quite simply, is to ask for them.

Are you asking God to move mountains in your life, or are you expecting Him to stumble over molehills? Whatever the size of your challenges, God is big enough to handle them. Ask for His help today, with faith and with fervor, and then watch in amazement as your mountains begin to move.

Today's Prayer

Dear Lord, today I will ask You for the things I need. In every circumstance, in every season of life, I will come to You in prayer. You know the desires of my heart, Lord; grant them, I ask. Yet not my will, Father, but Your will be done. Amen

A Life of Integrity

The man of integrity walks securely, but he who takes crooked paths will be found out.

Proverbs 10:9 NIV

Charles Swindoll correctly observed, "Nothing speaks louder or more powerfully than a life of integrity." Godly men and women agree.

Integrity is built slowly over a lifetime. It is a precious thing—difficult to build but easy to tear down. As believers in Christ, we must seek to live each day with discipline, honesty, and faith. When we do, at least two things happen: integrity becomes a habit, and God blesses us because of our obedience to Him.

Living a life of integrity isn't always the easiest way, but it is always the right way. And God clearly intends that it should be our way, too.

There's nothing like the power of integrity. It is a characteristic so radiant, so steady, so consistent, so beautiful, that it makes a permanent picture in our minds.

Franklin Graham

Today's Prayer

Heavenly Father, Your Word instructs me to walk in righteousness and with integrity. Make me Your worthy servant, Lord. Let my words be true, and let my actions influence my friends to trust You. Amen

Pats on the Back

So then, we must pursue what promotes peace and what builds up one another.

Romans 14:19 HCSB

Life is a team sport, and all of us need occasional pats on the back from our teammates. In the book of Ephesians, Paul writes, "Do not let any unwholesome talk come out of your mouths, but only what is helpful for building others up according to their needs, that it may benefit those who listen" (4:29 NIV). Paul reminds us that when we choose our words carefully, we can have a powerful impact on those around us.

Since we don't always know who needs our help, the best strategy is to encourage all the people who cross our paths. So today, be a world-class source of encouragement to everyone you meet. Never has the need been greater.

Make it a rule, and pray to God to help you to keep it, never to lie down at night without being able to say: "I have made at least one human being a little wiser, a little happier, or a little better this day."

Charles Kingsley

Today's Prayer

Dear Heavenly Father, just as You have lifted me up, let me lift up others in a spirit of encouragement and hope. And if I can help a fellow traveler, even in a small way, dear Lord, may the glory be Yours. Amen

God's Guidance

The steps of a good man are ordered by the LORD.

Psalm 37:23 KJV

God is intensely interested in each of us, and He will guide our steps if we serve Him obediently.

When we sincerely offer heartfelt prayers to our Heavenly Father, He will give direction and meaning to our lives—but He won't force us to follow Him. To the contrary, God has given us the free will to follow His commandments . . . or not.

When we stray from God's commandments, we invite bitter consequences. But, when we follow His commandments, and when we genuinely and humbly seek His will, He touches our hearts and leads us on the path of His choosing.

Will you trust God to guide your steps? You should. When you entrust your life to Him completely and without reservation, God will give you the strength to meet any challenge, the courage to face any trial, and the wisdom to live in His righteousness and in His peace. So trust Him today and seek His guidance. When you do, your next step will be the right one.

Today's Prayer

Dear Lord, You always stand ready to guide me. Let me accept your guidance, today and every day of my life. Lead me, Father, so that my life can be a tribute to Your grace, to Your mercy, to Your love, and to Your Son. Amen

The Best Policy

The godly are directed by their honesty.

Proverbs 11:5 NLT

From the time we are children, we are taught that honesty is the best policy, but sometimes, being honest is hard. So, we convince ourselves that it's alright to tell "little white lies." But there's a problem: Little white lies tend to grow up, and when they do, they cause havoc and pain in our lives.

For Christians, the issue of honesty is not a topic for debate. Honesty is not just the best policy, it is God's policy, pure and simple. And if we are to be servants worthy of our Savior, Jesus Christ, we must avoid all lies, white or otherwise. So, if you're tempted to sow the seeds of deception (perhaps in the form of a "harmless" white lie), resist that temptation. Truth is God's way, and a lie—of whatever color—is not.

———◉———

A little lie is like a little pregnancy. It doesn't take long before everyone knows.

C. S. Lewis

Today's Prayer

Dear Lord, give me the courage to speak honestly, and let me walk righteously with You so that others might see Your eternal truth reflected in my words and my deeds. Amen

An Awesome God

The fear of the Lord is a fountain of life, turning people from the snares of death.

Proverbs 14:27 HCSB

God's hand shapes the universe, and it shapes our lives. God maintains absolute sovereignty over His creation, and His power is beyond comprehension. As believers, we must cultivate a sincere respect for God's awesome power. God has dominion over all things, and until we acknowledge His sovereignty, we lack the humility we need to live righteously, and we lack the humility we need to become wise.

The fear of the Lord is, indeed, the beginning of knowledge. So today, as you face the realities of everyday life, remember this: until you acquire a healthy, respectful fear of God's power, your education is incomplete, and so is your faith.

When true believers are awed by the greatness of God and by the privilege of becoming His children, then they become sincerely motivated, effective evangelists.

Bill Hybels

Today's Prayer

Dear Lord, others have expectations of me, and I have hopes and desires for my life. Lord, bring all other expectations in line with Your plans for me. May my only fear be that of displeasing the One who created me. May I obey Your commandments and seek Your will this day and every day. Amen

Hope Is Contagious

Finally, all of you be of one mind, having compassion for one another; love as brothers, be tenderhearted, be courteous.

1 Peter 3:8 NKJV

One of the reasons that God placed you here on earth is so that you might become a beacon of encouragement to the world. As a faithful follower of the One from Galilee, you have every reason to be hopeful, and you have every reason to share your hopes with others. When you do, you will discover that hope, like other human emotions, is contagious.

As a follower of Christ, you are instructed to choose your words carefully so as to build others up through wholesome, honest encouragement (Ephesians 4:29). So look for the good in others and celebrate the good that you find. As the old saying goes, "When someone does something good, applaud—you'll make two people happy."

He climbs highest who helps another up.

Zig Ziglar

Today's Prayer

Dear Lord, You have loved me eternally, and cared for me faithfully. Just as You have lifted me up, Lord, let me also lift up others in a spirit of encouragement, optimism, and hope. Today and every day, let me share Your healing message so that I might encourage others. And, Lord, may the glory be Yours. Amen

A Shining Light

While ye have light, believe in the light, that ye may be the children of light.

John 12:36 KJV

The Bible says that you are "the light that gives light to the world." What kind of light have you been giving off? Hopefully, you've been a good example for everybody to see. Why? Because the world needs all the light it can get, and that includes your light, too!

Christ showed enduring love for you by willingly sacrificing His own life so that you might have eternal life. As a response to His sacrifice, you should love Him, praise Him, and share His message of salvation with your neighbors and with the world. So let your light shine today and every day. When you do, God will bless you now and forever.

———◦◦◦———

Whatever clouds you face today, ask Jesus, the light of the world, to help you look behind the cloud to see His glory and His plans for you.

Billy Graham

Today's Prayer

Heavenly Father, You are the way and the truth and the light. Today—as I follow Your way and share Your Good News—let me be a worthy example to others and a worthy servant to You. Amen

Now Is the Time

So, my son, throw yourself into this work for Christ.

2 Timothy 1:1 MSG

God's love for you is deeper and more profound than you can imagine. God's love for you is so great that He sent His only Son to this earth to die for your sins and to offer you the priceless gift of eternal life. Now, you must decide whether or not to accept God's gift. Will you ignore it or embrace it? Will you return it or neglect it? Will you accept Christ's love and build a lifelong relationship with Him, or will you turn away from Him and take a different path?

Your decision to allow Christ to reign over your heart is the pivotal decision of your life. It is a decision that you cannot ignore. It is a decision that is yours and yours alone. Accept God's gift now: allow His Son to preside over your heart, your thoughts, and your life, starting this very instant.

———

We have in Jesus Christ a perfect example of how to put God's truth into practice.

Bill Bright

Today's Prayer

Dear Lord, You are my Teacher—I will study Your Word, and I will seek Your will. Today, I will stand upon the truth that You reveal, and I will share Your wisdom with my family, with my friends, and with the world. Amen

Forgiving and Forgetting

But the wisdom from above is first pure, then peace-loving, gentle, compliant, full of mercy and good fruits, without favoritism and hypocrisy.

James 3:17 HCSB

Do you have a tough time forgiving and forgetting? If so, welcome to the club. Most of us find it difficult to forgive the people who have hurt us. And that's too bad because life would be much simpler if we could forgive people "once and for all" and be done with it. Yet forgiveness is seldom that easy. Usually, the decision to forgive is straightforward, but the process of forgiving is more difficult. Forgiveness is a journey that requires time, perseverance, and prayer.

If you sincerely wish to forgive someone, pray for that person. And then pray for yourself by asking God to heal your heart. Don't expect forgiveness to be easy or quick, but rest assured: with God as your partner, you can forgive . . . and you will.

———

There is no use in talking as if forgiveness were easy. For we find that the work of forgiveness has to be done over and over again.

C. S. Lewis

Today's Prayer

Dear Lord, today, I ask You to help me move beyond feelings of bitterness and anger. Jesus forgave those who hurt Him; let me walk in His footsteps by forgiving those who have injured me. Amen

The Answer to Adversity

I have heard your prayer, I have seen your tears; surely I will heal you.

2 Kings 20:5 NKJV

From time to time, all of us must endure discouragement and defeat. And, we sometimes experience life-changing personal losses that leave us reeling. When we do, God stands ready to protect us. When we are troubled, we must call upon God, and, in His own time and according to His own plan, He will heal us.

Are you anxious? Take those anxieties to God. Are you troubled? Take your troubles to Him. Does your world seem to be trembling beneath your feet? Seek protection from the One who cannot be moved. The same God who created the universe will protect you if you ask Him . . . so ask Him.

―――――――

We should not be upset when unexpected and upsetting things happen. God, in his wisdom, means to make something of us which we have not yet attained, and He is dealing with us accordingly.

J. I. Packer

Today's Prayer

Dear Heavenly Father, You are my strength and my protector. In times of adversity, let me trust Your plan for my life. Your love is infinite, as is Your wisdom. Whatever my circumstances, dear Lord, let me always give the praise, and the thanks, and the glory to You. Amen

Hope for Today

You have already heard about this hope in the message of truth, the gospel that has come to you. It is bearing fruit and growing all over the world, just as it has among you since the day you heard it and recognized God's grace in the truth.

Colossians 1:5-6 HCSB

Despite God's promises, despite Christ's love, and despite our countless blessings, we frail human beings can still lose hope from time to time. When we do, we need the encouragement of Christian friends, the life-changing power of prayer, and the healing truth of God's Holy Word. If we find ourselves falling into the spiritual traps of worry and discouragement, we should seek the healing touch of Jesus and the encouraging words of fellow Christians. Even though this world can be a place of trials and struggles, God has promised us peace, joy, and eternal life if we give ourselves to Him. And, of course, God keeps His promises today, tomorrow, and forever.

Hope is the power of being cheerful in circumstances which we know to be desperate.

G. K. Chesterton

Today's Prayer

Dear Lord, I will place my hope in You. If I become discouraged, I will turn to You. If I am afraid, I will seek strength in You. In every aspect of my life, I will trust You. You are my Father, and I will place my hope, my trust, and my faith in You. Amen

Love That Forgives

Whenever you stand praying, forgive, if you have anything against anyone, so that your Father in heaven will also forgive you your transgressions.

Mark 11:25 NASB

Genuine love is an exercise in forgiveness. If we wish to build lasting relationships, we must learn how to forgive. Why? Because our loved ones are imperfect (as are we). How often must we forgive our family and friends? More times than we can count. Why? Because that's what God wants us to do.

Perhaps granting forgiveness is hard for you. If so, you are not alone. Genuine, lasting forgiveness is often difficult to achieve—difficult but not impossible. Thankfully, with God's help, all things are possible, and that includes forgiveness. But, even though God is willing to help, He expects you to do some of the work. And make no mistake: forgiveness is work, which is okay with God. He knows that the payoffs are worth the effort.

Are you aware of the joy-stealing effect an unforgiving spirit is having on your life?

Charles Swindoll

Today's Prayer

Dear Lord, let forgiveness rule my heart, even when forgiveness is difficult. Let me be Your obedient servant, Lord, and let me be a person who forgives others just as You have forgiven me. Amen

A Passionate Life

Do not lack diligence; be fervent in spirit; serve the Lord.

Romans 12:11 HCSB

Are you passionate about your life, your loved ones, your work, and your faith? As a believer who has been saved by a risen Christ, you should be.

As a thoughtful Christian, you have every reason to be enthusiastic about life, but sometimes the inevitable struggles of life may cause you to feel decidedly unenthusiastic. If you feel that your enthusiasm is slowly fading away, it's time to slow down, to rest, to count your blessings, and to pray. When you feel worried or weary, you must pray fervently for God to renew your sense of wonderment and excitement.

Life with God is a glorious adventure; revel in it. When you do, God will most certainly smile upon your work and your life.

⸻

This is Christianity as God intended it—a passionate, willful, and fully emotional relationship.

Bill Hybels

Today's Prayer

Dear Lord, the life that I live and the words that I speak bear testimony to my faith. Make me a faithful and passionate servant of Your Son, and let my testimony be worthy of You. Let my words be sure and true, Lord, and let my actions point others to You. Amen

Face-to-face with Old Man Trouble

I will be with you when you pass through the waters . . . when you walk through the fire . . . the flame will not burn you. For I the Lord your God, the Holy One of Israel, and your Savior.

Isaiah 43:2-3 HCSB

As life-here-on-earth unfolds, all of us encounter occasional setbacks: Those occasional visits from Old Man Trouble are simply a fact of life, and none of us are exempt. When tough times arrive, we may be forced to rearrange our plans and our priorities. But even on our darkest days, we must remember that God's love remains constant.

The fact that we encounter adversity is not nearly so important as the way we choose to deal with it. When tough times arrive, we have a clear choice: we can begin the difficult work of tackling our troubles . . . or not. When we summon the courage to look Old Man Trouble squarely in the eye, an amazing thing usually happens: he blinks.

Today's Prayer

Heavenly Father, You are my refuge. As I journey through this day, I know that I may encounter disappointments and losses. When I am troubled, let me turn to You. Keep me steady, Lord, and renew a right spirit inside of me this day and forever. Amen

Friendships That Honor God

If your life honors the name of Jesus, he will honor you.

2 Thessalonians 1:12 MSG

Some friendships help us honor God; these friendships should be nurtured. Other friendships place us in situations where we are tempted to dishonor God by disobeying His commandments; friendships such as these have the potential to do us great harm.

Because we tend to become like our friends, we must choose our friends carefully. Because our friends influence us in ways that are both subtle and powerful, we must ensure that our friendships are pleasing to God. When we spend our days in the presence of godly believers, we are blessed, not only by those friends, but also by our Creator.

In a circle of true friends each man is simply what he is: stands for nothing but himself.

C. S. Lewis

Today's Prayer

Dear Lord, let my friendships honor You. Keep me mindful that I am Your servant in every aspect of my life. Let me be a worthy servant, Lord, and a worthy friend. And, may the love of Jesus shine in me and through me today and forever. Amen

Beyond Anxiety

In the multitude of my anxieties within me, Your comforts delight my soul.

Psalm 94:19 NKJV

God calls us to live above and beyond anxiety. God calls us to live by faith, not by fear. He instructs us to trust Him completely, this day and forever. But sometimes, trusting God is difficult, especially when we become caught up in the incessant demands of an anxious world.

When you feel anxious—and you will—return your thoughts to God's love. Then, take your concerns to Him in prayer, and to the best of your ability, leave them there. Whatever "it" is, God is big enough to handle it. Let Him. Now.

Worry and anxiety are sand in the machinery of life; faith is the oil.

E. Stanley Jones

Today's Prayer

Lord, sometimes this world is a difficult place, and, as a frail human being, I am fearful. When I am worried, restore my faith. When I am anxious, turn my thoughts to You. Amen.

Ask and Receive

Ask, and it will be given to you; seek, and you will find; knock, and it will be opened to you. For everyone who asks receives, and he who seeks finds, and to him who knocks it will be opened.

Matthew 7:7-8 NKJV

Are you a person who asks God for guidance and strength? If so, then you're continually inviting your Creator to reveal Himself in a variety of ways. As a follower of Christ, you must do no less.

Jesus made it clear to His disciples: they should petition God to meet their needs. So should we. Genuine, heartfelt prayer produces powerful changes in us and in our world. When we lift our hearts to God, we open ourselves to a never-ending source of divine wisdom and infinite love.

Do you have questions about your future that you simply can't answer? Do you have needs that you simply can't meet by yourself? Do you sincerely seek to know God's purpose for your life? If so, ask Him for direction, for protection, and for strength—and then keep asking Him every day that you live. Whatever your need, no matter how great or small, pray about it and never lose hope. God is not just near; He is here, and He's perfectly capable of answering your prayers. Now, it's up to you to ask.

Today's Prayer

Lord, today I will ask You for the things I need. In every situation, I will come to You in prayer. You know what I want, Lord, and more importantly, You know what I need. Yet even though I know that You know, I still won't be too timid—or too busy—to ask. Amen

In His Hands

Do not boast about tomorrow, for you do not know what a day may bring forth.

Proverbs 27:1 NKJV

The old saying is both familiar and true: "Man proposes and God disposes." Our world unfolds according to God's plans, not our wishes. Thus, boasting about future events is to be avoided by those who acknowledge God's sovereignty over all things.

Are you planning for a better tomorrow for yourself and your family? If so, you are to be congratulated: God rewards forethought in the same way that He often punishes impulsiveness. But as you make your plans, do so with humility, with gratitude, and with trust in your Heavenly Father. His hand directs the future; to think otherwise is both arrogant and naïve.

That we may not complain of what is, let us see God's hand in all events; and, that we may not be afraid of what shall be, let us see all events in God's hand.

Matthew Henry

Today's Prayer

Dear Lord, as I look to the future, I will place my trust in You. If I become discouraged, I will turn to You. If I am weak, I will seek strength in You. You are my Father, and I will place my hope, my trust, and my faith in You. Amen

Enthusiastic Discipleship

Do your work with enthusiasm. Work as if you were serving the Lord, not as if you were serving only men and women.

Ephesians 6:7 NCV

With whom will you choose to walk today? Will you walk with shortsighted people who honor the ways of the world, or will you walk with the Son of God? Jesus walks with you. Are you walking with Him? Hopefully, you will choose to walk with Him today and every day of your life.

Jesus has called upon believers of every generation (and that includes you) to follow in His footsteps. And God's Word promises that when you follow in Christ's footsteps, you will learn how to live freely and lightly (Matthew 11:28-30).

Jesus doesn't want you to be a run-of-the-mill, follow-the-crowd kind of person. Jesus wants you to be a "new creation" through Him. And that's exactly what you should want for yourself, too. Jesus deserves your extreme enthusiasm; the world deserves it; and you deserve the experience of sharing it.

Today's Prayer

Dear Lord, You have called me not to a life of mediocrity, but to a life of passion. Today, I will be an enthusiastic follower of Your Son, and I will share His Good News—and His love—with all who cross my path. Amen

The World's Best Friend

No one has greater love than this, that someone would lay down his life for his friends.

John 15:13 HCSB

Who's the best friend this world has ever had? Jesus, of course! When you invite Him into your heart, Jesus will be your friend, too . . . your friend forever.

Jesus has offered to share the gifts of everlasting life and everlasting love with the world . . . and with you. If you make mistakes, He'll still be your friend. If you behave badly, He'll still love you. If you feel sorry or sad, He can help you feel better.

Jesus wants you to have a happy, healthy life. He wants you to be generous and kind. He wants you to follow His example. And the rest is up to you. You can do it! And with a friend like Jesus, you will.

———————

The dearest friend on earth is but a mere shadow compared with Jesus Christ.

Oswald Chambers

Today's Prayer

Dear Jesus, You are my Savior and my protector. Give me the courage to trust You completely. Today, I will praise You, I will honor You, and I will live according to Your commandments. Amen

God's Lessons

Get all the advice and instruction you can, and be wise the rest of your life.

Proverbs 19:20 NLT

When it comes to learning life's lessons, we can either do things the easy way or the hard way. The easy way can be summed up as follows: when God teaches us a lesson, we learn it . . . the first time! Unfortunately, too many of us learn much more slowly than that.

When we resist God's instruction, He continues to teach, whether we like it or not. Our challenge, then, is to discern God's lessons from the experiences of everyday life. Hopefully, we learn those lessons sooner rather than later because the sooner we do, the sooner He can move on to the next lesson and the next, and the next . . .

Enjoy the adventure of receiving God's guidance. Taste it, revel in it, appreciate the fact that the journey is often a lot more exciting than arriving at the destination.

Bill Hybels

Today's Prayer

Dear Lord, I have so much to learn. Help me to watch, to listen, to think, and to learn, every day of my life. Amen

The Seeds of Generosity

Freely you have received, freely give.

Matthew 10:8 NKJV

Paul reminds us that when we sow the seeds of generosity, we reap bountiful rewards in accordance with God's plan for our lives. Thus, we are instructed to give cheerfully and without reservation: "But this I say, He which soweth sparingly shall reap also sparingly; and he which soweth bountifully shall reap also bountifully. Every man according as he purposeth in his heart, so let him give; not grudgingly, or of necessity: for God loveth a cheerful giver" (2 Corinthians 9:6, 7 KJV).

Today, make this pledge and keep it: Be a cheerful, generous, courageous giver. The world needs your help, and you need the spiritual rewards that will be yours when you give it.

All the blessings we enjoy are divine deposits, committed to our trust on this condition: that they should be dispensed for the benefit of our neighbors.

John Calvin

Today's Prayer

Lord, You have given me so much. Let me share my blessings with those in need. Make me a generous, humble Christian, Lord, and let the glory be Yours and Yours alone. Amen

A Helping Hand

The greatest among you will be your servant. Whoever exalts himself will be humbled, and whoever humbles himself will be exalted.

Matthew 23:11-12 HCSB

Jesus has much to teach us about generosity. He teaches that the most esteemed men and women are not the self-congratulatory leaders of society but are, instead, the humblest of servants. If you were being graded on generosity, how would you score? Would you earn "A"s in philanthropy and humility? Hopefully so. But if your grades could stand a little improvement, this is the perfect day to begin.

Today, you may feel the urge to hoard your blessings. Don't do it. Instead, give generously to your neighbors, and do so without fanfare. Find a need and fill it . . . humbly. Lend a helping hand and share a word of kindness . . . anonymously. This is God's way.

The happiest and most joyful people are those who give money and serve.

Dave Ramsey

Today's Prayer

Dear Lord, make me a sacrificial giver. Let me give of my possessions, my talents, my time, and my testimony. Let me give cheerfully, faithfully, and prayerfully. And make me a humble steward of my talents, Lord, so that the praise might be Yours, not mine. Amen

Why Bad Things?

They won't be afraid of bad news; their hearts are steady because they trust the Lord.

Psalm 112:7 NCV

If God is good, and if He made the world, why do bad things happen? Part of that question is easy to answer, and part of it isn't. Let's get to the easy part first: Sometimes, bad things happen because people disobey God's commandments and invite sadness and heartache into God's beautiful world.

But on other occasions, bad things happen, and it's nobody's fault. So who is to blame? Sometimes, nobody is to blame. Sometimes, things just happen and we simply cannot know why. Thankfully, all our questions will be answered . . . some day. The Bible promises that in Heaven we will understand all the reasons behind God's plans. But until then, we must simply trust that God is good, and that, in the end, He will make things right.

God's curriculum for all who sincerely want to know Him and do His will always includes lessons we wish we could skip. With an intimate understanding of our deepest needs and individual capacities, He chooses our curriculum.

Elisabeth Elliot

Today's Prayer

Lord, give me courage in every circumstance and in every stage of life. Give me the wisdom, Father, to place my hope and my trust in Your perfect plan and Your boundless love. Amen

Using Your Gifts

Do not neglect the gift that is in you.

1 Timothy 4:14 HCSB

God has given you talents and opportunities that are uniquely yours. Are you willing to use your gifts in the way that God intends? And are you willing to summon the discipline that is required to develop your talents and to hone your skills? That's precisely what God wants you to do, and that's precisely what you should desire for yourself.

As you seek to expand your talents, you will undoubtedly encounter stumbling blocks along the way, such as the fear of rejection or the fear of failure. When you do, don't stumble! Just continue to refine your skills, and offer your services to God. And when the time is right, He will use you—but it's up to you to be thoroughly prepared when He does.

There's a unique sense of fulfillment that comes when we submit our gifts to God's use and ask Him to energize them in a supernatural way—and then step back to watch what He does.

Lee Strobel

Today's Prayer

Lord, I praise You for Your priceless gifts. I give thanks for Your creation, for Your Son, and for the unique talents and opportunities that You have given me. Let me use my gifts for the glory of Your kingdom, this day and every day. Amen

Constant Praise

Through Him then, let us continually offer up a sacrifice of praise to God, that is, the fruit of lips that give thanks to His name.

Hebrews 13:15 NASB

The Bible makes it clear: it pays to praise God. But sometimes, we allow ourselves to become so preoccupied with the demands of daily life that we forget to say "Thank You" to the Giver of all good gifts.

Worship and praise should be a part of everything we do. Otherwise, we quickly lose perspective as we fall prey to the demands of the moment.

Do you sincerely desire to be a worthy servant of the One who has given you eternal love and eternal life? Then praise Him for who He is and for what He has done for you. Praise Him all day long, every day, for as long as you live . . . and then for all eternity.

Praise opens the window of our hearts, preparing us to walk more closely with God. Prayer raises the window of our spirit, enabling us to listen more clearly to the Father.

Max Lucado

Today's Prayer

Heavenly Father, I come to You today with hope in my heart and praise on my lips. I place my trust in You, dear Lord, knowing that with You as my Protector, I have nothing to fear. I thank You, Lord, for Your grace, for Your love, and for Your Son. Amen

The Bread of Life

"I am the bread of life," Jesus told them. "No one who comes to Me will ever be hungry, and no one who believes in Me will ever be thirsty again."

John 6:35 HCSB

He was the Son of God, but He wore a crown of thorns. He was the Savior of mankind, yet He was put to death on the cross. He offered His healing touch to an unsaved world, and yet the same hands that had healed the sick and raised the dead were pierced with nails.

Jesus Christ, the Son of God, was born into humble circumstances. He walked this earth, not as a ruler of men, but as the Savior of mankind. His crucifixion, a torturous punishment that was intended to end His life and His reign, instead became the pivotal event in the history of all humanity. Jesus is the bread of life. Accept His grace. Share His love. And follow in His footsteps.

Jesus came into the world so we could know, once and for all, that God is concerned about the way we live, the way we believe, and the way we die.

Billy Graham

Today's Prayer

Dear Jesus, You give me peace. Thank You, Lord, for the gift of eternal life and for the gift of eternal love. May I be ever grateful, and may I share Your Good News with a world that so desperately needs Your healing grace. Amen

Faith Versus Fear

So do not fear, for I am with you; do not be dismayed, for I am your God. I will strengthen you and help you; I will uphold you with my righteous right hand.

Isaiah 41:10 NIV

A terrible storm rose quickly on the Sea of Galilee, and the disciples were afraid. Although they had witnessed many miracles, the disciples feared for their lives, so they turned to Jesus, and He calmed the waters and the wind.

The next time you find yourself facing a fear-provoking situation, remember that the One who calmed the wind and the waves is also your personal Savior. Then ask yourself which is stronger: your faith or your fear. The answer should be obvious. So, when the storm clouds form overhead and you find yourself being tossed on the stormy seas of life, remember this: Wherever you are, God is there, too. And, because He cares for you, you are protected.

The Lord Jesus by His Holy Spirit is with me, and the knowledge of His presence dispels the darkness and allays any fears.

Bill Bright

Today's Prayer

Heavenly Father, when I am fearful, keep me mindful that You are my protector and my salvation. Give me strength, Lord, to face the challenges of this day as I gain my courage from You. Amen

The Inner Voice

Let us draw near with a true heart in full assurance of faith, our hearts sprinkled clean from an evil conscience and our bodies washed in pure water.

Hebrews 10:22 HCSB

American humorist Josh Billings observed, "Reason often makes mistakes, but conscience never does." How true. Even when we deceive our neighbors, and even when we attempt to deceive ourselves, God has given each of us a conscience, a small, quiet voice that tells us right from wrong. We must listen to that inner voice . . . or else we must accept the consequences that inevitably befall those who choose to rebel against God.

The voice of the subconscious argues with you, tries to convince you; but the inner voice of God does not argue; it does not try to convince you. It just speaks, and it is self-authenticating.

E. Stanley Jones

Today's Prayer

Dear Lord, today, I will honor the quiet voice that You have placed in my heart. I will strive to obey Your Word as I follow in the footsteps of Your Son today, tomorrow, and every day of my life. Amen

Working Faithfully

Take a lesson from the ants, you lazybones. Learn from their ways and be wise! Even though they have no prince, governor, or ruler to make them work, they labor hard all summer, gathering food for the winter. But you, lazybones, how long will you sleep? When will you wake up?

Proverbs 6:6-9 NLT

The Bible instructs us that we can learn an important lesson of a surprising source: ants. Ants are among nature's most industrious creatures. They do their work without supervision and without hesitation. We should do likewise.

God's Word is clear: We are instructed to work diligently and faithfully. We are told that the fields are ripe for the harvest, that the workers are few, and that the importance of our work is profound. Let us labor, then, for our Master without hesitation and without complaint. Nighttime is coming. Until it does, let us honor our Heavenly Father with grateful hearts and willing hands.

———

God provides the ingredients for our daily bread but expects us to do the baking. With our own hands!

Barbara Johnson

Today's Prayer

Dear Lord, make my work pleasing to You. Help me to sow the seeds of Your abundance everywhere I go. Let me be diligent in all my undertakings and give me patience to wait for Your harvest. Amen

Heeding God's Call

One thing I do, forgetting those things which are behind and reaching forward to those things which are ahead, I press toward the goal for the prize of the upward call of God in Christ Jesus.

Philippians 3:13-14 NKJV

It is vitally important that you heed God's call. In John 15:16, Jesus says, "You did not choose me, but I chose you and appointed you to go and bear fruit—fruit that will last" (NIV). In other words, you have been called by Christ, and now, it is up to you to decide precisely how you will answer.

Have you already found your special calling? If so, you're a very lucky person. If not, keep searching and keep praying until you discover it. And remember this: God has important work for you to do—work that no one else on earth can accomplish but you.

God never calls without enabling us. In other words, if he calls you to do something, he makes it possible for you to do it.

Luci Swindoll

Today's Prayer

Heavenly Father, You have called me to Your kingdom work, and I acknowledge that calling. In these quiet moments before this busy day unfolds, I come to You. I will study Your Word and seek Your guidance. Give me the wisdom to know Your will for my life and the courage to follow wherever You may lead me, today and forever. Amen

His Comforting Hand

Nevertheless God, who comforts the downcast, comforted us . . . .

2 Corinthians 7:6 NKJV

If you have been touched by the transforming hand of Jesus, then you have every reason to live courageously. Still, even if you are a dedicated Christian, you may find yourself discouraged by the inevitable disappointments and tragedies that occur in the lives of believers and non-believers alike.

The next time you find your courage tested to the limit, lean upon God's promises. Trust His Son. Remember that God is always near and that He is your protector and your deliverer. When you are worried, anxious, or afraid, call upon Him and accept the touch of His comforting hand. Remember that God rules both mountaintops and valleys—with limitless wisdom and love—now and forever.

When God allows extraordinary trials for His people, He prepares extraordinary comforts for them.

Corrie ten Boom

Today's Prayer

Dear Lord, thank You for Your comfort. You lift me up when I am disappointed. You protect me in times of trouble. Today, I will be mindful of Your love, Your wisdom, and Your grace. Amen

Conduct and Character

Lead a quiet and peaceable life in all godliness and honesty.

1 Timothy 2:2 KJV

Charles Stanley said, "The Bible teaches that we are accountable to one another for our conduct and character." Godly Christians agree.

As believers in Christ, we must seek to live each day with discipline, honesty, and faith. When we do, at least two things happen: integrity becomes a habit, and God blesses us because of our obedience to Him. Living a life of integrity isn't always the easiest way, but it is always the right way . . . and God clearly intends that it should be our way, too.

Character isn't built overnight; it is built slowly over a lifetime. It is the sum of every right decision and every honest word. It is forged on the anvil of honorable work and polished by the twin virtues of honesty and fairness. Character is a precious thing—difficult to build and wonderful to behold.

———

What lessons about honor did you learn from your childhood? Are you living what you learned today?

Dennis Swanberg

Today's Prayer

Dear Lord, make me a person whose conduct is honorable. Make me a person whose words are true. Give me the wisdom to know right from wrong, and give me the courage—and the skill—to do what needs to be done in the service of Your Son. Amen

Behavior Reflects Belief

As you have therefore received Christ Jesus the Lord, so walk in Him, rooted and built up in Him and established in the faith, as you have been taught, abounding in it with thanksgiving.

Colossians 2:6-7 NKJV

As Christians, we must do our best to make sure that our actions are accurate reflections of our beliefs. Our theology must be demonstrated, not only by our words but, more importantly, by our actions. In short, we should be practical believers, quick to act whenever we see an opportunity to serve God.

English clergyman Thomas Fuller observed, "He does not believe who does not live according to his beliefs." These words are most certainly true. Like it or not, your life is an accurate reflection of your creed. If this fact gives you cause for concern, don't bother talking about the changes that you intend to make—make them. And then, when your good deeds speak for themselves—as they most certainly will—don't interrupt.

Obedience is the natural outcome of belief.

C. H. Spurgeon

Today's Prayer

Lord, it is so much easier to speak of the righteous life than it is to live it. Let me live righteously, and let my actions be consistent with my beliefs. May every step that I take reflect Your truth and Your love, and may I live a life that is worthy of Your love and Your grace. Amen

Limitless Power, Limitless Love

I pray that the eyes of your heart may be enlightened so you may know what is the hope of His calling, what are the glorious riches of His inheritance among the saints, and what is the immeasurable greatness of His power to us who believe, according to the working of His vast strength.

Ephesians 1:18-19 HCSB

Because God's power is limitless, it is far beyond the comprehension of mortal minds. Yet even though we cannot fully understand the awesome power of God, we can praise it. When we worship God with faith and assurance, when we place Him at the absolute center of our lives, we invite His love into our hearts. In turn, we grow to love Him more deeply as we sense His love for us. St. Augustine wrote, "I love you, Lord, not doubtingly, but with absolute certainty. Your Word beat upon my heart until I fell in love with you, and now the universe and everything in it tells me to love you."

Let us pray that we, too, will turn our hearts to the Creator, knowing with certainty that His heart has ample room for each of us, and that we, in turn, must make room in our hearts for Him.

Today's Prayer

Father, You are all-knowing and all-powerful. Today, I praise You for Your love, and I marvel at the glory of Your creation. With You as my protector, Lord, I am secure, today and forever. Amen

The Attitude of a Leader

Those who are wise will shine like the brightness of the heavens, and those who lead many to righteousness, like the stars for ever and ever.

Daniel 12:3 NIV

John Maxwell writes, "Great leaders understand that the right attitude will set the right atmosphere, which enables the right response from others." If you are in a position of leadership, whether as a father—or as a leader at your work, your church, or your school—it's up to you to set the right tone by maintaining the right attitude.

Our world needs Christian leaders, and so do your family members and coworkers. You can become a trusted, competent, thoughtful leader if you learn to maintain the right attitude: one that is realistic, optimistic, forward looking, and Christ-centered.

When God wants to accomplish something, He calls dedicated men and women to challenge His people and lead the way.

Warren Wiersbe

Today's Prayer

Heavenly Father, when I find myself in a position of leadership, let me follow Your teachings and obey Your commandments. Make me a person of integrity and wisdom, Lord, and make me a worthy example to those whom I serve. Amen

The Direction of Your Thoughts

My cup runs over. Surely goodness and mercy shall follow me all the days of my life; and I will dwell in the house of the Lord Forever.

Psalm 23:5-6 NKJV

God has given you free will, including the ability to influence the direction and the tone of your thoughts. And, here's how God wants you to direct those thoughts: "Finally brothers, whatever is true, whatever is honorable, whatever is just, whatever is pure, whatever is lovely, whatever is commendable—if there is any moral excellence and if there is any praise—dwell on these things" (Philippians 4:8 HCSB).

The quality of your attitude will help determine the quality of your life, so you must guard your thoughts accordingly. So, the next time you find yourself dwelling upon the negative aspects of your life, refocus your attention on things positive. And, the next time you're tempted to waste valuable time gossiping or complaining, resist those temptations with all your might. And remember: You'll never whine your way to the top . . . so don't waste your breath.

Today's Prayer

Lord, I pray for an attitude that is Christlike. Whatever my circumstances, whether good or bad, triumphal or tragic, let my response reflect a God-honoring attitude of optimism, faith, and love for You. Amen

Trust Him to Guide You

Trust the Lord your God with all your heart and lean not on your own understanding; in all your ways acknowledge him, and he will make your paths straight.

Proverbs 3:5-6 NIV

As Christians whose salvation has been purchased by the blood of Christ, we have every reason to live joyously and courageously. After all, Christ has already fought and won our battle for us—He did so on the cross at Calvary. But despite Christ's sacrifice, and despite God's promises, we may become confused or disoriented by the endless complications and countless distractions of life.

If you're unsure of your next step, lean upon God's promises and lift your prayers to Him. Remember that God is your protector. Open yourself to His heart, and trust Him to guide you. When you do, God will direct your steps, and you will receive His blessings today, tomorrow, and throughout eternity.

God's plan for our guidance is for us to grow gradually in wisdom before we get to the crossroads.

Bill Hybels

Today's Prayer

Dear Lord, today I will trust You more completely. I will lean upon Your understanding, not mine. And I will trust You to guide my steps along a path of Your choosing. Amen

Offering Thanks

In everything give thanks; for this is the will of God in Christ Jesus for you.

1 Thessalonians 5:18 NKJV

Sometimes, life-here-on-earth can be complicated, demanding, and frustrating. When the demands of life leave us rushing from place to place with scarcely a moment to spare, we may fail to pause and thank our Creator for His gifts. But, whenever we neglect to give proper thanks to the Father, we suffer because of our misplaced priorities.

Today, begin making a list of your blessings. You most certainly will not be able to make a complete list, but take a few moments and jot down as many blessings as you can. Then, give thanks to the Giver of all good things: God. His love for you is eternal, as are His gifts. And it's never too soon—or too late—to offer Him thanks.

Grace is an outrageous blessing bestowed freely on a totally undeserving recipient.

Bill Hybels

Today's Prayer

Today, Lord, let me count my blessings with thanksgiving in my heart. You have cared for me, Lord, and I will give You the glory and the praise. Amen

His Intimate Love

As the Father loved Me, I also have loved you; abide in My love.

John 15:9 NKJV

St. Augustine observed, "God loves each of us as if there were only one of us." Do you believe those words? Do you seek an intimate, one-on-one relationship with your Heavenly Father, or are you satisfied to keep Him at a "safe" distance?

Sometimes, in the crush of our daily duties, God may seem far away, but He is not. God is everywhere we have ever been and everywhere we will ever go. He is with us night and day; He knows our thoughts and our prayers. And, when we earnestly seek Him, we will find Him because He is here, waiting patiently for us to reach out to Him. May we reach out to Him today and always. And may we praise Him for the glorious gifts that have transformed us today and forever.

God wants to emancipate his people; he wants to set them free. He wants his people to be not slaves but sons. He wants them governed not by law but by love.

Max Lucado

Today's Prayer

God, You are love. I love You, Lord, and as I love You more, I am able to love my family and friends more. Let me be Your loving servant, Heavenly Father, today and throughout eternity. Amen

Doubt and the True Believer

Immediately the father of the child cried out and said with tears, "Lord, I believe; help my unbelief!"

Mark 9:24 NKJV

Even the most faithful Christians are overcome by occasional bouts of fear and doubt. You are no different. When you feel that your faith is being tested to its limits, seek the comfort and assurance of the One who sent His Son as a sacrifice for you.

Have you ever felt your faith in God slipping away? If so, you are not alone. Every life—including yours—is a series of successes and failures, celebrations and disappointments, joys and sorrows, hopes and doubts. But even when you feel very distant from God, God is never distant from you. When you sincerely seek His presence, He will touch your heart, calm your fears, and restore your faith in the future . . . and your faith in Him.

All of us are forced to live with a measure of uncertainty, and we grow accustomed to weighing evidence, considering data, and making our decisions based on probability.

Bill Hybels

Today's Prayer

Dear Lord, when I am filled with uncertainty and doubt, give me faith. In the dark moments of life, keep me mindful of Your healing power and Your infinite love, so that I may live courageously and faithfully today and every day. Amen

Transcendent Love

Who can separate us from the love of Christ? Can affliction or anguish or persecution or famine or nakedness or danger or sword? . . . No, in all these things we are more than victorious through Him who loved us.

Romans 8:35, 37 HCSB

Where can we find God's love? Everywhere. God's love transcends space and time. It reaches beyond the heavens, and it touches the darkest, smallest corner of every human heart. When we become passionate in our devotion to the Father, when we sincerely open our minds and hearts to Him, His love does not arrive "some day"—it arrives immediately.

Today, take God at His word and welcome His Son into your heart. When you do, God's transcendent love will surround you and transform you, now and forever.

The grace of God transcends all our feeble efforts to describe it. It cannot be poured into any mental receptacle without running over.

Vance Havner

Today's Prayer

Thank You, Lord, for Your love. Your love is boundless, infinite, and eternal. Today, let me pause and reflect upon Your love for me, and let me share that love with all those who cross my path. Amen

Solving the Riddles

If you need wisdom—if you want to know what God wants you to do—ask him, and he will gladly tell you. He will not resent your asking.

James 1:5 NLT

Life presents each of us with countless questions, conundrums, doubts, and problems. Thankfully, the riddles of everyday living are not too difficult to solve if we look for answers in the right places. When we have questions, we should consult God's Word, we should seek the guidance of the Holy Spirit, and we should trust the counsel of God-fearing friends and family members.

Are you facing a difficult decision? Take your concerns to God and avail yourself of the messages and mentors that He has placed along your path. When you do, God will speak to you in His own way and in His own time, and when He does, you can most certainly trust the answers that He gives.

———※———

God does not give His counsel to the curious or the careless; He reveals His will to the concerned and to the consecrated.

Warren Wiersbe

Today's Prayer

Dear Lord, today I come to You seeking guidance. I will trust You to show me the path that I should take, and I will strive, as best I can, to follow in the footsteps of Your Son. Amen.

Your Way or God's Way

A man's heart plans his way, but the Lord directs his steps.

Proverbs 16:9 NKJV

The popular song "My Way" is a perfectly good tune, but it's not a perfect guide for life. If you're looking for life's perfect prescription, you'd better forget about doing things your way and start doing things God's way. The most important decision of your life is, of course, your commitment to accept Jesus as your personal Lord and Savior. And once your eternal destiny is secured, you will undoubtedly ask the question "What now, Lord?" If you earnestly seek God's will for your life, you will find it . . . in time.

Sometimes, God's plans are crystal clear; sometimes they are not. So be patient, keep searching, and keep praying. If you do, then in time, God will answer your prayers and make His plans known. You'll discover those plans by doing things His way . . . and you'll be eternally grateful that you did.

———◉———

Almost 2,000 years ago, Jesus Christ won the decisive battle against sin and Satan through His death and resurrection. Satan did his best to defeat God's plans, but he could not win against God's overwhelming power.

Billy Graham

Today's Prayer

Lord, today, I will seek Your will for my life. You have a plan for me, Father. Let me discover it and live it, knowing that when I trust in You, I am eternally blessed. Amen

Contentment That Lasts

But godliness with contentment is a great gain. For we brought nothing into the world, and we can take nothing out. But if we have food and clothing, we will be content with these. But those who want to be rich fall into temptation, a trap, and many foolish and harmful desires, which plunge people into ruin and destruction.

1 Timothy 6:6-9 HCSB

The preoccupation with happiness and contentment is an ever-present theme in the modern world. We are bombarded with messages that tell us where to find peace and pleasure in a world that worships materialism and wealth. But, lasting contentment is not found in material possessions; genuine contentment is a spiritual gift from God to those who trust in Him and follow His commandments. When God dwells at the center of our lives, peace and contentment will belong to us just as surely as we belong to God.

———

He is truly happy who has all that he wishes to have, and wishes to have nothing that he ought not to have.

St. Augustine

Today's Prayer

Heavenly Father, You are my contentment and my peace. I find protection when I seek Your healing hand; I discover joy when I welcome Your healing Spirit. Let me look to You, Lord, for the peace and contentment that You have offered me through the gift of Your Son. Amen

Feeding the Church

The church, you see, is not peripheral to the world; the world is peripheral to the church. The church is Christ's body, in which he speaks and acts, by which he fills everything with his presence.

Ephesians 1:23 MSG

One way that we come to know God is by involving ourselves in His church.

In the Book of Acts, Luke reminds us to "feed the church of God" (20:28). As Christians who have been saved by a loving, compassionate Creator, we are compelled not only to worship Him in our hearts but also to worship Him in the presence of fellow believers.

Do you feed the church of God? Do you attend regularly, and are you an active participant? The answer to these questions will have a profound impact on the quality and direction of your spiritual journey.

So do yourself a favor: become actively involved in your church. Don't just go to church out of habit. Go to church out of a sincere desire to know and worship God. When you do, you'll be blessed by the One who sent His Son to die so that you might have everlasting life.

Today's Prayer

Heavenly Father, I give thanks for my church and for the opportunity to worship there. Guide my steps, Lord, as I worship You in spirit and in truth, today and forever. Amen

Standing Up for Your Faith

Watch, stand fast in the faith, be brave, be strong.

1 Corinthians 16:13 NKJV

Are you a person whose faith is obvious to your family and to the world, or are you a spiritual shrinking violet? God needs more people who are willing to stand up and be counted for Him.

Genuine faith is never meant to be locked up in the heart of a believer; to the contrary, it is meant to be shared. And a person who wishes to share God's Good News with the world should begin by sharing that message with friends and family members.

Through every triumph and tragedy, God will stand by your side and strengthen you . . . if you have faith in Him. Jesus taught His disciples that if they had faith, they could move mountains. You can too, and so can your family . . . if you have faith.

Hope must be in the future tense. Faith, to be faith, must always be in the present tense.

Catherine Marshall

Today's Prayer

Dear Lord, make me Your obedient, faithful servant. You are with me always. Give me faith and let me remember that with Your love and Your power, I can live courageously and faithfully today and every day. Amen

Sensing His Presence

Where can I go from Your Spirit? Or where can I flee from Your presence? If I ascend into heaven, You are there; if I make my bed in hell, behold, You are there. If I take the wings of the morning, and dwell in the uttermost parts of the sea, even there Your hand shall lead me, and Your right hand shall hold me.

Psalm 139:7-10 NKJV

If God is everywhere, why does He sometimes seem so far away? The answer to that question, of course, has nothing to do with God and everything to do with us.

When we begin each day on our knees, in praise and worship to Him, God often seems very near indeed. But, if we ignore God's presence or—worse yet—rebel against it altogether, the world in which we live becomes a spiritual wasteland.

Today, and every day hereafter, thank God and praise Him. He is the Giver of all things good. Wherever you are, whether you are happy or sad, victorious or vanquished, celebrate God's presence. And be comforted. For He is here.

The Lord Jesus by His Holy Spirit is with me, and the knowledge of His presence dispels the darkness and allays any fears.

Bill Bright

Today's Prayer

Heavenly Father, even when it seems to me that You are far away, You never leave my side. Today and every day, I will strive to feel Your presence, and I will strive to sense Your love for me. Amen

Using Your Gifts

Based on the gift they have received, everyone should use it to serve others, as good managers of the varied grace of God.

1 Peter 4:10 HCSB

All people possess special gifts—bestowed from the Father above—and you are no exception. But, your gift is no guarantee of success; it must be cultivated and nurtured; otherwise, it will go unused . . . and God's gift to you will be squandered.

Today, make a promise to yourself that you will earnestly seek to discover the talents that God has given you. Then, nourish those talents and make them grow. Finally, vow to share your gifts with the world for as long as God gives you the power to do so. After all, the best way to say "Thank You" for God's gifts is to use them.

One thing taught large in the Holy Scriptures is that while God gives His gifts freely, He will require a strict accounting of them at the end of the road.

A. W. Tozer

Today's Prayer

Dear Lord, let me use my gifts, and let me help others discover theirs. Your gifts are priceless and eternal. May we, Your children, use them to the glory of Your kingdom, today and forever. Amen

He Deserves the Credit

By humility and the fear of the Lord are riches and honor and life.

Proverbs 22:4 NKJV

We have heard the phrase on countless occasions: "He's a self-made man." In truth, none of us are self-made. We all owe countless debts that we can never repay. Our first debt, of course, is to our Father in Heaven—Who has given us everything that we are and will ever be—and to His Son Who sacrificed His own life so that we might live eternally. We are also indebted to ancestors, parents, teachers, friends, spouses, family members, coworkers, fellow believers . . . and the list, of course, goes on.

Most of us, it seems, are more than willing to stick out our chests and say, "Look at me; I did that!" But in our better moments, in the quiet moments when we search the depths of our own hearts, we know better. Whatever "it" is, God did that. And He deserves the credit.

———

We can never have more of true faith than we have of true humility.

Andrew Murray

Today's Prayer

Heavenly Father, Jesus clothed Himself with humility when He chose to leave Heaven and come to earth to live and die for all creation. Christ is my Master and my example. Clothe me with humility, Lord, so that I might be more like Your Son. Amen

To Judge or Not to Judge

When they persisted in questioning Him, He stood up and said to them, "The one without sin among you should be the first to throw a stone at her."

John 8:7 HCSB

The warning of Matthew 7:1 is clear: "Judge not, that ye be not judged" (KJV). Yet even the most devoted Christians may fall prey to a powerful yet subtle temptation: the temptation to judge others. But as obedient followers of Christ, we are commanded to refrain from such behavior.

As Jesus came upon a young woman who had been condemned by the Pharisees, He spoke not only to the crowd that was gathered there, but also to all generations when He warned, "The one without sin among you should be the first to throw a stone at her." Christ's message is clear, and it applies not only to the Pharisees of ancient times, but also to us.

Christians think they are prosecuting attorneys or judges, when, in reality, God has called all of us to be witnesses.

Warren Wiersbe

Today's Prayer

Dear Lord, sometimes I am quick to judge others. But, You have commanded me not to judge. Keep me mindful, Father, that when I judge others, I am living outside of Your will for my life. You have forgiven me, Lord. Let me forgive others, let me love them, and let me help them . . . without judging them. Amen

Sufficient for Your Needs

And God is able to make all grace abound toward you, that you, always having all sufficiency in all things, may have an abundance for every good work.

2 Corinthians 9:8 NKJV

Of this you can be sure: the love of God is sufficient to meet your needs. Whatever dangers you may face, whatever heartbreaks you must endure, God is with you, and He stands ready to comfort you and to heal you.

The Psalmist writes, "Weeping may endure for a night, but joy comes in the morning" (Psalm 30:5 NKJV). But when we are suffering, the morning may seem very far away. It is not. God promises that He is "near to those who have a broken heart" (Psalm 34:18 NKJV).

If you are experiencing the intense pain of a recent loss, or if you are still mourning a loss from long ago, perhaps you are now ready to begin the next stage of your journey with God. If so, be mindful of this fact: the loving heart of God is sufficient to meet any challenge, including yours.

Today's Prayer

Dear Lord, whatever "it" is, You can handle it! Let me turn to You when I am fearful or worried. You are my loving Heavenly Father, sufficient in all things and I will always trust You. Amen

Ultimate Protection

The Lord is the One who will go before you. He will be with you; He will not leave you or forsake you. Do not be afraid or discouraged.

Deuteronomy 31:8 HCSB

God has promised to protect us, and He intends to fulfill His promise. In a world filled with dangers and temptations, God is the ultimate armor. In a world filled with misleading messages, God's Word is the ultimate truth. In a world filled with more frustrations than we can count, God's Son offers the ultimate peace.

Will you accept God's peace and wear God's armor against the dangers of our world? Hopefully so, because when you do, you can live courageously, knowing that you possess the ultimate protection: God's unfailing love for you.

———————

The promises of God's Word sustain us in our suffering, and we know Jesus sympathizes and empathizes with us in our darkest hour.

Bill Bright

Today's Prayer

Lord, You have promised to protect me, and I will trust You. Today, I will live courageously as I place my hopes, my faith, and life in Your hands. Let my life be a testimony to the transforming power of Your love, Your grace, and Your Son. Amen

Faith That Works

I can already hear one of you agreeing by saying, "Sounds good. You take care of the faith department, I'll handle the works department." Not so fast. You can no more show me your works apart from your faith than I can show you my faith apart from my works. Faith and works, works and faith, fit together hand in glove.

James 2:18 MSG

It is important to remember that the work required to build and sustain our faith is an ongoing process. Corrie ten Boom advised, "Be filled with the Holy Spirit; join a church where the members believe the Bible and know the Lord; seek the fellowship of other Christians; learn and be nourished by God's Word and His many promises. Conversion is not the end of your journey—it is only the beginning."

The work of nourishing your faith can and should be joyful work. The hours that you invest in Bible study, prayer, meditation, and worship should be times of enrichment and celebration. And, as you continue to build your life upon a foundation of faith, you will discover that the journey toward spiritual maturity lasts a lifetime. As a child of God, you are never fully "grown": instead, you can continue "growing up" every day of your life. And that's exactly what God wants you to do.

Today's Prayer

Lord, when I am filled with uncertainty and doubt, give me faith. Today, Lord, and forever, I will place my trust in You. Amen

Perfect Wisdom

Therefore, everyone who hears these words of Mine and acts on them will be like a sensible man who built his house on the rock. The rain fell, the rivers rose, and the winds blew and pounded that house. Yet it didn't collapse, because its foundation was on the rock.

Matthew 7:24-25 HCSB

Where will you place your trust today? Will you trust in the wisdom of fallible men and women, or will you place your faith God's perfect wisdom? Where you choose to place your trust will determine the direction and quality of your life.

Are you tired? Discouraged? Fearful? Be comforted and trust God. Are you worried or anxious? Be confident in God's power and trust His Holy Word. Are you confused? Listen to the quiet voice of your Heavenly Father. He is not a God of confusion. Talk with Him; listen to Him; trust Him. He is steadfast, and He is your protector . . . forever.

If you lack knowledge, go to school. If you lack wisdom, get on your knees.

Vance Havner

Today's Prayer

Dear Lord, You are my wise Teacher. Help me to learn from You. And then, let me show others what it means to be a kind, generous, loving Christian. Amen

God's Gift of Family

Choose for yourselves this day whom you will serve . . . as for me and my household, we will serve the LORD.

Joshua 24:15 NIV

In the life of every family, there are moments of frustration and disappointment. Lots of them. But, for those who are lucky enough to live in the presence of a close-knit, caring clan, the rewards far outweigh the frustrations.

No family is perfect, and neither is yours. But, despite the inevitable challenges and hurt feelings of family life, your clan is God's gift to you. That little band of men, women, kids, and babies is a priceless treasure on temporary loan from the Father above. Give thanks to the Giver for the gift of family . . . and act accordingly.

The only true source of meaning in life is found in love for God and his son Jesus Christ, and love for mankind, beginning with our own families.

James Dobson

Today's Prayer

Dear Lord, You have given me a wonderful gift: a loving family. Today and every day, let me show my family that I love them by the things that I say and the things that I do. Amen

A Pattern of Good Works

In all things showing yourself to be a pattern of good works; in doctrine showing integrity, reverence, incorruptibility . . . .

Titus 2:7 NKJV

It has been said that character is what we are when nobody is watching. How true. When we do things that we know aren't right, we try to hide them from our families and friends. But even then, God is watching.

If you sincerely wish to walk with God, you must seek, to the best of your ability, to follow His commandments. When you do, your character will take care of itself . . . and you won't need to look over your shoulder to see who, besides God, is watching.

A person's character is determined by his motives, and motive is always a matter of the heart.

John Eldredge

Today's Prayer

Lord, You are my Father in Heaven. You search my heart and know me far better than I know myself. May I be Your worthy servant, and may I live according to Your commandments. Let me be a person of integrity, Lord, and let my words and deeds be a testimony to You, today and always. Amen

Waiting for God

The Lord is good to those who wait for Him, to the soul who seeks Him. It is good that one should hope and wait quietly for the salvation of the Lord.

Lamentations 3:25–26 NKJV

We human beings are so impatient. We know what we want, and we know exactly when we want it: RIGHT NOW! But, God knows better. He has created a world that unfolds according to His own timetable, not ours.

As Christians, we must be patient as we wait for God to show us the wonderful plans that He has in store for us. And while we're waiting for God to make His plans clear, let's keep praying and keep giving thanks to the One who has given us more blessings than we can count.

———⚬———

God knows exactly how much you can take, and He will never permit you to reach a breaking point.

Barbara Johnson

Today's Prayer

Dear Lord, You have a plan for my life that is grander than I can imagine. When I am impatient, remind me that You are never early or late. You are always on time, Father, so let me trust in You. Amen

Defining Success

Commit your work to the LORD, and then your plans will succeed.

Proverbs 16:3 NLT

How do you define success? Do you define it as the accumulation of material possessions or the adulation of your neighbors? If so, you need to reorder your priorities. Genuine success has little to do with fame or fortune; it has everything to do with God's gift of love and His promise of salvation.

If you have accepted Christ as your personal Savior, you are already a towering success in the eyes of God, but there is still more that you can do. Your task—as a believer who has been touched by the Creator's grace—is to accept the spiritual abundance and peace that He offers through the person of His Son. Then, you can share the healing message of God's love and His abundance with a world that desperately needs both. When you do, you have reached the pinnacle of success.

Maintenance of the devotional mood is indispensable to success in the Christian life.

A. W. Tozer

Today's Prayer

Dear Lord, let Your plans be my plans. Let Your will be my will. And let Your Word be my guide as I focus not on the world's approval but on Your approval. Amen

Relying upon Him

Humble yourselves therefore under the mighty hand of God, so that He may exalt you in due time, casting all your care upon Him, because He cares about you.

1 Peter 5:6-7 HCSB

God is a never-ending source of support and courage for those of us who call upon Him. When we are weary, He gives us strength. When we see no hope, God reminds us of His promises. When we grieve, God wipes away our tears.

Do the demands of this day threaten to overwhelm you? If so, you must rely not only upon your own resources but also upon the promises of your Father in Heaven. God will hold your hand and walk with you every day of your life if you let Him. So even if your circumstances are difficult, trust the Father. His love is eternal and His goodness endures forever.

Faith is not merely you holding on to God—it is God holding on to you.

E. Stanley Jones

Today's Prayer

Heavenly Father, You never leave or forsake me. You are always with me, protecting me and encouraging me. Whatever this day may bring, I thank You for Your love and Your strength. Amen

The Courage to Live Boldly

For God has not given us a spirit of fearfulness, but one of power, love, and sound judgment.

2 Timothy 1:7 HCSB

Do you prefer to face your fears rather than run from them? If so, you will be blessed because of your willingness to live courageously.

When Paul wrote Timothy, he reminded his young protégé that the God they served was a bold God, and God's spirit empowered His children with boldness also. Like Timothy, we face times of uncertainty and fear. God's message is the same to us, today, as it was to Timothy: We can live boldly because the spirit of God resides in us.

So today, as you face the challenges of everyday living, remember that God is with you . . . and you are protected.

———————

The Holy Spirit is no skeptic, and the things He has written in our hearts are not doubts or opinions, but assertions—surer and more certain than sense or life itself.

Martin Luther

Today's Prayer

Lord, I'm only human, and sometimes I am afraid. But You are always with me, and when I turn to You, You give me courage. Let me be a faith-filled Christian, God, and keep me mindful that, with You as my protector, I am secure today . . . and throughout eternity. Amen

Additional Responsibilities

So he who had received five talents came and brought five other talents, saying, "Lord, you delivered to me five talents; look, I have gained five more talents besides them." His lord said to him, "Well done, good and faithful servant; you were faithful over a few things, I will make you ruler over many things. Enter into the joy of your lord."

Matthew 25:20-21 NKJV

God has promised us this: when we do our duties in small matters, He will give us additional responsibilities. Sometimes, those responsibilities come when God changes the course of our lives so that we may better serve Him. Sometimes, our rewards come in the form of temporary setbacks that lead, in turn, to greater victories. Sometimes, God rewards us by answering "no" to our prayers so that He can say "yes" to a far grander request that we, with our limited understanding, would never have thought to ask for.

If you seek to be God's servant in great matters, be faithful, be patient, and be dutiful in smaller matters. Then step back and watch as God surprises you with the spectacular creativity of His infinite wisdom and His perfect plan.

Today's Prayer

Lord, You have a plan for my life. Let me discover it and live it. Today, I will seek Your will, knowing that when I trust in You, dear Father, I am eternally blessed. Amen

Smiles and More Smiles

Jacob said, "For what a relief it is to see your friendly smile. It is like seeing the smile of God!"

Genesis 33:10 NLT

Life should never be taken for granted. Each day is a priceless gift from God and should be treated as such.

Hannah Whitall Smith observed, "How changed our lives would be if we could only fly through the days on wings of surrender and trust!" And Clement of Alexandria noted, "All our life is a celebration for us; we are convinced, in fact, that God is always everywhere. We sing while we work…we pray while we carry out all life's other occupations." These words remind us that this day is God's creation, a gift to be treasured and savored.

Today, let us celebrate life with smiles on our faces and kind words on our lips. After all, this is God's day, and He has given us clear instructions for its use. We are commanded to rejoice and be glad. So, with no further ado, let the celebration begin.

———

Christ and joy go together.

E. Stanley Jones

Today's Prayer

Lord, Your desire is that I be complete in Your joy. Joy begets celebration. Today, I celebrate the life and work You have given me, and I celebrate the lives of my friends and family. Thank You, Father, for Your love, for Your blessings, and for Your joy. Let me treasure Your gifts and share them this day and forever. Amen

Always with Us

For unto us a Child is born, unto us a Son is given; and the government will be upon His shoulder. And His name will be called Wonderful, Counselor, Mighty God, Everlasting Father, Prince of Peace.

Isaiah 9:6 NKJV

Are you facing uncertain circumstances or unwelcome changes? If so, please remember that God is far bigger than any problem you may face. So, instead of worrying about life's inevitable challenges, put your faith in the Father and His only begotten Son: "Jesus Christ is the same yesterday, today, and forever" (Hebrews 13:8 NKJV). And remember: it is precisely because your Savior does not change that you can face your challenges with courage for today and hope for tomorrow.

Life is often challenging, but as Christians, we should not be afraid. God loves us, and He will protect us. In times of hardship, He will comfort us; in times of change, He will guide our steps. When we are troubled, or weak, or sorrowful, God is always with us. We must build our lives on the rock that cannot be moved . . . we must trust in God. Always.

Today's Prayer

Dear Lord, our world is constantly changing. When I face the inevitable transitions of life, I will turn to You for strength and assurance. Thank You, Father, for love that is unchanging and everlasting. Amen

Thy Will Be Done

"Father, if it is Your will, take this cup away from Me; nevertheless not My will, but Yours, be done."

Luke 22:42 NKJV

As human beings with limited understanding, we can never fully comprehend the will of God. But as believers in a benevolent God, we must always trust the will of our Heavenly Father.

Before His crucifixion, Jesus went to the Mount of Olives and poured out His heart to God. Jesus knew of the agony that He was destined to endure, but He also knew that God's will must be done. We, like our Savior, face trials that bring fear and trembling to the very depths of our souls, but like Christ, we, too, must ultimately seek God's will, not our own. When we entrust our lives to Him completely and without reservation, He gives us the strength to meet any challenge, the courage to face any trial, and the wisdom to live in His righteousness.

Wherever you are, be all there. Live to the hilt every situation you believe to be the will of God.

Jim Elliot

Today's Prayer

Dear Lord, You are the Creator of the universe, and I know that Your plan for my life is grander than I can imagine. Let Your purposes be my purposes, and let me trust in the assurance of Your promises. Amen

Finding Encouragement

Haven't I commanded you: be strong and courageous? Do not be afraid or discouraged, for the Lord your God is with you wherever you go.

Joshua 1:9 HCSB

God offers us the strength to meet our challenges, and He offers us hope for the future. One way that He shares His message of hope is through the words of encouraging friends and family members.

Hope, like other human emotions, is contagious. If we associate with hope-filled, enthusiastic people, their enthusiasm will have a tendency to lift our spirits. But if we find ourselves spending too much time in the company of naysayers, pessimists, or cynics, our thoughts—like the naysayers'—will tend to be negative.

Are you a hopeful, optimistic Christian? And do you associate with like-minded people? If so, then you're both wise and blessed.

———————

The Christian life is not a constant high. I have my moments of deep discouragement. I have to go to God in prayer with tears in my eyes, and say, "O God, forgive me," or "Help me."

Billy Graham

Today's Prayer

Heavenly Father, when I am discouraged, I will turn to You, and I will also turn to my Christian friends. I thank You, Father, for friends and family members who are willing to encourage me. I will acknowledge their encouragement, and I will share it. Amen

Extreme Changes

Then he told them what they could expect for themselves: "Anyone who intends to come with me has to let me lead."

Luke 9:23 MSG

Jesus made an extreme sacrifice for you. Are you willing to make extreme changes in your life for Him? Can you honestly say that you're passionate about your faith and that you're really following Jesus? Hopefully so. But if you're preoccupied with other things—or if you're strictly a one-day-a-week Christian—then you're in need of an extreme spiritual makeover!

Nothing is more important than your wholehearted commitment to your Creator and to His only begotten Son. Your faith must never be an afterthought; it must be your ultimate priority, your ultimate possession, and your ultimate passion. You are the recipient of Christ's love. Accept it enthusiastically and share it passionately. Jesus deserves your extreme enthusiasm, the world deserves it, and you deserve the experience of sharing it.

Jesus Christ is not a security from storms. He is perfect security in storms.

Kathy Troccoli

Today's Prayer

Dear Lord, You sent Jesus to save the world and to save me. I thank You for Jesus, and I will do my best to follow Him, today and forever. Amen

A Light for the Path

Your word is a lamp to my feet and a light to my path.

Psalm 119:105 NKJV

Are you a person who trusts God's Word without reservation? Hopefully so, because the Bible is unlike any other book—it is a guidebook for life here on earth and for life eternal. The Psalmist describes God's Word as, "a light to my path." Is the Bible your lamp? If not, you are depriving yourself of a priceless gift from the Creator.

Vance Havner observed, "It takes calm, thoughtful, prayerful meditation on the Word to extract its deepest nourishment." How true. God's Word can be a roadmap to a place of righteous and abundance. Make it your roadmap. God's wisdom can be a light to guide your steps. Claim it as your light today, tomorrow, and every day of your life—and then walk confidently in the footsteps of God's only begotten Son.

The Scriptures were not given for our information, but for our transformation.

D. L. Moody

Today's Prayer

Heavenly Father, Your Word is a light unto the world; I will study it, trust it, and share it. In all that I do, help me be a worthy witness for You as I share the Good News of Your perfect Son and Your perfect Word. Amen

His Strength Is Sufficient

Now glory be to God! By his mighty power at work within us, he is able to accomplish infinitely more than we would ever dare to ask or hope.

Ephesians 3:20 NLT

Have you really tapped in to God's power? Have you turned your life and your heart over to Him, or are you still trying to do everything by yourself? The answer to these simple questions will determine the quality of your day and the direction of your life.

The Bible promises that you can do great things when you avail yourself of God's power. But how can you tap in? By allowing the Creator to work in you and through you—and by placing Him squarely at the center of your heart, that's how.

When you accept God's love and experience His power—when you trust Him to manage His world and yours—you will discover that He offers the strength to live victoriously today, tomorrow, and forever. So don't delay. Accept His strength now.

If God sends us on stony paths, He provides strong shoes.

Corrie ten Boom

Today's Prayer

Lord, You have promised never to leave me or forsake me. You are always with me, protecting me and encouraging me. Whatever this day may bring, I thank You for Your love and for Your strength. Let me lean upon You, Father, this day and forever. Amen

A Fresh Opportunity

When we were baptized, we were buried with Christ and shared his death. So, just as Christ was raised from the dead by the wonderful power of the Father, we also can live a new life.

Romans 6:4 NCV

God's Word is clear: When we genuinely invite Him to reign over our hearts, and when we accept His transforming love, we are forever changed. When we welcome Christ into our hearts, an old life ends and a new way of living—along with a completely new way of viewing the world—begins.

Each morning offers a fresh opportunity to invite Christ, yet once again, to rule over our hearts and our days. Each morning presents yet another opportunity to take up His cross and follow in His footsteps. Today, let us rejoice in the new life that is ours through Christ, and let us follow Him, step by step, on the path that He first walked.

When I met Christ, I felt that I had swallowed sunshine.

E. Stanley Jones

Today's Prayer

Heavenly Father, renew in me the passion to share the Good News of Jesus Christ. Make the experience of my conversion real and fresh so that I might be an effective witness for You. Amen

An Attitude of Gratitude

And let the peace of God rule in your hearts . . . and be ye thankful.

Colossians 3:15 KJV

For most of us, life is busy and complicated. We have countless responsibilities, some of which begin before sunrise and many of which end long after sunset. Amid the rush and crush of the daily grind, it is easy to lose sight of God and His blessings. But, when we forget to slow down and say "Thank You" to our Maker, we rob ourselves of His presence, His peace, and His joy.

Our task, as believing Christians, is to praise God many times each day. Then, with gratitude in our hearts, we can face our daily duties with the perspective and power that only He can provide.

Nobody who gets enough food and clothing in a world where most are hungry and cold has any business to talk about "misery."

C. S. Lewis

Today's Prayer

Lord, You have given me much; when I think of Your grace and goodness, I am humbled and thankful. Today, I will praise You with my words and my deeds . . . and may all the glory be Yours. Amen

Commissioned to Witness

Go, therefore, and make disciples of all nations, baptizing them in the name of the Father and of the Son and of the Holy Spirit, teaching them to observe everything I have commanded you. And remember, I am with you always, to the end of the age.

Matthew 28:19-20 HCSB

After His resurrection, Jesus addressed His disciples. As recorded in the 28th chapter of Matthew, Christ instructed His followers to share His message with the world. This "Great Commission" applies to Christians of every generation, including our own.

As believers, we are called to share the Good News of Jesus with our families, with our neighbors, and with the world. Christ commanded His disciples to become fishers of men. We must do likewise, and we must do so today. Tomorrow may indeed be too late.

Witnessing is not something that we do for the Lord; it is something that He does through us if we are filled with the Holy Spirit.

Warren Wiersbe

Today's Prayer

Heavenly Father, every man and woman, every boy and girl is Your child. You desire that all Your children know Jesus as their Lord and Savior. Father, let me be part of Your Great Commission. Let me give, let me pray, and let me go out into this world so that I might be a fisher of men . . . for You. Amen

God Is Love

God is love; and he that dwelleth in love dwelleth in God, and God in him.

1 John 4:16 KJV

The Bible makes this promise: God is love. It's a sweeping statement, a profoundly important description of what God is and how God works. God's love is perfect. When we open our hearts to His perfect love, we are touched by the Creator's hand, and we are transformed.

Today, even if you can only carve out a few quiet moments, offer sincere prayers of thanksgiving to your Creator. He loves you now and throughout all eternity. Open your heart to His presence and His love.

———◦———

Even when we cannot see the why and wherefore of God's dealings, we know that there is love in and behind them, so we can rejoice always.

J. I. Packer

Today's Prayer

Dear God, You are love. You love me, Father, and I love You. As I love You more, Lord, I am also able to love my family and friends more. I will be Your loving servant, Lord, today and throughout eternity. Amen

What Doesn't Change

Jesus Christ is the same yesterday, today, and forever.

Hebrews 13:8 HCSB

Our world is in a state of constant change. God is not. At times, the world seems to be trembling beneath our feet. But we can be comforted in the knowledge that our Heavenly Father is the rock that cannot be shaken. His Word promises, "I am the Lord, I do not change" (Malachi 3:6 NKJV).

Every day that we live, we mortals encounter a multitude of changes—some good, some not so good, some downright disheartening. On those occasions when us must endure life-changing personal losses that leave us breathless, there is a place we can turn for comfort and assurance—we can turn to God. When we do, our loving Heavenly Father stands ready to protect us, to comfort us, to guide us, and, in time, to heal us.

In a world kept chaotic by change, you will eventually discover, as I have, that this is one of the most precious qualities of the God we are looking for: He doesn't change.

Bill Hybels

Today's Prayer

Dear Lord, our world changes, but You are unchanging. When I face challenges that leave me discouraged or fearful, I will turn to You for strength and assurance. Let my trust in You—like Your love for me—be unchanging and everlasting. Amen

Growing in Christ

When I was a child, I spoke as a child, I understood as a child, I thought as a child; but when I became a man, I put away childish things.

1 Corinthians 13:11 NKJV

The journey toward spiritual maturity lasts a lifetime. As Christians, we can and should continue to grow in the love and the knowledge of our Savior as long as we live. Norman Vincent Peale had the following advice for believers of all ages: "Ask the God who made you to keep remaking you." That advice, of course, is perfectly sound, but often ignored.

When we cease to grow, either emotionally or spiritually, we do ourselves a profound disservice. But, if we study God's Word, if we obey His commandments, and if we live in the center of His will, we will not be "stagnant" believers; we will, instead, be growing Christians . . . and that's exactly what God wants for our lives.

———

Every great company, every great brand, and every great career has been built in exactly the same way: bit by bit, step by step, little by little.

John Maxwell

Today's Prayer

Dear Lord, I know that I still have so many things to learn. I won't stop learning, I won't give up, and I won't stop growing. Every day, I will do my best to become a little bit more like the person You intend for me to be. Amen

Beyond Guilt

There is therefore now no condemnation to those who are in Christ Jesus, who do not walk according to the flesh, but according to the Spirit.

Romans 8:1 NKJV

All of us have sinned. Sometimes our sins result from our own stubborn rebellion against God's commandments. And sometimes, we are swept up in events that are beyond our abilities to control. Under either set of circumstances, we may experience intense feelings of guilt. But God has an answer for the guilt that we feel. That answer, of course, is His forgiveness. When we confess our wrongdoings and repent from them, we are forgiven by the One who created us.

Are you troubled by feelings of guilt or regret? If so, you must repent from your misdeeds, and you must ask your Heavenly Father for His forgiveness. When you do so, He will forgive you completely and without reservation. Then, you must forgive yourself just as God has forgiven you: thoroughly and unconditionally.

Guilt is a healthy regret for telling God one thing and doing another.

Max Lucado

Today's Prayer

Dear Lord, thank You for the guilt that I feel when I disobey You. Help me confess my wrongdoings, help me accept Your forgiveness, and help me renew my passion to serve You. Amen

The Power of Perseverance

I do not consider myself yet to have taken hold of it. But one thing I do: Forgetting what is behind and straining toward what is ahead, I press on toward the goal to win the prize for which God has called me heavenward in Christ Jesus.

Philippians 3:13-14 NIV

A well-lived life calls for preparation, determination, and, of course, lots of perseverance. As an example of perfect perseverance, we Christians need look no further than our Savior, Jesus Christ. Jesus finished what He began. Despite His suffering, despite the shame of the cross, Jesus was steadfast in His faithfulness to God. We, too, must remain faithful, especially during times of hardship. Sometimes, God may answer our prayers with silence, and when He does, we must patiently persevere.

Are you facing a tough situation? If so, remember this: whatever your problem, God can handle it. Your job is to keep persevering until He does.

Today's Prayer

Lord, when life is difficult, I am tempted to abandon hope in the future. But You are my God, and I can draw strength from You. Let me trust You, Father, in good times and in bad times. Let me persevere—even if my soul is troubled—and let me follow Your Son Jesus Christ this day and forever. Amen

Protected

Be of good courage, and He shall strengthen your heart, all you who hope in the Lord.

Psalm 31:24 NKJV

Being a godly person in this difficult world is no easy task. Ours is a time of uncertainty and danger, a time when even the most courageous have legitimate cause for concern. But as believers we can live courageously, knowing that we have been saved by a loving Father and His only begotten Son.

Are you anxious? Take those anxieties to God. Are you troubled? Take your troubles to Him. Seek protection from the One who cannot be moved. And then live courageous, knowing that even in these troubled times, God is always as near as your next breath—and you are always protected.

—————

Faith is stronger than fear.

John Maxwell

Today's Prayer

Dear Lord, fill me with Your Spirit and help me face my challenges with courage and determination. Keep me mindful, Father, that You are with me always—and with You by my side, I have nothing to fear. Amen

The Power of Words

The wise store up knowledge, but the mouth of the fool hastens destruction.

Proverbs 10:14 HCSB

All too often, in the rush to have ourselves heard, we speak first and think next . . . with unfortunate results. God's Word reminds us that, "Reckless words pierce like a sword, but the tongue of the wise brings healing" (Proverbs 12:18 NIV). If we seek to be a source of encouragement to friends and family, then we must measure our words carefully. Words are important: they can hurt or heal. Words can uplift us or discourage us, and reckless words, spoken in haste, cannot be erased.

Today, measure your words carefully. Use words of kindness and praise, not words of anger or derision. Remember that you have the power to heal others or to injure them, to lift others up or to hold them back. When you lift them up, your wisdom will bring healing and comfort to a world that needs both.

———

Attitude and the spirit in which we communicate are as important as the words we say.

Charles Stanley

Today's Prayer

Dear Lord, You have commanded me to choose my words carefully so that I might be a source of encouragement and hope to all whom I meet. Let the words that I speak today be worthy of the One who has saved me forever. Amen

In Times of Adversity

For whatever is born of God overcomes the world. And this is the victory that has overcome the world—our faith.

1 John 5:4 NKJV

All of us face times of adversity. On occasion, we all must endure the disappointments and tragedies that befall believers and nonbelievers alike. The reassuring words of 1 John 5:4 remind us that when we accept God's grace, we overcome the passing hardships of this world by relying upon His strength, His love, and His promise of eternal life.

When we face the inevitable difficulties of life-here-on-earth, God stands ready to protect us. Our responsibility, of course, is to ask Him for protection. When we call upon Him in heartfelt prayer, He will answer—in His own time and according to His own plan—and He will heal us. And while we are waiting for God's plans to unfold and for His healing touch to restore us, we can be comforted in the knowledge that our Creator will can overcome any obstacle, even if we cannot. Let us take God at His word, and let us trust Him.

Today's Prayer

Dear Heavenly Father, when I am troubled, You heal me. When I am afraid, You protect me. When I am discouraged, You lift me up. In times of adversity, let me trust Your plan and Your will for my life. And whatever my circumstances, Lord, let me always give the thanks and the glory to You. Amen

Abundant Peace

The peace of God, which surpasses all understanding, will guard your hearts and minds through Christ Jesus.

Philippians 4:7 NKJV

If you are a thoughtful believer, you will open yourself to the spiritual abundance that your Savior offers by following Him completely and without reservation. When you do, you will receive the love, the peace, and the joy that He has promised.

Do you sincerely seek the riches that our Savior offers to those who give themselves to Him? Then follow Him. When you do, you will receive the love and the abundance that He has promised. Seek first the salvation that is available through a personal, passionate relationship with Christ, and then claim the joy, the peace, and the spiritual abundance that the Shepherd offers His sheep.

God's riches are beyond anything we could ask or even dare to imagine! If my life gets gooey and stale, I have no excuse.

Barbara Johnson

Today's Prayer

Heavenly Father, You have promised an abundant life through Your Son Jesus. Thank You, Lord, for Your abundance and Your peace. Your blessings endure forever, Lord, and I will praise You today, tomorrow, and throughout eternity. Amen

Taking Up the Cross

Then He said to them all, "If anyone wants to come with Me, he must deny himself, take up his cross daily, and follow Me."

Luke 9:23 HCSB

When we have been saved by Christ, we can, if we choose, become passive Christians. We can sit back, secure in our own salvation, and let other believers spread the healing message of Jesus. But to do so is wrong. Instead, we are commanded to become disciples of the One who has saved us, and to do otherwise is a sin of omission with terrible consequences.

When Jesus addressed His disciples, He warned them that each one must, "take up his cross daily and follow Me" (Luke 9:23 NIV). Christ's message was clear: in order to follow Him, Christ's disciples must deny themselves and, instead, trust Him completely. Nothing has changed since then.

Do you seek to fulfill God's purpose for your life? Then follow Christ. Follow Him by picking up His cross today and every day that you live. Then, you will quickly discover that Christ's love has the power to change everything, including you.

Being a disciple involves becoming a learner, a student of the Master.

Charles Stanley

Today's Prayer

Help me, Lord, to understand what cross I am to bear this day. Give me the strength and the courage to carry that cross along the path of Your choosing so that I may be a worthy disciple of Your Son. Amen

A Sacrificial Love

I am the good shepherd. The good shepherd lays down his life for the sheep.

John 10:11 NIV

How much does Christ love us? More than we, as mere mortals, can comprehend. His love is perfect and steadfast. Even though we are fallible and wayward, the Shepherd cares for us still. Even though we have fallen far short of the Father's commandments, Christ loves us with a power and depth that is beyond our understanding. The sacrifice that Jesus made upon the cross was made for each of us, and His love endures for eternity.

Christ's love changes everything. When you accept His gift of grace, you are transformed, not only for today, but also for all eternity. If you haven't already done so, accept Jesus Christ as your Savior. He's waiting patiently for you to invite Him into your heart. Please don't make Him wait a single minute longer.

Sacrificial love, giving-up love, is love that is willing to go to any lengths to provide for the well-being of the beloved.

Ed Young

Today's Prayer

Dear Jesus, I am humbled by Your love and mercy. You went to Calvary so that I might have eternal life. Thank You, Jesus, for Your priceless gift, and for Your love. You loved me first, Lord, and I will return Your love today and forever. Amen

Finding Hope

These things I have spoken to you, that in Me you may have peace. In the world you will have tribulation; but be of good cheer, I have overcome the world.

John 16:33 NKJV

There are few sadder sights on earth than the sight of a person who has lost all hope. In difficult times, hope can be elusive, but Christians need never lose it. After all, God is good; His love endures; He has promised His children the gift of eternal life.

If you find yourself falling into the spiritual traps of worry and discouragement, consider the words of Jesus. It was Christ who promised, "In the world you will have tribulation; but be of good cheer, I have overcome the world." This world is indeed a place of trials and tribulations, but as believers, we are secure. God has promised us peace, joy, and eternal life. And, of course, God always keeps His promises.

God is the only one who can make the valley of trouble a door of hope.

Catherine Marshall

Today's Prayer

Dear Lord, let my hopes always reside in You. If I become discouraged, let me turn to You. If I grow tired, let me find strength in You. You are my Father, and I will place my faith, my trust, and my hopes in You. Amen

Be Thankful

Let the peace of Christ rule in your hearts, since as members of one body you were called to peace. And be thankful.

Colossians 3:15 NIV

As Christians, we are blessed beyond measure. God sent His only Son to die for our sins. And, God has given us the priceless gifts of eternal love and eternal life. We, in turn, are instructed to approach our Heavenly Father with reverence and thanksgiving. But sometimes, in the crush of everyday living, we simply don't stop long enough to pause and thank our Creator for the countless blessings He has bestowed upon us.

When we slow down and express our gratitude to the One who made us, we enrich our own lives and the lives of those around us. Thanksgiving should become a habit, a regular part of our daily routines. God has blessed us beyond measure, and we owe Him everything, including our eternal praise. To paraphrase the familiar children's blessing, "God is great, God is good, let us thank Him for . . . everything!"

Today's Prayer

Dear Lord, sometimes, amid the demands of the day, I lose perspective, and I fail to give thanks for Your blessings and for Your love. Today, help me to count those blessings, and let me give thanks to You, Father, for Your love, for Your grace, for Your blessings, and for Your Son. Amen

To God Be the Glory

Clothe yourselves with humility toward one another, because God resists the proud, but gives grace to the humble.

1 Peter 5:5 HCSB

As Christians, we have a profound reason to be humble: We have been refashioned and saved by Jesus Christ, and that salvation came not because of our own good works but because of God's grace. Thus, we are not "self-made"; we are "God-made" and "Christ-saved." How, then, can we be boastful?

Dietrich Bonhoeffer observed, "It is very easy to overestimate the importance of our own achievements in comparison with what we owe others." In other words, reality breeds humility. So, instead of puffing out your chest and saying, "Look at me!", give credit where credit is due, starting with God. And, rest assured: There is no such thing as a self-made man. All of us are made by God . . . and He deserves the glory, not us.

The one true way of dying to self is the way of patience, meekness, humility, and resignation to God.

Andrew Murray

Today's Prayer

Heavenly Father, it is the nature of mankind to be prideful, and I am no exception. When I am boastful, Lord, keep me mindful that all my gifts come from You. Let me grow beyond my need for earthly praise, God, and let me look only to You for approval. Amen

Faith That Moves Mountains

I tell you the truth, you can say to this mountain, "Go, fall into the sea."
And if you have no doubts in your mind and believe that what you say
will happen, God will do it for you.

Mark 11:23 NCV

Because we live in a demanding world, all of us have mountains to climb and mountains to move. Moving those mountains requires faith.

Are you a mountain mover whose faith is evident for all to see? Hopefully so. God needs more men who are willing to move mountains for His glory and for His kingdom.

God walks with you, ready and willing to strengthen you. Accept His strength today. And remember—Jesus taught His disciples that if they had faith, they could move mountains. You can too . . . so with no further ado, let the mountain-moving begin.

Faith is a strong power, mastering any difficulty in the strength of the Lord who made Heaven and earth.

Corrie ten Boom

Today's Prayer

Lord, I want a faith that moves mountains. You are a big God with big plans for this world and for me. Help me to dream big and be ready for a mountain moving day. Amen.

Infinite Possibilities

Is anything too hard for the LORD?

Genesis 18:14 KJV

Ours is a God of infinite possibilities. But sometimes, because of limited faith and limited understanding, we wrongly assume that God cannot or will not intervene in the affairs of mankind. Such assumptions are simply wrong.

Are you afraid to ask God to do big things in your life? Is your faith threadbare and worn? If so, it's time to abandon your doubts and reclaim your faith in God's promises.

God's Holy Word makes it clear: absolutely nothing is impossible for the Lord. And since the Bible means what it says, you can be comforted in the knowledge that the Creator of the universe can do miraculous things in your own life and in the lives of your loved ones. Your challenge, as a believer, is to take God at His word, and to expect the miraculous.

So God's patience is His power over Himself. Great is that God who, having all power, yet keeps all power subject to Himself.

Jim Elliot

Today's Prayer

Dear God, nothing is impossible for You—keep me always mindful of Your strength. When I lose hope, give me faith; when others lose hope, let me tell them of Your glory and Your works. Today, Lord, let me expect the miraculous, and let me trust in You. Amen

The Self-fulfilling Prophecy

May He grant you according to your heart's desire, and fulfill all your purpose.

Psalm 20:4 NKJV

The self-fulfilling prophecy is alive, well, and living at your house. If you trust God and have faith for the future, your optimistic beliefs will give you direction and motivation. That's one reason that you should never lose hope, but certainly not the only reason. The primary reason that you, as a believer, should never lose hope, is because of God's unfailing promises.

Make no mistake about it: thoughts are powerful things; your thoughts have the power to lift you up or to hold you down. When you acquire the habit of hopeful thinking, you will have acquired a powerful tool for improving your life. So if you fall into the habit of negative thinking, think again. After all, God's Word teaches us that Christ can overcome every difficulty (John 16:33). And when God makes a promise, He keeps it.

———

Everything that is done in the world is done by hope.

Martin Luther

Today's Prayer

Dear Lord, make me a hope-filled Christian. If I become discouraged, let me turn to You. If I grow weary, let me seek strength in You. In every aspect of my life, I will trust You, Father, today and forever. Amen

A Passion for Life

But those who trust in the Lord will renew their strength; they will soar on wings like eagles; they will run and not grow weary; they will walk and not faint.

Isaiah 40:31 HCSB

Are you enthusiastic about your life and your faith? Hopefully so. But if your zest for life has waned, it is now time to redirect your efforts and recharge your spiritual batteries. And that means refocusing your priorities (by putting God first) and counting your blessings (instead of your troubles).

Nothing is more important than your wholehearted commitment to your Creator and to His only begotten Son. Your faith must never be an afterthought; it must be your ultimate priority, your ultimate possession, and your ultimate passion. When you become passionate about your faith, you'll become passionate about your life, too. And God will smile.

If your heart has grown cold, it is because you have moved away from the fire of His presence.

Beth Moore

Today's Prayer

Dear Lord, if the obligations of the day leave me exhausted or discouraged, I will turn to You for strength and for renewal. When I follow Your will for my life, You will renew my enthusiasm. Let Your will be my will, Lord, and let me find strength and courage in You. Amen

Lessons to Learn

Reverence for the Lord is the foundation of true wisdom. The rewards of wisdom come to all who obey him.

Psalm 111:10 NLT

Whether you're twenty-two or a hundred and two, you've still got lots to learn. Even if you're very wise, God isn't finished with you yet, and He isn't finished teaching you important lessons about life here on earth and life eternal.

God does not intend for you to remain stuck in one place. Far from it! God wants you to continue growing as a person and as a Christian every day that you live. And make no mistake: both spiritual and intellectual growth are possible during every stage of life—during the happiest days or the hardest ones.

Your Bible contains powerful prescriptions for overcoming tough times. When you study God's Word and live according to His commandments, adversity becomes a practical instructor. While you're enduring difficult days, you learn lessons you simply could not have learned any other way. And when you learn those lessons, you will serve as a shining example to your friends, to your family, and to the world.

Today's Prayer

Dear Lord, let me listen carefully to You. When I listen, I learn. Let me become a better listener today than I was yesterday, and let me become an even better listener tomorrow. Amen

Great Is Thy Faithfulness

God is faithful, by whom you were called into the fellowship of His Son,
Jesus Christ our Lord.

1 Corinthians 1:9 NKJV

God is faithful to us even when we are not faithful to Him. God keeps His promises to us even when we stray far from His will. He continues to love us even when we disobey His commandments. But God does not force His blessings upon us. If we are to experience His love and His grace, we must claim them for ourselves.

Are you tired, discouraged, or fearful? Be comforted: God is with you. Are you confused? Listen to the quiet voice of your Heavenly Father. Are you bitter? Talk with God and seek His guidance. Are you celebrating a great victory? Thank God and praise Him. He is the Giver of all things good. In whatever condition you find yourself, trust God and be comforted. The Father is with you now and forever.

The God of the galaxies is the God who knows when your heart is broken—and He can heal it!

Warren Wiersbe

Today's Prayer

Your faithfulness, Lord, is everlasting. You are faithful to me even when I am not faithful to You. Today, let me serve You with my heart, my soul, and my mind. And, then, let me rest in the knowledge of Your constant love for me. Amen

Forgive: It's God's Way

And be kind and compassionate to one another, forgiving one another, just as God also forgave you in Christ.

Ephesians 4:32 HCSB

To forgive others is difficult. Being frail, fallible, imperfect human beings, we are quick to anger, quick to blame, slow to forgive, and even slower to forget. No matter. Forgiveness, no matter how difficult, is God's way, and it must be our way, too.

God's commandments are not intended to be customized for the particular whims of particular believers. God's word is not a menu from which each of us may select items à la carte, according to our own desires. Far from it. God's Holy Word is a book that must be taken in its entirety; all of God's commandments are to be taken seriously. And, so it is with forgiveness. So, if you hold bitterness against even a single person, forgive. Then, to the best of your abilities, forget. It's God's way for you to live.

Looking back over my life, all I can see is mercy and grace written in large letters everywhere. May God help me have the same kind of heart toward those who wound or offend me.

Jim Cymbala

Today's Prayer

Heavenly Father, genuine forgiveness is difficult. Help me to forgive those who have injured me, and deliver me from the traps of anger and bitterness. Forgiveness is Your way, Lord; let it be mine. Amen

No Shortcuts

Those who work their land will have plenty of food, but the ones who chase empty dreams instead will end up poor.

Proverbs 28:19 NCV

The world often promises instant gratification: Get rich—today. Lose weight—this week. Have whatever you want—right now. Yet life's experiences and God's Word teach us that the best things in life require heaping helpings of both time and work.

It has been said, quite correctly, that there are no shortcuts to any place worth going. So it's important to remember that hard work is not simply a proven way to get ahead, it's also part of God's plan.

Today, do yourself this favor: Don't look for shortcuts (because there aren't any) and don't expect easy solutions to life's big challenges (because big rewards usually require lots of effort). You inhabit a world in which instant gratification is rare, but the rewards of hard work are not. Shape your expectations—and your work habits—accordingly.

Today's Prayer

Heavenly Father, I seek to be Your faithful servant. When I am tired, give me strength. When I become frustrated, give me patience. When I lose sight of Your purpose for my life, give me a passion for my daily responsibilities, and when I have completed my work, let all the honor and glory be Yours. Amen

In the Footsteps of Jesus

The one who loves his life will lose it, and the one who hates his life in this world will keep it for eternal life. If anyone serves Me, he must follow Me. Where I am, there My servant also will be. If anyone serves Me, the Father will honor him.

John 12:25-26 HCSB

Whom will you walk with today? Will you walk with people who worship the ways of the world? Or will you walk with the Son of God? Jesus walks with you. Are you walking with Him? Hopefully, you will choose to walk with Him today and every day of your life. God's Word promises that when you follow in Christ's footsteps, you will learn how to live freely and lightly (Matthew 11:28-30).

Are you worried about the day ahead? Be confident in God's power. He will never desert you. Are you concerned about the future? Be courageous and call upon God. He will protect you. Are you confused? Listen to the quiet voice of your Heavenly Father. He is not a God of confusion. So talk with God; listen to Him; and walk with His Son—starting now.

Today's Prayer

Dear Lord, You sent Your Son so that I might have abundant life and eternal life. Thank You, Father, for my Savior, Christ Jesus. I will follow Him, honor Him, and share His Good News, this day and every day. Amen

Behavior That Is Consistent with Your Beliefs

If the way you live isn't consistent with what you believe, then it's wrong.

Romans 14:23 MSG

In describing our beliefs, our actions are far better descriptors than our words. Yet far too many of us spend more energy talking about our beliefs than living by them—with predictably poor results.

As believers, we must beware: Our actions should always give credence to the changes that Christ can make in the lives of those who walk with Him.

Your beliefs shape your values, and your values shape your life. Is your life a clearly-crafted picture book of your creed? Are your actions always consistent with your beliefs? Are you willing to practice the philosophies that you preach? Hopefully so; otherwise, you'll be tormented by inconsistencies between your beliefs and your behaviors.

More depends on my walk than my talk.

D. L. Moody

Today's Prayer

Lord, it is so much easier to speak of the righteous life than it is to live it. Let me live righteously, and let my actions be consistent with my beliefs. Let every step that I take reflect Your truth, and let me live a life that is worthy of Your Son. Amen

A Book Unlike Any Other

For I am not ashamed of the gospel, because it is God's power for salvation to everyone who believes.

Romans 1:16 HCSB

God's Word is unlike any other book. A. W. Tozer wrote, "The purpose of the Bible is to bring men to Christ, to make them holy and prepare them for Heaven. In this it is unique among books, and it always fulfills its purpose."

George Mueller observed, "The vigor of our spiritual lives will be in exact proportion to the place held by the Bible in our lives and in our thoughts." As Christians, we are called upon to study God's Holy Word and then to share it with the world.

The Bible is a priceless gift, a tool for Christians to use as they share the Good News of their Savior, Christ Jesus. Too many Christians, however, keep their spiritual tool kits tightly closed and out of sight. Jonathan Edwards advised, "Be assiduous in reading the Holy Scriptures. This is the fountain whence all knowledge in divinity must be derived. Therefore let not this treasure lie by you neglected." God's Holy Word is, indeed, a priceless, one-of-a-kind treasure. Handle it with care, but, more importantly, handle it every day.

Today's Prayer

Dear Lord, the Bible is Your gift to me. Let me use, let me trust it, and let me obey it, today and every day that I live. Amen

Mid-Course Corrections

The wise see danger ahead and avoid it, but fools keep going and get into trouble.

Proverbs 27:12 NCV

In our fast-paced world, everyday life has become an exercise in managing change. Our circumstances change; our relationships change; our bodies change. We grow older every day, as does our world. Thankfully, God does not change. He is eternal, as are the truths that are found in His Holy Word.

Are you facing one of life's inevitable "mid-course corrections"? If so, you must place your faith, your trust, and your life in the hands of the One who does not change: your Heavenly Father. He is the unmoving rock upon which you must construct this day and every day. When you do, you are secure.

———

Sometimes your medicine bottle says, "Shake well before using." That is what God has to do with some of his people. He has to shake them well before they are usable.

Vance Havner

Today's Prayer

Heavenly Father, when the world seems to be spinning out of control, I will turn to You. I will trust Your wisdom, I will trust Your plans for my life, and I will trust Your Son, this day and every day. Amen

Always Forgiving

Then Peter came to Him and said, "Lord, how many times could my brother sin against me and I forgive him? As many as seven times?" "I tell you, not as many as seven," Jesus said to him, "but 70 times seven."

Matthew 18:21-22 HCSB

How often should we forgive other people? More times than we can count (Matthew 18:21-22). That's a mighty tall order, but we must remember that it's an order from God—an order that must be obeyed.

In God's curriculum, forgiveness isn't optional; it's a required course. Sometimes, of course, we have a very difficult time forgiving the people who have hurt us, but if we don't find it in our hearts to forgive them, we not only hurt ourselves, we also disobey our Father in Heaven. So we must forgive—and keep forgiving—as long as we live.

By not forgiving, by not letting wrongs go, we aren't getting back at anyone. We are merely punishing ourselves by barricading our own hearts.

Jim Cymbala

Today's Prayer

Heavenly Father, keep me mindful that forgiveness is Your commandment. You have forgiven me, Lord; let me show my thankfulness to You by offering forgiveness to others. And, when I do, may others see Your love reflected through my words and deeds. Amen

The Rule That's Golden

Don't be obsessed with getting your own advantage. Forget yourselves long enough to lend a helping hand.

Philippians 2:4 MSG

Sometimes, when we feel happy or generous, we find it easy to be kind. Other times, when we are discouraged or tired, we can scarcely summon the energy to utter a single kind word. But, God's commandment is clear: He intends that we make the conscious choice to treat others with kindness and respect, no matter our circumstances, no matter our emotions.

Today, as you consider all the things that Christ has done in your life, honor Him by following His commandment and obeying the Golden Rule. He expects no less, and He deserves no less.

The mark of a Christian is that he will walk the second mile and turn the other cheek. A wise man or woman gives the extra effort, all for the glory of the Lord Jesus Christ.

John Maxwell

Today's Prayer

Dear Lord, because I expect to be treated with kindness, let me be kind. Because I wish to be loved, let me love others. Because I need forgiveness, let me be merciful. In all things, Lord, let me live by the Golden Rule every day. Amen

The Voice of God

Be silent before Me.

Isaiah 41:1 HCSB

Sometimes God speaks loudly and clearly. More often, He speaks in a quiet voice—and if you are wise, you will be listening carefully when He does. To do so, you must carve out quiet moments each day to study His Word and sense His direction.

Can you quiet yourself long enough to listen to your conscience? Are you attuned to the subtle guidance of your intuition? Are you willing to pray sincerely and then to wait quietly for God's response. Hopefully so. Usually God refrains from sending His messages on stone tablets or city billboards. More often, He communicates in subtler ways. If you sincerely desire to hear His voice, you must listen carefully, and you must do so in the silent corners of your quiet, willing heart.

In the soul-searching of our lives, we are to stay quiet so we can hear Him say all that He wants to say to us in our hearts.

Charles Swindoll

Today's Prayer

Dear Lord, I have so much to learn and You have so much to teach me. Give me the wisdom to be still and the discernment to hear Your voice. Amen

Mentors That Matter

The lips of the righteous feed many.

Proverbs 10:21 HCSB

Here's a simple yet effective way to strengthen your faith: Choose role models whose faith in God is strong.

When you emulate godly people, you become a more godly person yourself. That's why you should seek out mentors who, by their words and their presence, make you a better person and a better Christian.

Today, as a gift to yourself, select, from your friends and family members, a mentor whose judgement you trust. Then listen carefully to your mentor's advice and be willing to accept that advice, even if accepting it requires effort, or pain, or both. Consider your mentor to be God's gift to you. Thank God for that gift, and use it for the glory of His kingdom.

God often keeps us on the path by guiding us through the counsel of friends and trusted spiritual advisors.

Bill Hybels

Today's Prayer

Dear Lord, thank You for family members, for friends, and for mentors. When I am troubled, let me turn to them for help, for guidance, for comfort, and for perspective. And Father, let me be a friend and mentor to others so that my love for You may be reflected in my genuine concern for them. Amen

The Wisdom to Forgive

Therefore, God's chosen ones, holy and loved, put on heartfelt compassion, kindness, humility, gentleness, and patience, accepting one another and forgiving one another if anyone has a complaint against another. Just as the Lord has forgiven you, so also you must forgive.

Colossians 3:12-13 HCSB

When people behave badly, it's hard to forgive them. How hard? Sometimes, it's very hard! But God tells us that we must forgive other people, even when we'd rather not. So, if you're angry with anybody (or if you're upset by something you yourself have done), it's now time to forgive.

God instructs you to treat other people exactly as you wish to be treated. And since you want to be forgiven for the mistakes that you make, you must be willing to extend forgiveness to other people for the mistakes that they have made. If you can't seem to forgive someone, you should keep asking God to help you until you do. And you can be sure of this: if you keep asking for God's help, He will give it.

Today's Prayer

Dear Lord, when I am bitter, You can change my unforgiving heart. And, when I am slow to forgive, Your Word reminds me that forgiveness is Your commandment. Let me be Your obedient servant, Lord, and let me forgive others just as You have forgiven me. Amen

The Importance of Prayer

Be anxious for nothing, but in everything by prayer and supplication, with thanksgiving, let your requests be made known to God.

Philippians 4:6 NKJV

Prayer is a powerful tool for communicating with our Creator; it is an opportunity to commune with the Giver of all things good. Prayer is not a thing to be taken lightly or to be used infrequently. Prayer should never be reserved for mealtimes or for bedtimes; it should be an ever-present focus in our daily lives.

In his first letter to the Thessalonians, Paul wrote, "Rejoice evermore. Pray without ceasing. In every thing give thanks: for this is the will of God in Christ Jesus concerning you" (5:17-18 KJV). Paul's words apply to every Christian of every generation. So, let us pray constantly about things great and small. God is listening, and He wants to hear from us. Now.

––––––––––

Each time, before you intercede, be quiet first and worship God in His glory. Think of what He can do and how He delights to hear the prayers of His redeemed people. Think of your place and privilege in Christ, and expect great things!

Andrew Murray

Today's Prayer

Dear Lord, I will open my heart to You. I will take my concerns, my fears, my plans, and my hopes to You in prayer. And, then, I will trust the answers that You give. You are my loving Father, and I will accept Your will for my life. Amen

With You Always

You reveal the path of life to me; in Your presence is abundant joy; in Your right hand are eternal pleasures.

Psalm 16:11 HCSB

Do you ever wonder if God is really here? If so, you're not the first person to think such thoughts. In fact, some of the biggest heroes in the Bible had their doubts—and so, perhaps, will you. But when questions arise and doubts begin to creep into your mind, remember this: You can talk with God any time. In fact, He's right here, right now, listening to your thoughts and prayers, watching over your every move.

Sometimes, you will allow yourself to become very busy, and that's when you may be tempted to ignore God. But, when you quiet yourself long enough to acknowledge His presence, God will touch your heart and restore your spirits. By the way, He's ready to talk right now. Are you?

———

What a comfort to know that God is present there in your life, available to meet every situation with you, that you are never left to face any problem alone.

Vonette Bright

Today's Prayer

Dear Lord, You are with me when I am strong and when I am weak. You never leave my side, even when it seems to me that You are far away. Today and every day, let me trust Your promises and let me feel Your love. Amen

Strength for the Day

I can do all things through Christ which strengtheneth me.

Philippians 4:13 KJV

Have you made God the cornerstone of your life, or is He relegated to a few hours on Sunday morning? Have you genuinely allowed God to reign over every corner of your heart, or have you attempted to place Him in a spiritual compartment? The answer to these questions will determine the direction of your day and your life.

God loves you. In times of trouble, He will comfort you; in times of sorrow, He will dry your tears. When you are weak or sorrowful, God is as near as your next breath. He stands at the door of your heart and waits. Welcome Him in and allow Him to rule. And then, accept the peace, and the strength, and the protection, and the abundance that only God can give.

The God we seek is a God who is intrinsically righteous and who will be so forever. With His example and His strength, we can share in that righteousness.

Bill Hybels

Today's Prayer

Lord, sometimes life is difficult. Sometimes, I am worried, weary, or discouraged. Life can be a struggle, but, when I lift my eyes to You, Father, You strengthen me. Today, I will turn to You, Lord, for strength, for hope, and for salvation. Amen

Cheerfulness 101

A happy heart is like a continual feast.

Proverbs 15:15 NCV

Few things in life are more sad, or, for that matter, more absurd, than a grumpy Christian. Christ promises us lives of abundance and joy, but He does not force His joy upon us. We must claim His joy for ourselves, and when we do, Jesus, in turn, fills our spirits with His power and His love.

How can we receive from Christ the joy that is rightfully ours? By giving Him what is rightfully His: our hearts and our souls.

When we earnestly commit ourselves to the Savior of mankind, when we place Jesus at the center of our lives and trust Him as our personal Savior, He will transform us, not just for today, but for all eternity. Then we, as God's children, can share Christ's joy and His message with a world that needs both.

If His presence does not cheer you, surely Heaven itself would not make you glad; for what is Heaven but the full enjoyment of His love?

C. H. Spurgeon

Today's Prayer

Dear Lord, You have given me so many reasons to be happy, and I want to be a cheerful Christian. Today and every day, I will do my best to share my happiness with my family and my friends. Amen

Nourished by the Word

You will be a good servant of Christ Jesus, nourished by the words of the faith and of the good teaching that you have followed.

1 Timothy 4:6 HCSB

Do you read your Bible a lot . . . or not? The answer to this simple question will determine, to a surprising extent, the quality of your life and the direction of your faith.

As you establish priorities for life, you must decide whether God's Word will be a bright spotlight that guides your path every day or a tiny nightlight that occasionally flickers in the dark. The decision to study the Bible—or not—is yours and yours alone. But make no mistake: how you choose to use your Bible will have a profound impact on you and your loved ones.

The Bible is the ultimate guide for life; make it your guidebook as well. When you do, you can be comforted in the knowledge that your steps are guided by a Source of wisdom and truth that never fails.

Some read the Bible to learn, and some read the Bible to hear from Heaven.

Andrew Murray

Today's Prayer

Lord, You've given me instructions for life here on earth and for life eternal. I will use the Bible as my guide. I will study it and meditate upon it as I trust You, Lord, to speak to me through Your Holy Word. Amen

Never-Ending Love

And we have this command from Him: the one who loves God must also love his brother.

1 John 4:21 HCSB

C. S. Lewis observed, "A man's spiritual health is exactly proportional to his love for God." If we are to enjoy the spiritual health that God intends for us, we must praise Him, we must love Him, and we must obey Him.

When we worship God faithfully and obediently, we invite His love into our hearts. When we truly worship God, we allow Him to rule over our days and our lives. In turn, we grow to love God even more deeply as we sense His love for us.

Today, open your heart to the Father. And let your obedience be a fitting response to His never-ending love.

I love Him because He first loved me, and He still does love me, and He will love me forever and ever.

Bill Bright

Today's Prayer

Dear Heavenly Father, You have blessed me with a love that is infinite and eternal. Let me love You, Lord, more and more each day. Make me a loving servant, Father, today and throughout eternity. And, let me show my love for You by sharing Your message and Your love with others. Amen

Problems in Perspective

It is important to look at things from God's point of view.

1 Corinthians 4:6 MSG

If a temporary loss of perspective has left you worried, exhausted, or both, it's time to readjust your thought patterns. Negative thoughts are habit-forming; thankfully, so are positive ones. With practice, you can form the habit of focusing on God's priorities and your possibilities. When you do, you'll soon discover that you will spend less time fretting about your challenges and more time praising God for His gifts.

When you call upon the Lord and prayerfully seek His will, He will give you wisdom and perspective. When you make God's priorities your priorities, He will direct your steps and calm your fears. So today and every day hereafter, pray for a sense of balance and perspective. And remember: no problems are too big for God— and that includes yours.

Earthly fears are no fears at all. Answer the big question of eternity, and the little questions of life fall into perspective.

Max Lucado

Today's Prayer

Lord, sometimes, the world's perspective can lead me astray. Help me, Lord, to see the world through Your eyes. Give me guidance and wisdom. And keep me ever mindful, Father, that Your reality is the ultimate reality, and that Your truth is the ultimate truth, now and forever. Amen

Taking Time to Ask

He granted their request because they trusted in Him.

1 Chronicles 5:20 HCSB

Sometimes, amid the demands and the frustrations of everyday life, we forget to slow ourselves down long enough to talk with God. Instead of turning our thoughts and prayers to Him, we rely upon our own resources. Instead of praying for strength and courage, we seek to manufacture it within ourselves. Instead of asking God for guidance, we depend only upon our own limited wisdom. The results of such behaviors are unfortunate and, on occasion, tragic.

Are you in need? Ask God to sustain you. Are you troubled? Take your worries to Him in prayer. Are you weary? Seek God's strength. In all things great and small, seek God's wisdom and His grace. He hears your prayers, and He will answer. All you must do is ask.

God's help is near and always available, but it is only given to those who seek it.

Max Lucado

Today's Prayer

Lord, when I have questions or fears, let me turn to You. When I am weak, let me seek Your strength. When I am discouraged, Father, keep me mindful of Your love and Your grace. In all things, let me seek Your will and Your way, dear Lord, today and forever. Amen

Love Is a Choice

Beloved, if God so loved us, we also ought to love one another.

1 John 4:11 NKJV

Love is always a choice. Sometimes, of course, we may "fall in love," but it takes work to stay there. Sometimes, we may be "swept off our feet," but the "sweeping" is only temporary; sooner or later, if love is to endure, one must plant one's feet firmly on the ground. The decision to love another person for a lifetime is much more than the simple process of "falling in" or "being swept up." It requires "reaching out," "holding firm," and "lifting up." Love, then, becomes a decision to honor and care for the other person, come what may.

How do you spell love? When you reach the point where the happiness, security, and development of another person is as much of a driving force to you as your own happiness, security, and development, then you have a mature love. True love is spelled G-I-V-E.

Josh McDowell

Today's Prayer

Dear Lord, You have given me the gift of love; let me share that gift with others. And, keep me mindful that the essence of love is not to receive it, but to give it, today and forever. Amen

The Miracle Worker

Jesus said to them, "I have shown you many great miracles from the Father."

John 10:32 NIV

God is a miracle worker. Throughout history He has intervened in the course of human events in ways that cannot be explained by science or human rationale. And He's still doing so today.

God's miracles are not limited to special occasions, nor are they witnessed by a select few. God is crafting His wonders all around us: the miracle of the birth of a new baby; the miracle of a world renewing itself with every sunrise; the miracle of lives transformed by God's love and grace. Each day, God's handiwork is evident for all to see and experience.

Today, seize the opportunity to inspect God's hand at work. His miracles come in a variety of shapes and sizes, so keep your eyes and your heart open. Be watchful, and you'll soon be amazed.

Throughout history, when God's people found themselves facing impossible odds, they reminded themselves of God's limitless power.

Bill Hybels

Today's Prayer

Dear Lord, absolutely nothing is impossible for You. Let me trust in Your power and in Your miracles. When I lose hope, give me faith; when others lose hope, let me tell them of Your glorious works. Today, Lord, keep me mindful that You are a God of infinite possibilities and infinite love. Amen

What Kind of Example?

In everything set them an example by doing what is good.

Titus 2:7 NIV

What kind of example are you? Are you the kind of person whose life serves as a powerful example of decency and morality? Are you a person whose behavior serves as a positive role model for others? Are you the kind of person whose actions, day in and day out, are based upon integrity, fidelity, and a love for the Lord? If so, you are not only blessed by God, you are also a powerful force for good in a world that desperately needs positive influences such as yours.

Phillips Brooks advised, "Be such a man, and live such a life, that if every man were such as you, and every life a life like yours, this earth would be God's Paradise." And that's sound advice because our families and friends are watching . . . and so, for that matter, is God.

⸺⸺⸺

A holy life will produce the deepest impression. Lighthouses blow no horns; they only shine.

D. L. Moody

Today's Prayer

Lord, make me a worthy example to my family and friends. And, let my words and my actions show people how my life has been changed by You. I will praise You, Father, by following in the footsteps of Your Son. Let others see Him through me. Amen

The Greatest of These

And now abide faith, hope, love, these three; but the greatest of these is love.

1 Corinthians 13:13 NKJV

The beautiful words of 1st Corinthians 13 remind us that love is God's commandment: Faith is important, of course. So, too, is hope. But, love is more important still. We are commanded (not advised, not encouraged . . . commanded!) to love one another just as Christ loved us (John 13:34). That's a tall order, but as Christians, we are obligated to follow it.

Christ showed His love for us on the cross, and we are called upon to return Christ's love by sharing it. Today, let us spread Christ's love to families, friends, and even strangers, so that through us, others might come to know Him.

———

It is important to know that you have to work to keep love alive; you have to protect it and maintain it, just like you would a delicate flower.

James Dobson

Today's Prayer

Lord, love is Your commandment. Help me always to remember that the gift of love is a precious gift indeed. Let me nurture love and treasure it, today and forever. Amen

On a Mission for God

But you are a chosen race, a royal priesthood, a holy nation, a people for His possession, so that you may proclaim the praises of the One who called you out of darkness into His marvelous light.

1 Peter 2:9 HCSB

Whether you realize it or not, you are on a personal mission for God. As a Christian, that mission is straightforward: Honor God, accept Christ as your personal Savior, and serve God's children.

Of course, you will encounter impediments as you attempt to discover the exact nature of God's purpose for your life, but you must never lose sight of the overriding purposes that God has established for all believers. You will encounter these overriding purposes again and again as you worship your Creator and study His Word.

Every day offers countless opportunities to serve God and to worship Him. When you do so, He will bless you in miraculous ways. May you continue to seek God's will, may you trust His Word, and may you place Him where He belongs: at the very center of your life.

Today's Prayer

Dear Lord, I know that You have a purpose for my life, and I will seek that purpose today and every day that I live. Let my actions be pleasing to You, and let me share Your Good News with a world that so desperately needs Your healing hand and the salvation of Your Son. Amen

Faith to Share

This and this only has been my appointed work: getting this news to those who have never heard of God, and explaining how it works by simple faith and plain truth.

1 Timothy 2:7 MSG

Genuine faith is never meant to be locked up in the heart of a believer; to the contrary, it is meant to be shared with the world. But, if you sincerely seek to share your faith, you must first find it.

When a suffering woman sought healing by merely touching the hem of His cloak, Jesus replied, "Daughter, be of good comfort; thy faith hath made thee whole" (Matthew 9:22 KJV). The message to believers of every generation is clear: live by faith every day.

How can you strengthen your faith? Through praise, through worship, through Bible study, and through prayer. And, as your faith becomes stronger, you will find ways to share it with your friends, your family, and with the world.

Our faith grows by expression. If we want to keep our faith, we must share it. We must act.

Billy Graham

Today's Prayer

Lord, help me to be a person whose faith is evident to my family and friends. Help me to remember that You are always near and that You can overcome any challenge. With Your love and Your power, Lord, I will live courageously and share my faith with others, today and every day. Amen

The Lessons of Tough Times

I waited patiently for the Lord, and He turned to me and heard my cry for help. He brought me up from a desolate pit, out of the muddy clay, and set my feet on a rock, making my steps secure. He put a new song in my mouth, a hymn of praise to our God.

Psalm 40:1-3 HCSB

Have you experienced a recent setback? If so, look for the lesson that God is trying to teach you. Instead of complaining about life's sad state of affairs, learn what needs to be learned, change what needs to be changed, and move on. View failure as an opportunity to reassess God's will for your life. View life's inevitable disappointments as opportunities to learn more about yourself and your world.

Life can be difficult at times. And everybody makes mistakes. Your job is to make them only once.

Lord, when we are wrong, make us willing to change; and when we are right, make us easy to live with.

Peter Marshall

Today's Prayer

Lord, I know that I am imperfect and that I fail You in many ways. Thank You for Your forgiveness and for Your unconditional love. Show me the error of my ways, Lord, that I might confess my wrongdoing and correct my mistakes. And, let me grow each day in wisdom, in faith, and in my love for You. Amen

New Beginnings

I will give you a new heart and put a new spirit in you....

Ezekiel 36:26 NIV

If we sincerely want to change ourselves for the better, we must start on the inside and work our way out from there. Lasting change doesn't occur "out there"; it occurs "in here." It occurs, not in the shifting sands of our own particular circumstances, but in quiet depths of our own hearts.

Are you in search of a new beginning or, for that matter, a new you? If so, don't expect changing circumstances to miraculously transform you into the person you want to become. Transformation starts with God, and it starts in the silent center of a humble human heart—like yours.

If we trust God and depend on His grace, we can grow in personal character as we go through trials.

Warren Wiersbe

Today's Prayer

Dear God, conform me to Your image. Create in me a new heart—a heart that reflects the love that You lavish upon me. When I need to change, Lord, change me, and make me new again. Amen

The Wisdom to Obey

And the world with its lust is passing away, but the one who does God's will remains forever.

1 John 2:17 HCSB

Since God created Adam and Eve, we human beings have been rebelling against our Creator. Why? Because we are unwilling to trust God's Word, and we are unwilling to follow His commandments. God has given us a guidebook for righteous living called the Holy Bible. It contains thorough instructions which, if followed, lead to fulfillment, righteousness, and salvation. But, if we choose to ignore God's commandments, the results are as predictable as they are tragic.

Talking about God is easy; living by His commandments is considerably harder. But, unless we are willing to abide by God's laws, all of our righteous proclamations ring hollow. How can we best proclaim our love for the Lord? By obeying Him. And, for further instructions, read the manual.

———

Happiness is obedience, and obedience is happiness.

C. H. Spurgeon

Today's Prayer

Dear Heavenly Father, You have blessed me with a love that is infinite and eternal. I will demonstrate my love for You by obeying Your commandments. Amen

Glorious Opportunities

Make the most of every opportunity.

Colossians 4:5 NIV

Are you excited about the opportunities of today and thrilled
by the possibilities of tomorrow? Do you confidently expect
God to lead you to a place of abundance, peace, and joy? And, when
your days on earth are over, do you expect to receive the priceless
gift of eternal life? If you trust God's promises, and if you have
welcomed God's Son into your heart, then you believe that your
future is intensely and eternally bright.

Today, as you prepare to meet the duties of everyday life, pause
and consider God's promises. And then think for a moment about
the wonderful future that awaits all believers, including you. God
has promised that your future is secure. Trust that promise, and
celebrate the life of abundance and eternal joy that is now yours
through Christ.

———

With the right attitude and a willingness to pay the price, almost
anyone can pursue nearly any opportunity and achieve it.

John Maxwell

Today's Prayer

Lord, as I take the next steps on my life's journey, let me take
them with You. Whatever this day may bring, I thank You for the
opportunity to live abundantly. Let me lean upon You, Father—and
trust You—this day and forever. Amen

Being an Optimistic Christian

Make me hear joy and gladness.

Psalm 51:8 NKJV

To be a pessimistic Christian is a contradiction in terms, yet sometimes even the most devout Christians fall prey to fear, doubt, and discouragement. But, God has a different plan for our lives. The comforting words of the 23rd Psalm remind us of God's blessings. In response to His grace, we should strive to focus our thoughts on things that are pleasing to Him, not upon things that are evil, discouraging, or frustrating.

So, the next time you find yourself mired in the pit of pessimism, remember God's Word and redirect your thoughts. This world is God's creation; look for the best in it, and trust Him to take care of the rest.

Keep your feet on the ground, but let your heart soar as high as it will. Refuse to be average or to surrender to the chill of your spiritual environment.

A. W. Tozer

Today's Prayer

Lord, give me faith, optimism, and hope. Let me expect the best from You, and let me look for the best in others. Let me trust You, Lord, to direct my life. And, let me be Your faithful, hopeful, optimistic servant every day that I live. Amen

Give Me Patience, Lord

We urge you, brethren, admonish the unruly, encourage the fainthearted,
help the weak, be patient with everyone.

1 Thessalonians 5:14 NASB

Most of us are impatient for God to grant us the desires of our heart. Usually, we know what we want, and we know precisely when we want it: right now, if not sooner. But God may have other plans. And when God's plans differ from our own, we must trust in His infinite wisdom and in His infinite love.

As busy people living in a fast-paced world, many of us find that waiting quietly for God is difficult. But God instructs us to be patient in all things. We must be patient with our families, our friends, and our associates. We must also be patient with our Creator as He unfolds His plan for our lives. And that's as it should be. After all, think how patient God has been with us.

It is wise to wait because God gives clear direction only when we are willing to wait.

Charles Stanley

Today's Prayer

Dear Lord, let me live according to Your plan and according to Your timetable. When I am hurried, Lord, slow me down. When I become impatient with others, give me empathy. Today, Lord, let me be a patient Christian, and let me trust in You and in Your master plan. Amen

Making Peace with Your Past

The Lord says, "Forget what happened before, and do not think about the past. Look at the new thing I am going to do. It is already happening. Don't you see it? I will make a road in the desert and rivers in the dry land."

Isaiah 43:18-19 NCV

Have you made peace with your past? If so, congratulations. But, if you are mired in the quicksand of regret, it's time to plan your escape. How can you do so? By accepting what has been and by trusting God for what will be.

Because you are human, you may be slow to forget yesterday's disappointments. But, if you sincerely seek to focus your hopes and energies on the future, then you must find ways to accept the past, no matter how difficult it may be. If you have not yet made peace with the past, today is the day to declare an end to all hostilities. When you do, you can then turn your thoughts to wondrous promises of God and to the glorious future that He has in store for you.

Today's Prayer

Heavenly Father, free me from anger, resentment, and envy. When I am bitter, I cannot feel the peace that You intend for my life. Keep me mindful that forgiveness is Your commandment, and help me accept the past, treasure the present, and trust the future . . . to You. Amen

Choosing Wisely

But the wisdom that is from above is first pure, then peaceable, gentle, willing to yield, full of mercy and good fruits, without partiality and without hypocrisy.

James 3:17 NKJV

Because we are creatures of free will, we make choices—lots of them. When we make choices that are pleasing to our Heavenly Father, we are blessed. When we make choices that cause us to walk in the footsteps of God's Son, we enjoy the abundance that Christ has promised to those who follow Him. But when make choices that are displeasing to God, we sow seeds that have the potential to bring forth a bitter harvest.

Today, as you encounter the challenges of everyday living, you will make hundreds of choices. Choose wisely. Make your thoughts and your actions pleasing to God. And remember: every choice that is displeasing to Him is the wrong choice—no exceptions.

Good and evil both increase at compound interest. That is why the little decisions you and I make every day are of such infinite importance.

C. S. Lewis

Today's Prayer

Dear Lord, today I will focus my thoughts on Your will for my life. I will strive to make decisions that are pleasing to You, and I will strive to follow in the footsteps of Your Son. Amen

Quality Time

So teach us to number our days, that we may gain a heart of wisdom.

Psalm 90:12 NKJV

Make no mistake: caring for your family requires time—lots of time. You've probably heard about "quality time" and "quantity time." Your family needs both. So, as a responsible Christian, you should willingly invest large quantities of your time and energy in the care and nurturing of your clan.

While caring for your family, you should do your best to ensure that God remains squarely at the center of your household. When you do, God will bless you and yours in ways that you could have scarcely imagined.

———◦———

Never give your family the leftovers and crumbs of your time.

Charles Swindoll

Today's Prayer

Father, help me to treasure those moments that I spend with my family—and let me demonstrate, through my words and my actions, how much love I feel in my heart for them. Amen

Being Patient with Ourselves

Knowing God leads to self-control. Self-control leads to patient endurance, and patient endurance leads to godliness.

2 Peter 1:6 NLT

Being patient with other people can be difficult. But sometimes, we find it even more difficult to be patient with ourselves. We have high expectations and lofty goals. We want to accomplish things now, not later. And, of course, we want our lives to unfold according to our own timetables, not God's.

Throughout the Bible, we are instructed that patience is the companion of wisdom. God's message, then, is clear: we must be patient with all people, beginning with that particular person who stares back at us each time we gaze into the mirror.

———

Be patient. God is using today's difficulties to strengthen you for tomorrow. He is equipping you. The God who makes things grow will help you bear fruit.

Max Lucado

Today's Prayer

Dear Lord, You have been so patient with me, and I praise You for Your forgiveness. Let me be patient with myself, Father, even when I fall short of my own expectations. You have forgiven me, Lord— now I must forgive myself. Amen

Sharing the Good News

For Christ did not send me to baptize, but to preach the gospel—not with clever words, so that the cross of Christ will not be emptied of its effect.

1 Corinthians 1:17 HCSB

In his second letter to Timothy, Paul offers a message to believers of every generation when he writes, "God has not given us a spirit of timidity" (1:7 NASB). Paul's meaning is crystal clear: When sharing our testimonies, we, as Christians, must be courageous, forthright, and unashamed.

We live in a world that desperately needs the healing message of Christ Jesus. Every believer, each in his or her own way, bears a personal responsibility for sharing that message. If you are a believer in Christ, you know how He has touched your heart and changed your life. Now it's your turn to share the Good News with others. And remember: today is the perfect time to share your testimony because tomorrow may quite simply be too late.

If I can love folks the way they are, we have greater chance of winning them to the kingdom.

Dennis Swanberg

Today's Prayer

Lord, the life that I live and the words that I speak will tell the world how I feel about You. Today and every day, let my testimony be worthy of You. Let my words be sure and true, and let my actions point others to You. Amen

A Series of Choices

But seek first the kingdom of God and His righteousness, and all these things will be provided for you.

Matthew 6:33 HCSB

Face facts: your life is a series of choices. From the instant you wake up in the morning until the moment you nod off to sleep at night, you make countless decisions—decisions about the things you do, decisions about the words you speak, and decisions about the way that you choose to direct your thoughts.

As a believer who has been transformed by the love of Jesus, you have every reason to make wise choices. But sometimes, when the daily grind threatens to grind you up and spit you out, you may make choices that are displeasing to God. When you do, you'll pay a price because you'll forfeit the happiness and the peace that might otherwise have been yours.

So, as you pause to consider the kind of Christian you are—and the kind of Christian you want to become—ask yourself whether you're sitting on the fence or standing in the light. The choice is yours . . . and so are the consequences.

Today's Prayer

Heavenly Father, I have many choices to make. Help me choose wisely as I follow in the footsteps of Your only begotten Son. Amen

God's Plan for Your Family

Unless the Lord builds the house, they labor in vain who build it; unless the Lord guards the city, the watchman stays awake in vain.

Psalm 127:1 NKJV

As you consider God's purpose for your own life, you must also consider how your plans will effect the most important people that God has entrusted to your care: your loved ones.

A loving family is a treasure from God. If you happen to be a member of a close knit, supportive clan, offer a word of thanks to your Creator. He has blessed you with one of His most precious earthly possessions. Your obligation, in response to God's gift, is to treat your family in ways that are consistent with His commandments. So, as you prayerfully seek God's direction, remember that He has important plans for your home life as well as your professional life. It's up to you to act—and to plan—accordingly.

Living life with a consistent spiritual walk deeply influences those we love most.

Vonette Bright

Today's Prayer

Lord, You have given me a family that cares for me and loves me. Thank You, Father. Let me love all the members of my family despite their imperfections, and let them love me despite mine. Amen

The Prince of Peace

Peace I leave with you, my peace I give unto you: not as the world giveth, give I unto you. Let not your heart be troubled, neither let it be afraid.

John 14:27 KJV

Have you found the genuine peace that can be yours through Jesus Christ? Or are you still rushing after the illusion of "peace and happiness" that the world promises but cannot deliver? The beautiful words of John 14:27 remind us that Jesus offers us peace, not as the world gives, but as He alone gives. Our challenge is to accept Christ's peace into our hearts and then, as best we can, to share His peace with our neighbors.

Today, as a gift to yourself, to your family, and to your friends, claim the inner peace that is your spiritual birthright: the peace of Jesus Christ. It is offered freely; it has been paid for in full; it is yours for the asking. So ask. And then share.

God's peace is like a river, not a pond. In other words, a sense of health and well-being, both of which are expressions of the Hebrew shalom, can permeate our homes even when we're in white-water rapids.

Beth Moore

Today's Prayer

Dear Lord, I will open my heart to You. And I thank You, God, for Your love, for Your peace, and for Your Son. Amen

Aim at Heaven,
Not the World

Do not love the world or the things in the world. If anyone loves the world, the love of the Father is not in him.

1 John 2:15 NKJV

If you wish to possess a comfortable conscience and a peaceful soul, you must distance yourself, at least in part, from the temptations and distractions of modern-day society. But distancing yourself isn't easy, especially when so many societal forces are struggling to capture your attention, your participation, and your money.

C. S. Lewis said, "Aim at Heaven and you will get earth thrown in; aim at earth and you will get neither." That's good advice. You're likely to hit what you aim at, so aim high . . . aim at Heaven. When you do, you'll be strengthening your character as you improve every aspect of your life. And God will demonstrate His approval as He showers you with more spiritual blessings than you can count.

———◦◦◦———

Christians don't fail to live as they should because they are in the world; they fail because the world has gotten into them.

Billy Graham

Today's Prayer

Dear Lord, when I look to the world for approval, I suffer. But, when I look to You for approval, I am blessed. Today, Father, help me focus less on the world and more on You. Amen

His Healing Touch

I am the Lord that healeth thee.

Exodus 15:26 KJV

Are you concerned about your spiritual, physical, or emotional health? If so, there is a timeless source of comfort and assurance that is as near as your bookshelf. That source is the Holy Bible.

God's Word has much to say about every aspect of your life, including your health. And, when you face concerns of any sort—including health-related challenges—God is with you. So trust your medical doctor to do his or her part, but place your ultimate trust in your benevolent Heavenly Father. His healing touch, like His love, endures forever.

———

Ultimate healing and the glorification of the body are certainly among the blessings of Calvary for the believing Christian. Immediate healing is not guaranteed.

Warren Wiersbe

Today's Prayer

Dear Lord, place Your healing hand upon me. Heal my body and my soul. Let me trust Your promises, Father, and let me turn to You for hope, for restoration, for renewal, and for salvation. Amen

At Peace with Your Purpose

But now in Christ Jesus you who once were far off have been brought near by the blood of Christ. For He Himself is our peace.

Ephesians 2:13–14 NKJV

Are you at peace with the direction of your life? If you're a Christian, you should be. Perhaps you seek a new direction or a sense of renewed purpose, but those feelings should never rob you of the genuine peace that can and should be yours through a personal relationship with Jesus.

Have you found the lasting peace that can be yours through Jesus, or are you still rushing after the illusion of "peace and happiness" that our world promises but cannot deliver? Today, as a gift to yourself, to your family, and to your friends, claim the inner peace that is your spiritual birthright: the peace of Jesus Christ.

That peace, which has been described and which believers enjoy, is a participation of the peace which their glorious Lord and Master himself enjoys.

Jonathan Edwards

Today's Prayer

Dear Lord, let me accept the peace and abundance that You offer through Your Son Jesus. You are the Giver of all things good, Father, and You give me peace when I draw close to You. Help me to trust Your will, to follow Your commands, and to accept Your peace, today and forever. Amen

Lost in the Crowd

The fear of man is a snare, but the one who trusts in the Lord is protected.

Proverbs 29:25 HCSB

Rick Warren observed, "Those who follow the crowd usually get lost in it." We know these words to be true, but oftentimes we fail to live by them. Instead of trusting God for guidance, we imitate our neighbors and suffer the consequences. Instead of seeking to please our Father in Heaven, we strive to please our peers, with decidedly mixed results.

Whom will you try to please today: your God or your associates? Your obligation is most certainly not to neighbors, to friends, or even to family members. Your obligation is to an all-knowing, all-powerful God. You must seek to please Him first and always. No exceptions.

———

People who constantly, and fervently, seek the approval of others live with an identity crisis. They don't know who they are, and they are defined by what others think of them.

Charles Stanley

Today's Prayer

Dear Lord, other people may encourage me to stray from Your path, but I wish to follow in the footsteps of Your Son. Give me the vision to see the right path—and the wisdom to follow it—today and every day of my life. Amen

The Chains of Perfectionism

Those who wait for perfect weather will never plant seeds; those who look at every cloud will never harvest crops.

Ecclesiastes 11:4 NCV

The media delivers an endless stream of messages that tell you how to look, how to behave, and how to dress. The media's expectations are impossible to meet—God's are not. God doesn't expect perfection . . . and neither should you.

If you find yourself bound up by the chains of perfectionism, it's time to ask yourself who you're trying to impress, and why. If you're trying to impress other people, it's time to reconsider your priorities. Your first responsibility is to the Heavenly Father who created you and to His Son who saved you. Then, you bear a powerful responsibility to your family. But, when it comes to meeting society's unrealistic expectations, forget it! After all, pleasing God is simply a matter of obeying His commandments and accepting His Son. But as for pleasing everybody else? That's impossible!

The greatest destroyer of good works is the desire to do great works.

C. H. Spurgeon

Today's Prayer

Lord, this world has so many expectations of me, but today I will not seek to meet the world's expectations; I will do my best to meet Your expectations. I will make You my ultimate priority, Lord, by serving You, by praising You, by loving You, and by obeying You. Amen

Your Traveling Companion

But thanks be to God, who gives us the victory through our Lord Jesus Christ. Therefore, my beloved brethren, be steadfast, immovable, always abounding in the work of the Lord, knowing that your labor is not in vain in the Lord.

1 Corinthians 15:57-58 NKJV

As you continue to seek God's purpose for your life, you will undoubtedly experience your fair share of disappointments, detours, false starts, and failures. When you do, don't become discouraged: God is not finished with you yet.

The old saying is as true today as it was when it was first spoken: "Life is a marathon, not a sprint." That's why wise travelers select a traveling companion who never tires and never falters. That partner, of course, is your Heavenly Father. So pray as if everything depended upon God, and work as if everything depended upon you. And trust God to do the rest.

───※───

Often God shuts a door in our face so that he can open the door through which he wants us to go.

Catherine Marshall

Today's Prayer

Dear Lord, when I want to give up, help me remember how important it is to keep trying. And when I'm worried or upset, help me remember to talk to You. Amen

A Thankful Heart

Since we are receiving a Kingdom that cannot be destroyed, let us be thankful and please God by worshiping him with holy fear and awe.

Hebrews 12:28 NLT

Sometimes, life here on earth can be complicated, demanding, and frustrating. When the demands of life leave us rushing from place to place with scarcely a moment to spare, we may fail to pause and thank our Creator for the countless blessings He bestows upon us. But, whenever we neglect to give proper thanks to the Giver of all things good, we suffer because of our misplaced priorities.

As believers who have been saved by a risen Christ, we are blessed beyond human comprehension. We who have been given so much should make thanksgiving a habit, a regular part of our daily routines. Of course, God's gifts are too numerous to count, but we should attempt to count them nonetheless. We owe our Heavenly Father everything, including our eternal praise . . . starting right now.

Today's Prayer

Heavenly Father, Your gifts are greater than I can imagine. May I live each day with thanksgiving in my heart and praise on my lips. Thank You for the gift of Your Son and for the promise of eternal life. Let me share the joyous news of Jesus Christ, and let my life be a testimony to His love and His grace. Amen

The Greatest Among Us

Therefore, get your minds ready for action, being self-disciplined, and set your hope completely on the grace to be brought to you at the revelation of Jesus Christ.

1 Peter 1:13 HCSB

Jesus teaches that the most esteemed men and women are not the leaders of society or the captains of industry. To the contrary, Jesus teaches that the greatest among us are those who choose to minister and to serve.

Today, you may feel the temptation to build yourself up in the eyes of your neighbors. Resist that temptation. Instead, serve your neighbors quietly and without fanfare. Then, when you have done your best to serve your community and to serve your God, you can rest comfortably knowing that in the eyes of God you have achieved greatness. And God's eyes, after all, are the only ones that really count.

God will open up places of service for you as He sees you are ready. Meanwhile, study the Bible and give yourself a chance to grow.

Warren Wiersbe

Today's Prayer

Dear Lord, let me help others in every way that I can. Jesus served others; I can too. I will serve other people with my good deeds and with my prayers. And I will give thanks for all those who help me. Amen

God's Guidance

Trust in the LORD with all your heart; do not depend on your own understanding. Seek his will in all you do, and he will direct your paths.

Proverbs 3:5-6 NLT

Proverbs 3:5-6 makes this promise: if you acknowledge God's sovereignty over every aspect of your life, He will guide your path. And, as you prayerfully consider the path that God intends for you to take, here are things you should do: You should study His Word and be ever-watchful for His signs. You should associate with fellow believers who will encourage your spiritual growth. You should listen carefully to that inner voice that speaks to you in the quiet moments of your daily devotionals. And you should be patient. Your Heavenly Father may not always reveal Himself as quickly as you would like, but rest assured that God intends to use you in wonderful, unexpected ways. Your challenge is to watch, to listen, to learn . . . and to follow.

———

Only by walking with God can we hope to find the path that leads to life.

John Eldredge

Today's Prayer

Dear Lord, let my plans and hopes be pleasing to You. Let me live according to Your commandments. Direct my path far from the temptations and distractions of this world. And, let me discover Your will and follow it, Father, this day and always. Amen

The Source of All Comfort

When doubts filled my mind, your comfort gave me renewed hope and cheer.

Psalm 94:19 NLT

In times of adversity, we are wise to remember the words of Jesus, who, when He walked on the waters, reassured His disciples, saying, "Take courage! It is I. Don't be afraid" (Matthew 14:27 NIV). Then, with Christ on His throne—and with trusted friends and loving family members at our sides—we can face our fears with courage and with faith.

Are you facing a difficult challenge? If so, remember that no problem is too big for God . . . not even yours.

No journey is complete that does not lead through some dark valleys. We can properly comfort others only with the comfort we ourselves have been given by God.

Vance Havner

Today's Prayer

Dear Lord, when I am troubled, You comfort me. When I am discouraged, You lift me up. Whatever my circumstances, Lord, I will trust Your plan for my life. And, when my family and friends are troubled, I will remind them of Your love, Your wisdom, and Your grace. Amen

One Mouth, Two Ears

So then, my beloved brethren, let every man be swift to hear, slow to speak, slow to wrath; for the wrath of man does not produce the righteousness of God.

James 1:19-20 NKJV

Perhaps God gave each of us one mouth and two ears in order that we might listen twice as much as we speak. Unfortunately, many of us do otherwise, especially when we become angry.

Anger is a natural human emotion that is sometimes necessary and appropriate. Even Jesus Himself became angered when He confronted the moneychangers in the temple. But, more often than not, our frustrations are of the more mundane variety. When you are tempted to lose your temper over the minor inconveniences of life, don't. Turn away from anger, and turn instead to God.

When you strike out in anger, you may miss the other person, but you will always hit yourself.

Jim Gallery

Today's Prayer

Dear Lord, when I am angry, I cannot feel the peace that You intend for my life. When I am bitter, I cannot sense Your love. Heavenly Father, keep me mindful that forgiveness is Your commandment and Your will for my life. Let me turn away from anger and instead claim the spiritual abundance that You offer through the priceless gift of Your Son Jesus. Amen

Our Thoughts Shape Us

Be careful what you think, because your thoughts run your life.

Proverbs 4:23 NCV

Our thoughts have the power to shape our lives—for better or worse. Thoughts have the power to lift our spirits, to improve our circumstances, to enhance our self-esteem, and to strengthen our relationship with the Creator. But, our thoughts also have the power to cause us great harm if we focus too intently upon the negative aspects of our lives or ourselves.

When we allow negative thinking to hijack our emotions, we do harm to our friends, to our families, and to ourselves. So we must guard our hearts against the negativity and cynicism that seems to have become the hallmark of this troubled generation.

Today, make your thoughts an offering to God. Seek—by the things you think and the actions you take—to honor Him and serve Him. He deserves no less. And neither, for that matter, do you.

Today's Prayer

Dear Lord, keep my thoughts focused on Your love, Your power, Your promises, and Your Son. When I am worried, I will turn to You for comfort; when I am weak, I will turn to You for strength; when I am troubled, I will turn to You for patience and perspective. Help me guard my thoughts, Father, so that I may honor You today and every day that I live. Amen

Caring for Your Family

Now if anyone does not provide for his own relatives, and especially for his household, he has denied the faith and is worse than an unbeliever.

1 Timothy 5:8 HCSB

The words of 1 Timothy 5:8 are unambiguous: if God has blessed us with families, then He expects us to care for them. Sometimes, this profound responsibility seems daunting. And sometimes, even for the most dedicated Christians, family life holds moments of frustration and disappointment. But, for those who are lucky enough to live in the presence of a close-knit, caring clan, the rewards far outweigh the demands.

No family is perfect, and neither is yours. Despite the inevitable challenges of providing for your family, and despite the occasional hurt feelings of family life, your clan is God's gift to you. Give thanks to the Giver for the gift of family . . . and act accordingly.

The secret of a happy home life is that the members of the family learn to give and receive love.

Billy Graham

Today's Prayer

Dear Lord, I am part of Your family, and I praise You for Your gifts and for Your love. You have also blessed me with my earthly family, and I pray for them, that they might be protected and blessed by You. Let me show love and acceptance for my family, Lord, so that through me, they might come to know and to love You. Amen

Celebrating Others

Therefore encourage one another and build each other up as you are already doing.

1 Thessalonians 5:11 HCSB

Do you delight in the victories of others? You should. Each day provides countless opportunities to encourage others and to praise their good works. When you do so, you not only spread seeds of joy and happiness, you also obey the commandments of God's Holy Word.

As Christians, we are called upon to spread the Good News of Christ, and we are also called to spread a message of encouragement and hope to the world.

Today, let us be cheerful Christians with smiles on our faces and encouraging words on our lips. By blessing others, we also bless ourselves, and, at the same time, we do honor to the One who gave His life for us.

You can't light another's path without casting light on your own.

John Maxwell

Today's Prayer

Dear Lord, let me celebrate the accomplishments of others. Make me a source of genuine, lasting encouragement to my family and friends. And let my words and deeds be worthy of Your Son, the One who gives me strength and salvation, this day and for all eternity. Amen

A Promise to Count On

God blesses the people who patiently endure testing. Afterward they will receive the crown of life that God has promised to those who love him.

James 1:12 NLT

Throughout the seasons of life, we must all endure life-altering personal losses that leave us breathless. When we do, we may be overwhelmed by fear, by doubt, or by both. Thankfully, God has promised that He will never desert us. And God keeps His promises.

Life is often challenging, but as Christians, we must trust the promises of our Heavenly Father. God loves us, and He will protect us. In times of hardship, He will comfort us; in times of sorrow, He will dry our tears. When we are troubled, or weak, or sorrowful, God is with us. His love endures, not only for today, but also for all of eternity.

God helps those who help themselves, but there are times when we are quite incapable of helping ourselves. That's when God stoops down and gathers us in His arms like a mother lifts a sick child, and does for us what we cannot do for ourselves.

Ruth Bell Graham

Today's Prayer

Dear Lord, when I face the inevitable disappointments of life, give me perspective and faith. When I am discouraged, give me the strength to trust Your promises and follow your will. Then, when I have done my best, Father, let me live with the assurance that You are firmly in control, and that Your love endures forever. Amen

Let the Celebration Begin

These things I have spoken to you, that My joy may remain in you, and that your joy may be full.

John 15:11 NKJV

Oswald Chambers correctly observed, "Joy is the great note all throughout the Bible." C. S. Lewis echoed that thought when he wrote, "Joy is the serious business of Heaven." But, even the most dedicated Christians can, on occasion, forget to celebrate each day for what it is: a priceless gift from God.

Today, let us be joyful Christians with smiles on our faces and kind words on our lips. After all, this is God's day, and He has given us clear instructions for its use. We are commanded to rejoice and be glad. So, with no further ado, let the celebration begin…

———————

Joy cannot be pursued. It comes from within. It is a state of being. It does not depend on circumstances, but triumphs over circumstances. It produces a gentleness of spirit and a magnetic personality.

Billy Graham

Today's Prayer

Dear Lord, You have given me so many blessings; let me celebrate Your gifts. Make me thankful, loving, responsible, and wise. Make me be a joyful Christian, a worthy example to others, and a dutiful servant to You this day and forever. Amen

A Dose of Laughter

A joyful heart is good medicine, but a broken spirit dries up the bones.

Proverbs 17:22 NASB

Laughter is medicine for the soul, but sometimes, amid the stresses of the day, we forget to take our medicine. Instead of viewing our world with a mixture of optimism and humor, we allow worries and distractions to rob us of the joy that God intends for our lives. Today, as you go about your daily activities, approach life with a smile and a chuckle. After all, God created laughter for a reason . . . and Father indeed knows best. So laugh!

When you have good, healthy relationships with your family and friends you're more prompted to laugh and not to take yourself so seriously.

Dennis Swanberg

Today's Prayer

Dear Lord, laughter is Your gift. Today and every day, put a smile on my face, and let me share that smile with all who cross my path . . . and let me laugh. Amen

The Power of Prayer

When a believing person prays, great things happen.

James 5:16 NCV

"The power of prayer": these words are so familiar, yet sometimes we forget what they mean. Prayer is a powerful tool for communicating with our Creator; it is an opportunity to commune with the Giver of all things good. Prayer helps us find strength for today and hope for the future. Prayer is not a thing to be taken lightly or to be used infrequently.

The quality of your spiritual life will be in direct proportion to the quality of your prayer life. Prayer changes things, and it changes you. Today, instead of turning things over in your mind, turn them over to God in prayer. Instead of worrying about your next decision, ask God to lead the way. Pray constantly about things great and small. God is listening, and He wants to hear from you now.

———

Our prayers are the link between God's inexhaustible resources and people's need. When we intercede, we stand in the gap between the need and the satisfaction of that need.

Charles Stanley

Today's Prayer

Dear Lord, let me raise my hopes and my dreams, my worries and my fears to You. Let me be a worthy example to family and friends, showing them the importance and the power of prayer. Let me take everything to You in prayer, Lord, and when I do, let me trust in Your answers. Amen

Your Partnership with God

Make a joyful noise unto the LORD, all ye lands. Serve the LORD with gladness: come before his presence with singing.

Psalm 100:1-2 KJV

If you want to be successful—genuinely successful in the things that really matter—you need a partner. That Partner is God. And the good news is this: When you humbly and sincerely ask God to become your partner, He will grant your request and transform your life.

Is your life a testimony to the personal relationship that you enjoy with your Heavenly Father? Or have you compartmentalized your faith to a few hours on Sunday morning? If you genuinely wish to make God your fulltime partner, you must allow Him to reign over every aspect of your life and every day of your week. When you do, you'll be amazed at the things that the two of you, working together, can accomplish.

***

God wants us to serve Him with a willing spirit, one that would choose no other way.

Beth Moore

Today's Prayer

Dear Lord, today I come to You seeking guidance. I will trust You to show me the path that I should take, and I will try, as best I can, to follow in the footsteps of Your Son. Amen

No Is an Answer

He granted their request because they trusted in Him.

1 Chronicles 5:20 HCSB

God answers our prayers. What God does not do is this: He does not always answer our prayers as soon as we might like, and He does not always answer our prayers by saying "Yes." God isn't an order-taker, and He's not some sort of cosmic vending machine. Sometimes—even when we want something very badly—our loving Heavenly Father responds to our requests by saying "No," and we must accept His answer, even if we don't understand it.

God answers prayers not only according to our wishes but also according to His master plan. We cannot know that plan, but we can know the Planner . . . and we must trust His wisdom, His righteousness, and His love. Always.

Let's never forget that some of God's greatest mercies are His refusals. He says no in order that He may, in some way we cannot imagine, say yes. All His ways with us are merciful. His meaning is always love.

Elisabeth Elliot

Today's Prayer

Dear Lord, Your Holy Word commands me to pray without ceasing. Let me take everything to You. When I am discouraged, let me pray. And when I am joyful, let me offer up prayers of thanksgiving. In all things great and small, at all times, whether happy or sad, let me seek Your wisdom and Your grace . . . in prayer. Amen

So Many Temptations

No temptation has seized you except what is common to man. And God is faithful; he will not let you be tempted beyond what you can bear. But when you are tempted, he will also provide a way out so that you can stand up under it.

1 Corinthians 10:13 NIV

This world is filled to the brim with temptations. Some of these temptations are small; eating a second scoop of ice cream, for example, is tempting, but not very dangerous. Other temptations, however, are not nearly so harmless. The devil is working 24/7, and he's causing pain and heartache in more ways than ever before. Thankfully, in the battle against Satan, we are never alone. God is always with us, and He gives us the power to resist temptation whenever we ask Him for the strength to do so.

In a letter to believers, Peter offered a stern warning: "Your adversary, the devil, prowls around like a roaring lion, seeking someone to devour" (1 Peter 5:8 NASB). As Christians, we must take that warning seriously, and we must behave accordingly.

Today's Prayer

Dear Lord, this world is filled with temptations, distractions, and frustrations. When I turn my thoughts away from You and Your Word, Lord, I suffer bitter consequences. But, when I trust in Your commandments, I am safe. Direct my path far from the temptations of the world, Father, this day and always. Amen

First Things First

Steep your life in God-reality, God-initiative, God-provisions. Don't worry about missing out. You'll find all your everyday human concerns will be met.

Matthew 6:33 MSG

Have you fervently asked God to help prioritize your life? Have you asked Him for guidance and for the courage to do the things that you know need to be done? If so, then you're continually inviting your Creator to reveal Himself in a variety of ways. As a follower of Christ, you must do no less.

When you make God a full partner in every aspect of your life, He will lead you along the proper path: His path. When you allow God to reign over your heart, He will honor you with spiritual blessings that are simply too numerous to count. So, as you plan for the day ahead, make God's will your ultimate priority. When you do, your daily to-do list will take care of itself.

―――――――――

Give to us clear vision that we may know where to stand and what to stand for. Let us not be content to wait and see what will happen, but give us the determination to make the right things happen.

Peter Marshall

Today's Prayer

Lord, let Your priorities be my priorities. Let Your will be my will. Let Your Word be my guide, and let me grow in faith and in wisdom this day and every day. Amen

Solving Problems

People who do what is right may have many problems, but the Lord will solve them all.

Psalm 34:19 NCV

Life is an exercise in problem-solving. The question is not whether we will encounter problems; the real question is how we will choose to address them. When it comes to solving the problems of everyday living, we often know precisely what needs to be done, but we may be slow in doing it—especially if what needs to be done is difficult or uncomfortable for us. So we put off till tomorrow what should be done today.

The words of Psalm 34 remind us that the Lord solves problems for "people who do what is right." And usually, doing "what is right" means doing the uncomfortable work of confronting our problems sooner rather than later. So with no further ado, let the problem-solving begin . . . now.

We are all faced with a series of great opportunities, brilliantly disguised as unsolvable problems. Unsolvable without God's wisdom, that is.

Charles Swindoll

Today's Prayer

Lord, sometimes my problems are simply too big for me, but they are never too big for You. Let me turn my troubles over to You, Lord, and let me trust in You today and for all eternity. Amen

The Shepherd's Gift

My cup runs over. Surely goodness and mercy shall follow me all the days of my life; and I will dwell in the house of the Lord forever.

Psalm 23:5-6 NKJV

The Word of God is clear: Christ came in order that we might have life abundant and life eternal. Eternal life is priceless possession of all who invite Christ into their hearts, but God's abundance is optional: He does not force it upon us.

When we entrust our hearts and our days to the One who created us, we experience abundance through the grace and sacrifice of His Son. But, when we turn our thoughts and direct our energies away from God's commandments, we inevitably forfeit the spiritual abundance that might otherwise be ours.

Do you sincerely seek the riches that our Savior offers to those who give themselves to Him? Then follow Him completely and obey Him without reservation. When you do, you will receive the love and the abundance that He has promised. Seek first the salvation that is available through a personal relationship with Jesus Christ, and then claim the joy, the peace, and the spiritual abundance that the Shepherd offers His sheep.

Today's Prayer

Good Shepherd, thank You for the abundant life that is mine through Christ Jesus. Guide me according to Your will, and help me to be a worthy servant in all that I say and do. Give me courage, Lord, to claim the rewards You have promised, and when I do, let the glory be Yours. Amen

Thy Will Be Done

Shall I not drink from the cup the Father has given me?

John 18:11 NLT

All of us must, from time to time, endure days filled with suffering and pain. And as human beings with limited understanding, we can never fully understand the plans of our Father in Heaven. But as believers in a benevolent God, we must always trust Him.

When Jesus went to the Mount of Olives, He poured out His heart to God (Luke 22). Jesus knew of the agony that He was destined to endure, but He also knew that God's will must be done.

We, like our Savior, face trials that bring fear and trembling to the very depths of our souls, but like Christ, we, too, must seek God's will, not our own. When we learn to accept God's will without reservation, we experience the peace that He offers to wise believers who trust Him completely.

Our Lord never asks us to decide for Him; He asks us to yield to Him—a very different matter.

Oswald Chambers

Today's Prayer

Dear Lord, let me live in the present, not the past. Let me focus on my blessings, not my sorrows. Give me the wisdom to be thankful for the gifts that I do have, not bitter about the things that I don't have. Let me accept what was, let me give thanks for what is, and let me have faith in what most surely will be: the promise of eternal life with You. Amen

Our Rock in Turbulent Times

And he said: "The Lord is my rock and my fortress and my deliverer; the God of my strength, in whom I will trust."

2 Samuel 22:2-3 NKJV

Psalm 145 promises, "The Lord is near to all who call on him, to all who call on him in truth. He fulfills the desires of those who fear him; he hears their cry and saves them." (vv. 18-20 NIV). And the words of Jesus offer us comfort: "These things I have spoken to you, that in Me you may have peace. In the world you will have tribulation; but be of good cheer, I have overcome the world" (John 16:33 NKJV).

As believers, we know that God loves us and that He will protect us. In times of hardship, He will comfort us; in times of sorrow, He will dry our tears. When we are troubled, or weak, or sorrowful, God is always with us. We must build our lives on the rock that cannot be shaken: we must trust in God. And then, we must get on with the hard work of tackling our problems . . . because if we don't, who will? Or should?

Today's Prayer

Heavenly Father, You are my strength. I can face the difficulties of this day because You are my Rock. As I stand with You, Father, I can overcome adversity just as Jesus overcame this world. Amen

Asking for Directions

Now if any of you lacks wisdom, he should ask God, who gives to all generously and without criticizing, and it will be given to him.

James 1:5 HCSB

Jesus made it clear to His disciples: they should petition God to meet their needs. So should we. Genuine, heartfelt prayer produces powerful changes in us and in our world. When we lift our hearts to God, we open ourselves to a never-ending source of divine wisdom and infinite love.

Do you have questions about your future that you simply can't answer? Do you have needs that you simply can't meet by yourself? Do you sincerely seek to know God's unfolding plans for your life? If so, ask Him for direction, for protection, and for strength—and then keep asking Him every day that you live. Whatever your need, no matter how great or small, pray about it and never lose hope. God is not just near; He is here, and He's perfectly capable of answering your prayers. Now, it's up to you to ask.

Today's Prayer

Lord, when I have questions about my purpose in life, I will turn to You. When I am weak, I will seek Your strength. When I am discouraged, Father, I will be mindful of Your love and Your grace. I will ask You for the things I need, Father, and I will trust Your answers, today and forever. Amen

Forgiveness at Home

Let all bitterness, wrath, anger, clamor, and evil speaking be put away from you, with all malice. And be kind to one another, tenderhearted, forgiving one another, just as God in Christ forgave you.

Ephesians 4:31-32 NKJV

Sometimes, it's easy to become angry with the people we love most, and sometimes it's hard to forgive them. After all, we know that our family will still love us no matter how angry we become. But while it's easy to become angry at home, it's wrong.

The next time you're tempted to lose your temper or to remain angry at a close family member, ask God to help you find the wisdom to forgive. And while you're at it, do your best to calm down sooner rather than later because peace is always beautiful, especially when it's peace at your house.

When something robs you of your peace of mind, ask yourself if it is worth the energy you are expending on it. If not, then put it out of your mind in an act of discipline. Every time the thought of "it" returns, refuse it.

Kay Arthur

Today's Prayer

Lord, sometimes, I am quick to anger and slow to forgive. But, I know that You seek abundance and peace for my life. You command us to forgive; let me obey You as I follow the example of Your Son Jesus who forgave His persecutors. As I turn away from anger, Father, let me claim the peace that You intend for my life. Amen

He Renews Our Strength

Have you not known? Have you not heard? The everlasting God, the Lord, the Creator of the ends of the earth, neither faints nor is weary. His understanding is unsearchable. He gives power to the weak, and to those who have no might He increases strength.

Isaiah 40:28-29 NKJV

When we genuinely lift our hearts and prayers to God, He renews our strength. Are you almost too weary to lift your head? Then bow it. Offer your concerns and your fears to your Father in Heaven. He is always at your side, offering His love and His strength.

Are you troubled or anxious? Take your anxieties to God in prayer. Are you weak or worried? Delve deeply into God's Holy Word and sense His presence in the quiet moments of the day. Are you spiritually exhausted? Call upon fellow believers to support you, and call upon Christ to renew your spirit and your life. Your Savior will never let you down. To the contrary, He will always lift you up if you ask Him to. So what, dear friend, are you waiting for?

Today's Prayer

Heavenly Father, sometimes I am troubled, and sometimes I grow weary. When I am weak, Lord, give me strength. When I am discouraged, renew me. When I am fearful, let me feel Your healing touch. Let me always trust in Your promises, Lord, and let me draw strength from those promises and from Your unending love. Amen

Thanksgiving Yes . . . Envy No!

Stop your anger! Turn from your rage! Do not envy others—it only leads to harm.

Psalm 37:8 NLT

As the recipient of God's grace, you have every reason to celebrate life. After all, God has promised you the opportunity to receive His abundance and His joy—in fact, you have the opportunity to receive those gifts right now. But if you allow envy to gnaw away at the fabric of your soul, you'll find that joy remains elusive. So do yourself an enormous favor: Rather than succumbing to the sin of envy, focus on the marvelous things that God has done for you—starting with Christ's sacrifice. Thank the Giver of all good gifts, and keep thanking Him for the wonders of His love and the miracles of His creation. Count your own blessings and let your neighbors count theirs. It's the godly way to live.

What God asks, does, or requires of others is not my business; it is His.

Kay Arthur

Today's Prayer

Dear Lord, deliver me from the needless pain of envy. You have given me countless blessings. Let me be thankful for the gifts I have received, and let me never be resentful of the gifts You have given others. Amen

A Time to Rest

Are you tired? Worn out? Burned out on religion? Come to me. Get away with me and you'll recover your life. I'll show you how to take a real rest. Walk with me and work with me…watch how I do it. Learn the unforced rhythms of grace. I won't lay anything heavy or ill-fitting on you. Keep company with me and you'll learn to live freely and lightly.

Matthew 11:28-30 MSG

Sometimes, the struggles of life can drain us of our strength. When we find ourselves tired, discouraged, or worse, there is a source from which we can draw the power needed to recharge our spiritual batteries. That source, of course, is God.

Is your spiritual battery running low? Is your energy on the wane? Are your emotions frayed? If so, it's time to turn your thoughts and your prayers to God. And when you're finished, it's time to rest.

———◦———

One reason so much American Christianity is a mile wide and an inch deep is that Christians are simply tired. Sometimes you need to kick back and rest for Jesus' sake.

Dennis Swanberg

Today's Prayer

Dear Lord, when I'm tired, give me the wisdom to do the smart thing: give me the wisdom to put my head on my pillow and rest! Amen

Keeping Up Appearances

We justify our actions by appearances; God examines our motives.

Proverbs 21:2 MSG

The world sees you as you appear to be; God sees you as you really are . . . He sees your heart, and He understands your intentions. The opinions of others should be relatively unimportant to you; however, God's view of you—His understanding of your actions, your thoughts, and your motivations—should be vitally important.

Few things in life are more futile than "keeping up appearances" for the sake of neighbors. What is important, of course, is pleasing your Father in Heaven. You please Him when your intentions are pure and your actions are just.

———————

If the narrative of the Scriptures teaches us anything, from the serpent in the Garden to the carpenter in Nazareth, it teaches us that things are rarely what they seem, that we shouldn't be fooled by appearances.

John Eldredge

Today's Prayer

Heavenly Father, examine my heart and show me ways that I can become a better person. Let my motives be pure, Lord, and let my actions please You, today and every day of my life. Amen

He Is Faithful

It is better to trust in the Lord than to put confidence in man. It is better to trust in the Lord than to put confidence in princes.

Psalm 118:8-9 NKJV

Are you tired? Discouraged? Fearful? Be comforted and trust God. Are you worried or anxious? Be confident in God's power. He will never desert you. Do you see no hope for the future? Be courageous and call upon God. He will protect you and then use you according to His purposes. Are you grieving? Know that God hears your suffering. He will comfort you and, in time, He will dry your tears. Are you confused? Listen to the quiet voice of your Heavenly Father. He is not a God of confusion. Talk with Him; listen to Him; trust Him. He is steadfast, and He is your Protector . . . forever.

———

This hard place in which you perhaps find yourself is the very place in which God is giving you opportunity to look only to Him, to spend time in prayer, and to learn long-suffering, gentleness, meekness—in short, to learn the depths of the love that Christ Himself has poured out on all of us.

Elisabeth Elliot

Today's Prayer

Today, Lord, I will trust You and seek Your will for my life. You have a plan for me, Father. Let me discover it and live it, knowing that when I trust in You, I am eternally blessed. Amen

Self-Esteem According to God

For you made us only a little lower than God, and you crowned us with glory and honor.

Psalm 8:5 NLT

What are you telling yourself about yourself? When you look in the mirror, are you staring back at your biggest booster or your harshest critic? If you can learn to give yourself the benefit of the doubt—if you can learn how to have constructive conversations with the person you see in the mirror—then your self-respect will tend to take care of itself. But, if you're constantly berating yourself—if you're constantly telling yourself that you can't measure up—then you'll find that self-respect is always in short supply.

So the next time you find yourself being critical of the person you see in the mirror, ask yourself if the criticism is really valid. If it is valid, make changes . . . if not, lighten up.

Being loved by Him whose opinion matters most gives us the security to risk loving, too—even loving ourselves.

Gloria Gaither

Today's Prayer

Lord, I'm certainly not perfect, but You love me just as I am. Thank You for Your love and for Your Son. And, help me to become the person that You want me to become. Amen

The Son of Encouragement

Bright eyes cheer the heart; good news strengthens the bones.

Proverbs 15:30 HCSB

Barnabas, a man whose name meant "Son of Encouragement," was a leader in the early Christian church. He was known for his kindness and for his ability to encourage others. Because of Barnabas, many people were introduced to Christ. And today, as believers living in a difficult world, we must seek to imitate the "Son of Encouragement."

We imitate Barnabas when we speak kind words to our families and to our friends. We imitate Barnabas when our actions give credence to our beliefs. We imitate Barnabas when we are generous with our possessions and with our praise. We imitate Barnabas when we give hope to the hopeless and encouragement to the downtrodden.

Today, be like Barnabas: become a source of encouragement to those who cross your path. When you do so, you will quite literally change the world, one person—and one moment—at a time.

Today's Prayer

Make me sensitive, O Lord, to the many gifts of encouragement I receive each day. And, let me be a source of encouragement to all who cross my path. The Bible tells of Your servant Barnabas. Like Barnabas, I, too, want to be an encourager to my family and friends so that I might do Your work and share Your love. Amen

The Trap of Addiction

Therefore submit to God. Resist the devil and he will flee from you. Draw near to God and He will draw near to you. Cleanse your hands, you sinners; and purify your hearts, you double-minded.

James 4:7-8 NKJV

The dictionary defines addiction as "the compulsive need for a habit-forming substance; the condition of being habitually and compulsively occupied with something." That definition is accurate, but incomplete. For Christians, addiction has an additional meaning: it means compulsively worshipping something other than God.

Unless you're living on a deserted island, you know people who are full-blown addicts—probably lots of people. If you, or someone you love, is suffering from the blight of addiction, remember this: Help is available.

And if you're one of those fortunate people who has never experimented with addictive substances, congratulations. You have just spared yourself a lifetime of headaches and heartaches.

Evidence of new birth is that we see the rule of God.

Oswald Chambers

Today's Prayer

Dear Lord, You have instructed me to care for my body, and I will obey You. I will be mindful of the destructive power of addiction, and I will avoid the people, the places, and the substances that can entrap my sprit and destroy my life. Amen

Be Still

Be still, and know that I am God.

Psalm 46:10 NKJV

Do you take time each day for an extended period of silence? And during those precious moments, do you sincerely open your heart to your Creator? If so, you are wise and you are blessed.

The world can be a noisy place, a place filled to the brim with distractions, interruptions, and frustrations. And if you're not careful, the struggles and stresses of everyday living can rob you of the peace that should rightfully be yours because of your personal relationship with Christ. So take time each day to quietly commune with your Savior. When you do, those moments of silence will enable you to participate more fully in the only source of peace that endures: God's peace.

Growth takes place in quietness, in hidden ways, in silence and solitude. The process is not accessible to observation.

Eugene Peterson

Today's Prayer

Dear Lord, in the quiet moments of this day, I will turn my thoughts and prayers to You. In silence I will sense Your presence, and I will seek Your will for my life, knowing that when I accept Your peace, I will be blessed today and throughout eternity. Amen

God Knows...and Cares

But with me it is a very small thing that I should be judged by you or by a human court. In fact, I do not even judge myself. For I know nothing against myself, yet I am not justified by this; but He who judges me is the Lord.

1 Corinthians 4:3-4 NKJV

If you're like most people, you seek the admiration of your neighbors, your coworkers, and your family members. But the eagerness to please others should never overshadow your eagerness to please God. If you seek to fulfill the purposes that God has in store for you, then you must be a "doer of the word." And how can you do so? By putting God first.

Martin Luther issued this stern warning: "You may as well quit reading and hearing the Word of God and give it to the devil if you do not desire to live according to it." Luther understood that obedience leads to abundance just as surely as disobedience leads to disaster; you should understand it, too.

Would you like a time-tested formula for successful living? Here it is: Don't just listen to God's Word, live by it. Does this sound too simple? Perhaps it is simple, but it is also the only way to reap the marvelous riches that God has in store for you.

Today's Prayer

Lord, there is a right way and a wrong way to live. Let me live according to Your rules, not the world's rules. Your path is right for me, God; let me follow it every day of my life. Amen

Too Busy

Careful planning puts you ahead in the long run; hurry and scurry puts you further behind.

Proverbs 21:5 MSG

Are you one simply too busy for your own good? Has the hectic pace of life robbed you of the peace that might otherwise be yours through Jesus Christ? If so, you're doing a disservice to yourself and your family.

Through His Son Jesus, God offers you a peace that passes human understanding, but He won't force His peace upon you; in order to experience it, you must slow down long enough to sense His presence and His love.

Today, as a gift to yourself, to your family, and to the world, be still and claim the inner peace that is your spiritual birthright—the peace of Jesus Christ. It is offered freely; it has been paid for in full; it is yours for the asking. So ask. And then share.

We often become mentally and spiritually barren because we're so busy.

Franklin Graham

Today's Prayer

Dear Lord, when the quickening pace of life leaves me with little time for worship or for praise, help me to reorder my priorities, and let me turn to Jesus for the peace that only He can give. Amen

Unbending Truth

Therefore, putting away lying, "Let each one of you speak truth with his neighbor," for we are members of one another.

Ephesians 4:25 NKJV

Oswald Chambers advised, "Never support an experience which does not have God as its source, and faith in God as its result." These words serve as a powerful reminder that as Christians we are called to walk with God and to obey His commandments. But, we live in a world that presents us with countless temptations to wander far from God's path. These temptations have the potential to destroy us, in part, because they cause us to be dishonest with ourselves and with others.

Dishonesty is a habit. Once we start bending the truth, we're likely to keep bending it. A far better strategy, of course, is to acquire the habit of being completely forthright with God, with other people, and with ourselves.

Honesty is also a habit, a habit that pays powerful dividends for those who place character above convenience. So, the next time you're tempted to bend the truth—or to break it—ask yourself this simple question: "What does God want to do?" Then listen carefully to your conscience. When you do, your actions will be honorable, and your character will take care of itself.

Today's Prayer

Heavenly Father, help me see the truth, help me speak the truth, and help me live the truth—today and every day of my life. Amen

Choices, Choices, Choices

But neither exile nor homecoming is the main thing. Cheerfully pleasing God is the main thing, and that's what we aim to do, regardless of our conditions.

2 Corinthians 5:9 MSG

Your life is a series of choices. From the instant you wake up in the morning until the moment you nod off to sleep at night, you make lots of decisions: decisions about the things you do, decisions about the words you speak, and decisions about the thoughts you choose to think. Simply put, the quality of those decisions determines the quality of your life.

So, if you sincerely want to lead a life that is pleasing to God, you must make choices that are pleasing to Him. He deserves no less . . . and neither, for that matter, do you.

Life is a series of choices between the bad, the good, and the best. Everything depends on how we choose.

Vance Havner

Today's Prayer

Dear Lord, help me to make choices that are pleasing to You. Help me to be honest, patient, and kind. And above all, help me to follow the teachings of Jesus, not just today, but every day. Amen

A Clear Conscience

If then you were raised with Christ, seek those things which are above, where Christ is, sitting at the right hand of God. Set your mind on things above, not on things on the earth.

Colossians 3:1-2 NKJV

Few things in life torment us more than a guilty conscience. And, few things in life provide more contentment than the knowledge that we are obeying God's commandments.

A clear conscience is one of the rewards we earn when we obey God's Word and follow His will. When we follow God's will and accept His gift of salvation, our earthly rewards are never-ceasing, and our heavenly rewards are everlasting.

———

One of the ways God has revealed Himself to us is in the conscience. Conscience is God's lamp within the human breast.

Billy Graham

Today's Prayer

Lord, You have given me a conscience that tells me right from wrong. Let me listen to that quiet voice so that I might do Your will and follow Your Word today and every day. Amen

Finding Contentment

I've learned by now to be quite content whatever my circumstances. I'm just as happy with little as with much, with much as with little. I've found the recipe for being happy whether full or hungry, hands full or hands empty.

Philippians 4:11-12 MSG

Where can we find contentment? Is it a result of wealth, or power, or beauty, or fame? Hardly. Genuine contentment is a gift from God to those who trust Him and follow His commandments.

Our modern world seems preoccupied with the search for happiness. We are bombarded with messages telling us that happiness depends upon the acquisition of material possessions. These messages are false. Enduring peace is not the result of our acquisitions; it is a spiritual gift from God to those who obey Him and accept His will.

If we don't find contentment in God, we will never find it anywhere else. But, if we seek Him and obey Him, we will be blessed with an inner peace that is beyond human understanding. When God dwells at the center of our lives, peace and contentment will belong to us just as surely as we belong to God.

Today's Prayer

Father, let me find contentment and balance. Let Your priorities be my priorities. And when I have done my best, give me the wisdom to place my faith and my trust in You. Amen

Diligence Now

Never be lacking in zeal, but keep your spiritual fervor, serving the Lord.

Romans 12:11 NIV

God's Word reminds us again and again that our Creator expects us to lead disciplined lives. God doesn't reward laziness, misbehavior, or apathy. To the contrary, He expects believers to behave with dignity and discipline.

We live in a world in which leisure is glorified and indifference is often glamorized. But God has other plans. He did not create us for lives of mediocrity; He created us for far greater things.

Life's greatest rewards seldom fall into our laps; to the contrary, our greatest accomplishments usually require lots of work, which is perfectly fine with God. After all, He knows that we're up to the task, and He has big plans for us; may we, as disciplined believers, always be worthy of those plans.

He will clothe you in rags if you clothe yourself with idleness.

C. H. Spurgeon

Today's Prayer

Dear Lord, You expect Your children to be diligent and disciplined. You have told us that the fields are ripe and the workers are few. Lead me to Your fields, Lord, and make me a disciplined worker in the service of Your Son. Amen

God's Ally

Be self-controlled and alert. Your enemy the devil prowls around like a
roaring lion looking for someone to devour. Resist him, standing firm
in the faith. . . .

1 Peter 5:8-9 NIV

Nineteenth century clergyman Edwin Hubbel Chapin warned, "Neutral men are the devil's allies." His words were true then, and they're true now. Neutrality in the face of evil is a sin. Yet all too often, we fail to fight evil, not because we are neutral, but because we are shortsighted: we don't fight the devil because we don't recognize his handiwork.

If we are to recognize evil and fight it, we must pay careful attention. We must pay attention to God's Word, and we must pay attention to the realities of everyday life. When we observe life objectively, and when we do so with eyes and hearts that are attuned to God's Holy Word, we can no longer be neutral believers. And when we are no longer neutral, God rejoices while the devil despairs.

———◈———

The worst evils which have ever come upon the world have been brought upon her by an unholy church.

C. H. Spurgeon

Today's Prayer

Protect us, Lord, from the evils and temptations of this difficult age. Help us to trust You, Father, and to obey Your Word, knowing that Your ultimate victory over evil is both inevitable and complete. Amen

His Calling

But as God has distributed to each one, as the Lord has called each one, so let him walk.

1 Corinthians 7:17 NKJV

It is terribly important that you heed God's calling by discovering and developing your talents and your spiritual gifts. If you seek to make a difference—and if you seek to bear eternal fruit—you must discover your gifts and begin using them for the glory of God.

Every believer has at least one gift. In John 15:16, Jesus says, "You did not choose Me, but I chose you and appointed you that you should go and bear fruit, and that your fruit should remain, that whatever you ask the Father in My name He may give you." Have you found your special calling? If not, keep searching and keep praying until you find it. God has important work for you to do, and the time to begin that work is now.

———

If God's Word, your circumstances, and the counsel of others line up, and if you sense his provision, I'd say go for it.

Luci Swindoll

Today's Prayer

Dear Lord, You created me, and You have called me to do Your work here on earth. Today, I choose to seek Your will and to live it, knowing that when I trust in You, I am eternally blessed. Amen

Obey and Be Blessed

Now by this we know that we know Him, if we keep His commandments.

1 John 2:3 NKJV

God gave us His commandments for a reason: so that we might obey them and be blessed. Oswald Chambers, the author of the Christian classic devotional text *My Utmost for His Highest*, advised, "Never support an experience which does not have God as its source, and faith in God as its result." These words serve as a powerful reminder that, as Christians, we are called to walk with God and obey His commandments. But, we live in a world that presents us with countless temptations to stray far from God's path. We Christians, when confronted with sin, have clear instructions: Walk—or better yet run—in the opposite direction.

———◆———

Let us remember therefore this lesson: That to worship our God sincerely we must evermore begin by hearkening to His voice, and by giving ear to what He commands us. For if every man goes after his own way, we shall wander. We may well run, but we shall never be a whit nearer to the right way, but rather farther away from it.

John Calvin

Today's Prayer

Lord, let me live by Your commandments and let me help others do the same. Give me the wisdom to walk righteously in the footsteps of Your Son, dear Father. And let me place my trust in You, today and forever. Amen

Defeating Stress
One Day at a Time

This is the day which the Lord hath made; we will rejoice and be glad in it.

Psalm 118:24 KJV

Face facts: just getting by can be stressful . . . very stressful. You live in a world that is brimming with demands, distractions, and deadlines (not to mention temptations, timetables, requirements, and responsibilities). Whew! No wonder you may be stressed.

What can you do in response to the stressors of everyday life? A wonderful place to start is by turning things over to God.

Psalm 118:24 reminds us that this day, like every other, is a glorious gift from the Father. How will you use that gift? Will you celebrate it and use it for His purposes? If so, you'll discover that when you turn things over to Him—when you allow God to rule over every corner of your life—He will calm your fears and guide your steps.

So today, make sure that you focus on God and upon His will for your life. Then, ask for His help. And remember: No challenge is too great for Him. Not even yours.

Today's Prayer

Dear Lord, sometimes the stresses of the day leave me tired and frustrated. Renew my energy, Father, and give me perspective and peace. Let me draw comfort and courage from Your promises, from Your love, and from Your Son. Amen

Abandoning Bad Habits

Do not be deceived: "Evil company corrupts good habits."

1 Corinthians 15:33 NKJV

It's an old saying and a true one: First, you make your habits, and then your habits make you. Some habits will inevitably bring you closer to God; other habits will lead you away from the path He has chosen for you. If you sincerely desire to improve your spiritual health, you must honestly examine the habits that make up the fabric of your day. And you must abandon those habits that are displeasing to God.

If you trust God, and if you keep asking for His help, He can transform your life. If you sincerely ask Him to help you, the same God who created the universe will help you defeat the harmful habits that have heretofore defeated you. So, if at first you don't succeed, keep praying. God is listening, and He's ready to help you become a better person if you ask Him . . . so ask today.

———

You will never change your life until you change something you do daily.

John Maxwell

Today's Prayer

Dear Lord, help me break bad habits and form good ones. And let me make a habit of sharing the things that I own and the love that I feel in my heart. Amen

Dealing with Disappointment

For we do not want you to be ignorant, brethren, of our trouble which came to us in Asia: that we were burdened beyond measure, above strength, so that we despaired even of life. Yes, we had the sentence of death in ourselves, that we should not trust in ourselves but in God who raises the dead, who delivered us from so great a death, and does deliver us; in whom we trust that He will still deliver us.

2 Corinthians 1:8-10 NKJV

From time to time, all of us face life-altering disappointments that leave us breathless. Oftentimes, these disappointments come unexpectedly, leaving us with more questions than answers. But even when we don't have all the answers—or, even when we don't seem to have any of the answers—God does. Whatever our circumstances, whether we stand atop the highest mountain or wander through the darkest valley, God is ready to protect us, to comfort us, and to heal us. Our task is to let Him.

What may seem defeat to us may be victory to him.

C. H. Spurgeon

Today's Prayer

Dear Lord, when I face the inevitable disappointments of life, remind me that You are in control. You are the Giver of all good things, Father, and You will bless me today, tomorrow, and forever. Amen

The Wisdom to Be Humble

When you do things, do not let selfishness or pride be your guide. Instead, be humble and give more honor to others than to yourselves.

Philippians 2:3 NCV

God's Word clearly instructs us to be humble. And that's good because, as fallible human beings, we have so very much to be humble about! Yet some of us continue to puff ourselves up, seeming to say, "Look at me!" To do so is wrong.

As Christians, we have been refashioned and saved by Jesus Christ, and that salvation came not because of our own good works but because of God's grace. How, then, can we be prideful? The answer, of course, is that, if we are honest with ourselves and with our God, we simply can't be boastful . . . we must, instead, be eternally grateful and exceedingly humble. The good things in our lives, including our loved ones, come from God. He deserves the credit—and we deserve the glorious experience of giving it to Him.

Because Christ Jesus came to the world clothed in humility, he will always be found among those who are clothed with humility. He will be found among the humble people.

A. W. Tozer

Today's Prayer

Dear Lord, keep me humble. When I am boastful, keep me mindful that all my gifts come from You. You are the Giver of all things good; let me give all the glory to You. Amen

Look Before You Leap

An impulsive vow is a trap; later you'll wish you could get out of it.

Proverbs 20:25 MSG

Are you, at times, just a little bit impulsive? Do you sometimes look before you leap? If so, God wants to have a little chat with you.

God's Word is clear: as believers, we are called to lead lives of discipline, diligence, moderation, and maturity. But the world often tempts us to behave otherwise. Everywhere we turn, or so it seems, we are faced with powerful temptations to behave in undisciplined, ungodly ways.

God's Word instructs us to be disciplined in our thoughts and our actions; God's Word warns us against the dangers of impulsive behavior. As believers in a just God, we should act and react accordingly.

Plan ahead—it wasn't raining when Noah built the ark.

Anonymous

Today's Prayer

Lord, sometimes I can be an impulsive person. Slow me down, calm me down, and help me make wise decisions . . . today and every day of my life. Amen

Your Spiritual Journey

Know the love of Christ which surpasses knowledge, that you may be filled up to all the fullness of God.

Ephesians 3:19 NASB

The journey toward spiritual maturity lasts a lifetime. As Christians, we can and should continue to grow in the love and the knowledge of our Savior as long as we live. When we cease to grow, either emotionally or spiritually, we do ourselves a profound disservice. But, if we study God's Word, if we obey His commandments, and if we live in the center of His will, we will not be "stagnant" believers; we will, instead, be healthy, growing Christians.

Life is a series of decisions. Each day, we make countless decisions that can bring us closer to God . . . or not. When we live according to the principles contained in God's Holy Word, we embark upon a journey of spiritual maturity that results in life abundant and life eternal.

The Holy Spirit was given to guide us into all truth, but He doesn't do it all at once.

Elisabeth Elliot

Today's Prayer

Thank You, Lord, that I am not yet what I am to become. The Holy Scripture tells me that You are at work in my life, continuing to help me grow and to mature in the faith. Show me Your wisdom, Father, and let me live according to Your Word and Your will. Amen

Where Is God Leading?

Consider it a great joy, my brothers, whenever you experience various trials, knowing that the testing of your faith produces endurance. But endurance must do its complete work, so that you may be mature and complete, lacking nothing.

James 1:2-4 HCSB

Whether we realize it or not, times of adversity can be times of intense personal and spiritual growth. Our difficult days are also times when we can learn and relearn some of life's most important lessons.

The next time you experience a difficult moment, a difficult day, or a difficult year, ask yourself this question: Where is God leading me? In times struggle and sorrow, you can be certain that God is leading you to a place of His choosing. Your duty is to watch, to pray, to listen, and to follow.

Every misfortune, every failure, every loss may be transformed. God has the power to transform all misfortunes into "God-sends."

Mrs. Charles E. Cowman

Today's Prayer

Lord, sometimes life is difficult. But even when I can't see any hope for the future, You are always with me. And, I can live courageously because I know that You are leading me to a place where I can accomplish Your kingdom's work . . . and where You lead, I will follow. Amen

Beyond the Difficulties

When you are in distress and all these things have happened to you, you will return to the Lord your God in later days and obey Him. He will not leave you, destroy you, or forget the covenant with your fathers that He swore to them by oath, because the Lord your God is a compassionate God.

Deuteronomy 4:30-31 HCSB

Sometimes the traffic jams, and sometimes the dog gobbles the homework. But, when we find ourselves overtaken by the minor frustrations of life, we must catch ourselves, take a deep breath, and lift our thoughts upward. Although we are here on earth struggling to rise above the distractions of the day, we need never struggle alone. God is here—eternally and faithfully, with infinite patience and love—and, if we reach out to Him, He will restore perspective and peace to our souls.

If you find yourself enduring difficult circumstances, remember that God remains in His Heaven. If you become discouraged with the direction of your day or your life, lift your thoughts and prayers to Him. He will guide you through your difficulties and beyond them.

Today's Prayer

Lord, on difficult days, I will turn to You for my strength. In times of sadness, I will put my trust in You. In times of frustration, I will find peace in You. And every day, whether I am happy or sad, I will praise You for Your glorious works and for the gift of Your Son. Amen

Choosing the Good Life

And in that day you will ask Me nothing. Most assuredly, I say to you, whatever you ask the Father in My name He will give you. Until now you have asked nothing in My name. Ask, and you will receive, that your joy may be full.

John 16:23-24 NKJV

God offers us abundance through His Son, Jesus. Whether or not we accept God's abundance is, of course, up to each of us. When we entrust our hearts and our days to the One who created us, we experience abundance through the grace and sacrifice of His Son, Jesus. But, when we turn our thoughts and our energies away from God's commandments, we inevitably forfeit the spiritual abundance that might otherwise be ours.

What is your focus today? Are you focused on God's Word and His will for your life? Or are you focused on the distractions and temptations of the world. The answer to this question will, to a surprising extent, determine the quality and the direction of your day.

If you sincerely seek the spiritual abundance that your Savior offers, then follow Him completely and without reservation. When you do, you will receive the love, the life, and the abundance that He has promised.

Today's Prayer

Dear Lord, thank You for the abundant life that is mine through Christ Jesus. Give me courage to claim the spiritual riches that You have promised, and lead me according to Your plan for my life, today and always. Amen

Good Pressures, Bad Pressures

For am I now trying to win the favor of people, or God? Or am I striving to please people? If I were still trying to please people, I would not be a slave of Christ.

Galatians 1:10 HCSB

Our world is filled with pressures: some good, some bad. The pressures that we feel to follow God's will and obey His commandments are positive pressures. God places them on our hearts, and He intends that we act in accordance with His leadings. But we also face different pressures, ones that are definitely not from God. When we feel pressured to do things—or even to think thoughts—that lead us away from God, we must beware.

Society seeks to mold us into more worldly beings; God seeks to mold us into new beings that are most certainly not conformed to this world. If we are to please God, we must resist the pressures that society seeks to impose upon us, and we must conform ourselves, instead, to God's will, to His path, and to His Son.

Today's Prayer

Thank You Lord, for the people who enrich my life. I pray for them today, and ask Your blessings upon them . . . and upon me. Amen

Pleasing God

But neither exile nor homecoming is the main thing. Cheerfully pleasing God is the main thing, and that's what we aim to do, regardless of our conditions.

2 Corinthians 5:9 MSG

When God made you, He equipped you with an array of talents and abilities that are uniquely yours. It's up to you to discover those talents and to use them, but sometimes the world will encourage you to do otherwise. At times, society will attempt to cubbyhole you, to standardize you, and to make you fit into particular, preformed mold. Sometimes, because you're an imperfect human being, you may become so wrapped up in meeting society's expectations that you fail to focus on God's expectations. To do so is a mistake of major proportions—don't make it.

Who will you try to please today: God or man? Your primary obligation is not to please imperfect men and women. Your obligation is to strive diligently to meet the expectations of an all-knowing and perfect God. Trust Him always. Love Him always. Praise Him always. And seek to please Him. Always.

Today's Prayer

Dear Lord, today I will honor You with my thoughts, my actions, and my prayers. I will seek to please You, and I will strive to serve You. Your blessings are as limitless as Your love. And because I have been so richly blessed, I will worship You, Father, with thanksgiving in my heart and praise on my lips, this day and forever. Amen

Keep Possessions in Perspective

And He told them, "Watch out and be on guard against all greed, because one's life is not in the abundance of his possessions."

Luke 12:15 HCSB

All too often, we focus our thoughts and energies on the accumulation of earthly treasures, leaving precious little time to accumulate the only treasures that really matter: the spiritual kind. Our material possessions have the potential to do great good or terrible harm, depending upon how we choose to use them. As believers, our instructions are clear: we must use our possessions in accordance with God's commandments, and we must be faithful stewards of the gifts He has seen fit to bestow upon us.

Today, let us honor God by placing no other gods before Him. God comes first; everything else comes next—and "everything else" most certainly includes all of our earthly possessions.

What we possess often possesses us—we are possessed by possessions.

Oswald Chambers

Today's Prayer

Dear Lord, Your Word teaches me to seek first Your kingdom and Your righteousness. Today, I will trust You completely for my needs, both spiritual and material. Thank You, Father, for Your protection, for Your love, and for Your Son. Amen

Living Righteously

Flee also youthful lusts; but pursue righteousness, faith, love, peace with those who call on the Lord out of a pure heart.

2 Timothy 2:22 NKJV

A life of righteousness is lived in accordance with God's commandments. A righteous person strives to be faithful, honest, generous, disciplined, loving, kind, humble, and grateful, to name only a few of the more obvious qualities which are described in God's Word.

If we seek to follow the steps of the Jesus, we must seek to live according to His teachings. In short, we must, to the best of our abilities, live according to the principles contained in the Holy Bible. When we do, we become powerful examples to our families and friends of the blessings that God bestows upon righteous men.

———

We must appropriate the tender mercy of God every day after conversion, or problems quickly develop. We need his grace daily in order to live a righteous life.

Jim Cymbala

Today's Prayer

Dear Lord, this world is filled with so many temptations, distractions, and frustrations. When I turn my thoughts away from You and Your Word, I suffer. But when I turn my thoughts, my faith, and my prayers to You, I am safe. Direct my path, Father, and let me discover Your will for me today and every day that I live. Amen

His Transforming Power

Your old life is dead. Your new life, which is your real life—even though invisible to spectators—is with Christ in God. He is your life.

Colossians 3:3 MSG

God's hand has the power to transform your day and your life. Your task is to accept Christ's grace with a humble, thankful heart as you receive the "new life" that can be yours through Him.

Righteous believers who fashion their days around Jesus see the world differently; they act differently, and they feel differently about themselves and their neighbors. Hopefully, you, too, will be such a believer.

Do you desire to improve some aspect of your life? If so, don't expect changing circumstances to miraculously transform you into the person you want to become. Transformation starts with God, and it starts in the quiet corners of a willing human heart—like yours.

Unparalleled joy and victory come from allowing Christ to do "the hard thing" with us.

Beth Moore

Today's Prayer

Dear Lord, let my thoughts and my actions demonstrate the difference that Your Son has made in my life. Let me live righteously, and let my actions be consistent with my beliefs. Let every step that I take reflect Your truth, and let me live a life that is worthy of Your Son. Amen

Doing It Now

We can't afford to waste a minute, must not squander these precious daylight hours in frivolity and indulgence. . . . Don't loiter and linger, waiting until the very last minute. Dress yourselves in Christ, and be up and about!

Romans 13:13-14 MSG

The habit of procrastination takes a two-fold toll on its victims. First, important work goes unfinished; second (and more importantly), valuable energy is wasted in the process of putting off the things that remain undone. Procrastination results from an individual's short-sighted attempt to postpone temporary discomfort. What results is a senseless cycle of 1. delay, followed by 2. worry followed by 3. a panicky and often futile attempt to "catch up." Procrastination is, at its core, a struggle against oneself; the only antidote is action.

Once you acquire the habit of doing what needs to be done when it needs to be done, you will avoid untold trouble, worry, and stress. So learn to defeat procrastination by paying less attention to your fears and more attention to your responsibilities. God has created a world that punishes procrastinators and rewards men who "do it now." Life doesn't procrastinate—neither should you.

Today's Prayer

Dear Lord, today is a new day. Help me tackle the important tasks immediately, even if those tasks are unpleasant. Don't let me put off until tomorrow what I should do today. Amen

Serve Him

Based on the gift they have received, everyone should use it to serve others, as good managers of the varied grace of God.

1 Peter 4:10 HCSB

How will you serve God? Will you give Him the firstfruits of your harvest? Will you honor Him with the best you have to offer? Will you praise the Creator not only with your words but also with your deeds?

Every day is a fresh opportunity to honor God with your prayers, with your praise, with your deeds, and with your testimony. Your Heavenly Father deserves no less.

Does the level of your stewardship honor the One who has given you everything? If so, God will bless you because of your obedience. And if your stewardship has been somehow deficient, the best day to begin serving Him more faithfully is today.

Everything that we own belongs to God—including money—and He will use it to direct our lives.

Larry Burkett

Today's Prayer

Dear Lord, make me a faithful steward of my possessions, my talents, my time, and my testimony. In every aspect of my life, Father, let me Your humble, obedient servant. I trust, Father, that You will provide for me now and throughout eternity. And I will obey Your commandment that I give sacrificially to the needs of Your Church. Amen

Community Life

Regarding life together and getting along with each other, you don't need me to tell you what to do. You're God-taught in these matters. Just love one another!

1 Thessalonians 4:9 MSG

As we travel along life's road, we build lifelong relationships with a small, dear circle of family and friends. And how best do we build and maintain these relationships? By following the Word of God. Healthy relationships are built upon honesty, compassion, responsible behavior, trust, and optimism. Healthy relationships are built upon the Golden Rule. Healthy relationships are built upon sharing and caring. All of these principles are found time and time again in God's Holy Word. When we read God's Word and follow His commandments, we enrich our own lives and the lives of those who are closest to us.

———

Horizontal relationships—relationships between people—are crippled at the outset unless the vertical relationship—the relationship between each person and God—is in place.

Ed Young

Today's Prayer

Dear Lord, You have brought family members and friends into my life. Let me love them, let me help them, let me treasure them, and let me lead them to You. Amen

Real Repentance

I preached to those in Damascus first, and to those in Jerusalem and in all the region of Judea, and to the Gentiles, that they should repent and turn to God, and do works worthy of repentance.

Acts 26:20 HCSB

Who among us has sinned? All of us. But the good news is this: When we do ask God's forgiveness and turn our hearts to Him, He forgives us absolutely and completely.

Genuine repentance requires more than simply offering God apologies for our misdeeds. Real repentance may start with feelings of sorrow and remorse, but it ends only when we turn away from the sin that has heretofore distanced us from our Creator. In truth, we offer our most meaningful apologies to God, not with our words, but with our actions. As long as we are still engaged in sin, we may be "repenting," but we have not fully "repented." So, if there is an aspect of your life that is distancing you from your God, ask for His forgiveness, and—just as importantly—stop sinning. Now.

Today's Prayer

When I stray from Your commandments, Lord, I must not only confess my sins, I must also turn from them. When I fall short, help me to change. Forgive my sins, Dear Lord, and help me live according to Your plan for my life. Your plan is perfect, Father; I am not. Let me trust in You. Amen

A Priceless Treasure

Man shall not live by bread alone, but by every word that proceeds from the mouth of God.

Matthew 4:4 NKJV

The Bible is a priceless gift, a tool for Christians to use as they share the Good News of their Savior, Christ Jesus. Too many Christians, however, keep their spiritual tool kits tightly closed and out of sight.

Jonathan Edwards advised, "Be assiduous in reading the Holy Scriptures. This is the fountain whence all knowledge in divinity must be derived. Therefore let not this treasure lie by you neglected."

God's Holy Word is, indeed, a priceless, one-of-a-kind treasure. Handle it with care, but more importantly, handle it every day . . . starting today.

The Bible is the treasure map that leads us to God's highest treasure: eternal life.

Max Lucado

Today's Prayer

Heavenly Father, Your Holy Word is a treasure to me; I will study it, trust it, and share it. In all that I do, help me be a worthy witness for You as I share the Good News of Your perfect Son and Your perfect Word. Amen

Excuses and More Excuses

And now, children, stay with Christ. Live deeply in Christ. Then we'll be ready for him when he appears, ready to receive him with open arms, with no cause for red-faced guilt or lame excuses when he arrives.

1 John 2:28-29 MSG

We live in a world where excuses are everywhere. And it's precisely because excuses are so numerous that they are also so ineffective. When we hear the words, "I'm sorry but . . . ," most of us know exactly what is to follow: the excuse. The dog ate the homework. Traffic was terrible. It's the company's fault. The boss is to blame. The equipment is broken. We're out of that. And so forth, and so on.

Because we humans are such creative excuse-makers, all of the really good excuses have already been taken. In fact, the high-quality excuses have been used, re-used, over-used, and ab-used. That's why excuses don't work—we've heard them all before.

So, if you're wasting your time trying to concoct a new and improved excuse, don't bother. It's impossible. A far better strategy is this: do the work. Now. And let your excellent work speak loudly and convincingly for itself.

Today's Prayer

Heavenly Father, how easy it is to make excuses. But, I want to be a person who accomplishes important work for You. Help me, Father, to strive for excellence, not excuses. Amen

Blessed Obedience

Return to the Lord your God and obey His voice, according to all that I command you today, you and your children, with all your heart and with all your soul, that the Lord your God will bring you back from captivity, and have compassion on you.

Deuteronomy 30:2-3 NKJV

We live in a world filled with temptations, distractions, and countless opportunities to disobey God. But as Christians who seek to be godly role models for our families, we must turn our thoughts and our hearts away from the evils of this world. We must turn instead to God.

Talking about God is easy; living by His laws is considerably harder. But unless we are willing to live obediently, all our righteous words ring hollow.

How can we best proclaim our love for the Lord? By obeying Him. We must seek God's counsel and trust the counsel He gives. And, when we invite God into our hearts and live according to His commandments, we are blessed today, and tomorrow, and forever.

Today's Prayer

Dear Lord, when I am tempted to disobey Your commandments, correct my errors and guide my path. Make me a faithful steward of my talents, my opportunities, and my possessions so that Your kingdom may be glorified, now and forever. Amen

Becoming Wise

The one who walks with the wise will become wise, but a companion of fools will suffer harm.

Proverbs 13:20 HCSB

Wisdom does not spring up overnight—it takes time. To become wise, we must seek God's wisdom and live according to His Word. And, we must not only learn the lessons of the Christian life, we must also live by them.

Do you seek to live a life of righteousness and wisdom? If so, you must study the ultimate source of wisdom: the Word of God. You must seek out worthy mentors and listen carefully to their advice. You must associate, day in and day out, with godly men and women. And, you must act in accordance with your beliefs. When you do these things, you will become wise . . . and you will be a blessing to your friends, to your family, and to the world.

––––––––––

Wise people listen to wise instruction, especially instruction from the Word of God.

Warren Wiersbe

Today's Prayer

Dear Lord, when I depend upon the world's wisdom, I make many mistakes. But when I trust in Your wisdom, I build my life on a firm foundation. Today and every day I will trust Your Word and follow it, knowing that the ultimate wisdom is Your wisdom and the ultimate truth is Your truth. Amen

Humbled by His Sacrifice

But God forbid that I should boast except in the cross of our Lord Jesus Christ, by whom the world has been crucified to me, and I to the world.

Galatians 6:14 NKJV

As we consider Christ's sacrifice on the cross, we should be profoundly humbled. And today, as we come to Christ in prayer, we should do so in a spirit of humble devotion.

Christ humbled Himself on a cross—for you. He shed His blood—for you. He has offered to walk with you through this life and throughout all eternity. As you approach Him today in prayer, think about His sacrifice and His grace. And be humble.

The sacrifice of the Lamb is absolutely sufficient in itself to take away our sin and reconcile us to God.

Anne Graham Lotz

Today's Prayer

Dear Lord, when I am called upon to make sacrifices for causes that are just, give me courage. Let my words and deeds be pleasing to You, and let my service to others be worthy of the One who sacrificed His life for mine. Amen

Beyond Worldliness

Don't copy the behavior and customs of this world, but let God transform you into a new person by changing the way you think.

Romans 12:2 NLT

We live in the world, but we must not worship it. Our duty is to place God first and everything else second. But because we are fallible beings with imperfect faith, placing God in His rightful place is often difficult. In fact, at every turn, or so it seems, we are tempted to do otherwise.

The 21st-century world is a noisy, distracting place filled with countless opportunities to stray from God's will. The world seems to cry, "Worship me with your time, your money, your energy, and your thoughts!" But God commands otherwise: He commands us to worship Him and Him alone; everything else must be secondary.

A fish would never be happy living on land, because it was made for water. An eagle could never feel satisfied if it wasn't allowed to fly. You will never feel completely satisfied on earth, because you were made for more.

Rick Warren

Today's Prayer

Dear Lord, I am an imperfect human being living in an imperfect world. Direct my path far from the temptations and distractions of this world, and let me follow in the footsteps of Your Son today and forever. Amen

Beyond Worry

*The one who understands a matter finds success, and the one who trusts
in the Lord will be happy.*

Proverbs 16:20 HCSB

Because we are imperfect human beings, we worry. Even though we are Christians who have been given the assurance of salvation—even though we are Christians who have received the promise of God's love and protection—we find ourselves fretting over the countless details of everyday life. Jesus understood our concerns when He spoke the reassuring words found in Matthew 6: "Therefore I tell you, do not worry about your life . . ."

As you consider the promises of Jesus, remember that God still sits in His Heaven and you are His beloved child. Then, perhaps, you will worry a little less and trust God a little more, and that's as it should be because God is trustworthy . . . and you are protected.

Worry makes you forget who's in charge.

Max Lucado

Today's Prayer

Forgive me, Lord, when I worry. Worry reflects a lack of trust in You. Help me to work, Lord, and not to worry. And, keep me mindful, Father, that nothing, absolutely nothing, will happen this day that You and I cannot handle together. Amen

This Is His Day

This is the day the LORD has made. We will rejoice and be glad in it.

Psalm 118:24 NLT

The 118th Psalm reminds us that today, like every other day, is a cause for celebration. God gives us this day; He fills it to the brim with possibilities, and He challenges us to use it for His purposes. The day is presented to us fresh and clean at midnight, free of charge, but we must beware: Today is a non-renewable resource—once it's gone, it's gone forever. Our responsibility, of course, is to use this day in the service of God's will and according to His commandments.

Today, treasure the time that God has given you. Give Him the glory and the praise and the thanksgiving that He deserves. And search for the hidden possibilities that God has placed along your path. This day is a priceless gift from God, so use it joyfully and encourage others to do likewise.

With each new dawn, life delivers a package to your front door, rings your doorbell, and runs.

Charles Swindoll

Today's Prayer

Dear Lord, You have given me so many blessings, and as a way of saying "Thank You," I will celebrate. I will be a joyful Christian, Lord, quick to smile and slow to frown. And, I will share my joy with my family, with my friends, and with my neighbors, this day and every day. Amen

Accepting God's Gifts

For God so loved the world, that he gave his only begotten Son, that whosoever believeth in him should not perish, but have everlasting life.

John 3:16 KJV

God loves you—His love for you is deeper and more profound than you can imagine. God's love for you is so great that He sent His only Son to this earth to die for your sins and to offer you the priceless gift of eternal life.

You must decide whether or not to accept God's gift. Will you ignore it or embrace it? Will you return it or neglect it? Will you invite Christ to dwell in the center of your heart, or will you relegate Him to a position of lesser importance? The decision is yours, and so are the consequences. So choose wisely . . . and choose today.

The most profound essence of my nature is that I am capable of receiving God.

St. Augustine

Today's Prayer

Dear Lord, You sent Your Son to this earth that we might have the gift of eternal life. Thank You, Father, for that priceless gift. Help me to share the wondrous message of Jesus with others so that they, too, might accept Him as their Savior. And, let me praise You always for the new life You have given me, a life that is both abundant and eternal. Amen

Notes

Notes